The Transformation of the Workers' Party in Brazil, 1989–2009

Drawing on historical institutionalism and strategic frameworks, this book analyzes the evolution of the Workers' Party between 1989, the year of Lula's first presidential bid, and 2009, when his second presidential term entered its final stretch. The book's primary purpose is to understand why and how the once-radical *Partido dos Trabalhadores* (PT) moderated the programmatic positions it endorsed and adopted other aspects of a more catchall electoral strategy, thereby increasing its electoral appeal. At the same time, the book seeks to shed light on why some of the PT's distinctive normative commitments and organizational practices have endured in the face of adaptations aimed at expanding the party's vote share. The conclusion asks whether, in the face of these changes and continuities, the PT can still be considered a mass organized party of the left.

Wendy Hunter is Associate Professor of Government at the University of Texas, Austin. Her early work focused on Latin American militaries during the transition from authoritarian rule. A second phase of her research career was devoted to social policy decision making and human capital formation in Latin America. Recently, she has been engaged in understanding the growth and transformation of the Workers' Party in Brazil from 1989 until the present. She is the author of *Eroding Military Influence in Brazil*, and her articles have appeared in *Comparative Politics*, *Comparative Political Studies*, *Political Science Quarterly*, *American Political Science Review*, *American Journal of Political Science*, *Journal of Democracy*, and *World Politics*. She earned her doctorate from the University of California at Berkeley.

The Transformation of the Workers' Party in Brazil, 1989–2009

WENDY HUNTER
University of Texas, Austin

CAMBRIDGE
UNIVERSITY PRESS

CAMBRIDGE UNIVERSITY PRESS
Cambridge, New York, Melbourne, Madrid, Cape Town, Singapore,
São Paulo, Delhi, Dubai, Tokyo, Mexico City

Cambridge University Press
32 Avenue of the Americas, New York, NY 10013-2473, USA

www.cambridge.org
Information on this title: www.cambridge.org/9780521733007

© Wendy Hunter 2010

This publication is in copyright. Subject to statutory exception
and to the provisions of relevant collective licensing agreements,
no reproduction of any part may take place without the written
permission of Cambridge University Press.

First published 2010

Printed in the United States of America

A catalog record for this publication is available from the British Library.

Library of Congress Cataloging in Publication data

Hunter, Wendy.
The transformation of the Workers' Party in Brazil, 1989–2009 / Wendy Hunter.
   p.   cm.
Includes bibliographical references and index.
ISBN 978-0-521-51455-2 (hardback) – ISBN 978-0-521-73300-7 (pbk.)
   1. Partido dos Trabalhadores (Brazil)   2. Brazil – Politics and government – 2002–
I. Title.
JL2498.T7H86   2010
324.281′07–dc22   2010033070

ISBN 978-0-521-51455-2 Hardback
ISBN 978-0-521-73300-7 Paperback

Cambridge University Press has no responsibility for the persistence or accuracy of URLS
for external or third-party Internet Web sites referred to in this publication and does not
guarantee that any content on such Web sites is, or will remain, accurate or appropriate.

Contents

Tables, Charts, and Figure in Text		*page* vi
Tables and Chart in the Appendix		vii
Acronyms		ix
Acknowledgments		xiii
1	Introduction: Understanding the Normalization of the Workers' Party	1
2	Strategic Change or Organizational Persistence? Evolution of the Workers' Party	13
3	Opposition Politics: The PT in the Chamber of Deputies	45
4	The PT in Municipal Government: The Pragmatic Face of the Party	79
5	Striving for the Presidency: From Opposition to Government	106
6	New Challenges and Opportunities: The PT in Government, 2003–2009	146
7	Analytical Implications and Comparative Perspectives	177
Appendix		201
References		211
Interviews		229
Index		231

Tables, Charts, and Figure in Text

TABLES

3.1. Ideological Blocs in the Chamber of Deputies: 1982–2006	page 48
5.1. Regional Breakdown of Second-Round Presidential Election Results: 1989 versus 2002	141
6.1. Regional Breakdown of Second-Round Presidential Election Results: 1989, 2002, and 2006	170

CHARTS

3.1. Growth of the PT in the Chamber of Deputies, 1982–2006	47
3.2. Percentage of party label votes for principal parties in lower house elections, 1990–2006	59
4.1. Mayoral PT wins by region, 1988–2008	82
4.2. Mayoral PT wins by city size, 1988–2008	82
6.1. Evolution of vote shares by region: Lula vs. the PT	172

FIGURE

3.1. Brazil's political landscape, 1989–2002	53

Tables and Chart in the Appendix

TABLES

A.1.	Lula's Record in Presidential Elections: 1989–2006	*page* 201
A.2.	Congressional Election Results: 1982–2006	202
A.3.	Municipal Election Results: 1982–2008	202
A.4.	PT Mayoral Victories by Region and City Size: 1988–2008	203
A.5.	Presidential Vote Intentions by Education Level: 1989–2006	204
A.6.	Presidential Vote Intentions by Income Level: 1989–2006	205
A.7.	Presidential Vote Intentions by City Size: 1994–2006	206
A.8.	Cabinet Distribution among Coalition Members: The Cardoso and Lula Administrations Compared	207

CHART

A.1.	Evolution of Party Preferences: 1988–2006	210

Acronyms

ABC region: A = Santo André, B = São Bernardo do Campo, C = São Caetano do Sul
AD: *Acción Democrática*, Democratic Action (Venezuela)
APRA: *Alianza Popular Revolucionaria Americana*, American Popular Revolutionary Alliance (Peru)
ARENA: *Aliança de Renovação Nacional*, National Renovating Alliance
BF: *Bolsa Família*, Family Stipend
BNDES: *Banco Nacional de Desenvolvimento Econômico e Social*, Brazilian Social and Economic Development Bank
CDES: *Conselho de Desenvolvimento Econômico e Social*, Council of Economic and Social Development
CNI: *Confederação Nacional da Indústria*, National Confederation of Industry
CNT: *Confederação Nacional do Transporte*, National Confederation of Transportation
COPEI: *Comité de Organización Política Electoral Independiente*, Social Christian Party of Venezuela
CPI: *Comissão Parlamentar de Inquérito*, Parliamentary Investigatory Committee
CUT: *Central Única dos Trabalhadores*, Unified Workers' Confederation
CVRD: *Companhia Vale do Rio Doce*
DF: *Distrito Federal*, Federal District (Brasília)
DIAP: *Departamento Intersindical de Assessoria Parlamentar*, Inter-Union Department of Parliamentary Assistance

EMBRAPA: *Empresa Brasileira de Pesquisa Agropecuária*, Brazilian Company of Agribusiness Research
FA: *Frente Amplio*, Broad Front (Uruguay)
FARC: *Fuerzas Armadas Revolucionarias de Colombia*, Revolutionary Armed Forces of Colombia
FHC: Fernando Henrique Cardoso
FIESP: *Federação das Industrias do Estado de São Paulo*, Federation of Industries of the State of São Paulo
FPA: *Fundação Perseu Abramo*, Perseu Abramo Foundation
FREPASO: *Frente por un País Solidario*, Front for a Country in Solidarity (Argentina)
FTAA: Free Trade Area of the Americas
IBAMA: *Instituto Brasileiro do Meio Ambiente e dos Recursos Naturais Renováveis*, Brazilian Institute of Environment and Renewable Natural Resources
IBGE: *Instituto Brasileiro de Geografia e Estatística*, Brazilian Institute of Geography and Statistics
IBOPE: *Instituto Brasileiro de Opinião Pública e Estatística*, Brazilian Institute of Public Opinion and Statistics
IC: *Instituto Cidadania*, Citizenship Institute
IDB: Inter-American Development Bank
IDESP: *Instituto de Estudos Econômicos, Sociais, e Políticos de São Paulo*, São Paulo Institute for Economic, Social, and Political Studies
IMF: International Monetary Fund
INCRA: *Instituto Nacional de Colonização e Reforma Agrária*, National Institute of Colonization and Land Reform
IPTU: *Imposto Predial e Territorial Urbano*, Urban Property and Building Tax
ISI: Import Substitution Industrialization
IU: *Izquierda Unida*, United Left (Peru)
LCR: *La Causa R*, The Radical Cause (Venezuela)
MERCOSUL: *Mercado Comum do Sul*, Southern Common Market
MDS: *Ministério do Desenvolvimento Social*, Ministry of Social Development
MST: *Movimento dos Trabalhadores Rurais Sem Terra*, Movement of Landless Rural Workers
PAN: *Partido Acción Nacional*, National Action Party (Mexico)
PCB: *Partido Comunista Brasileiro*, Brazilian Communist Party

PCdoB: *Partido Comunista do Brasil*, Communist Party of Brazil
PDS: *Partido Democrático Social*, Democratic Social Party
PDT: *Partido Democrático Trabalhista*, Democratic Labor Party
PDVSA: *Petróleos de Venezuela, S.A.*
PED: *Processo de Eleições Diretas*, Process of Direct Elections
PFL: *Partido da Frente Liberal*, Party of the Liberal Front
PJ: *Partido Justicialista*, Justicialist Party (Argentina)
PL: *Partido Liberal*, Liberal Party
PMDB: *Partido do Movimento Democrático Brasileiro*, Party of the Brazilian Democratic Movement
PMN: *Partido da Mobilização Nacional*, Party of National Mobilization
PPA: Plano Plurianual, Multiyear Plan
PPB: *Partido Progressista Brasileiro*, Brazilian Progressive Party
PPR: *Partido Progressista Renovador*, Reformist Progressive Party
PPS: *Partido Popular Socialista*, Popular Socialist Party
PRD: *Partido de la Revolución Democrática*, Party of the Democratic Revolution (Mexico)
PRI: *Partido Revolucionario Institucional*, Institutional Revolutionary Party (Mexico)
PRN: *Partido da Reconstrução Nacional*, Party of National Reconstruction
PRONA: *Partido da Reedificação da Ordem Nacional*, National Order Reconstruction Party
PRP: *Partido Republicano Progressista*, Progressive Republican Party
PSB: *Partido Socialista Brasileiro*, Brazilian Socialist Party
PSDB: *Partido da Social Democracia Brasileira*, Party of Brazilian Social Democracy
PSOE: *Partido Socialista Obrero Español*, Spanish Socialist Workers' Party
PSOL: *Partido Socialismo e Liberdade*, Party for Socialism and Liberty
PST: *Partido Social Trabalhista*, Social Labor Party
PSTU: *Partido Socialista dos Trabalhadores Unificado*, Unified Socialist Workers' Party
PT: *Partido dos Trabalhadores*, Workers' Party
PTB: *Partido Trabalhista Brasileiro*, Brazilian Labor Party
PUM *Partido Unificado Mariateguista*, Unified Mariateguista Party (Peru)
PV: *Partido Verde*, Green Party
SMs: *salários minimos*, minimum wage levels

STF: *Supremo Tribunal Federal*, Supreme Court
TSE: *Tribunal Superior Eleitoral*, Supreme Electoral Court
UAMPA: *União das Associações de Moradores de Porto Alegre*, Union of Neighborhood Associations of Porto Alegre
WTO: World Trade Organization

Acknowledgments

I have incurred many debts in the process of researching and writing this book. I am glad to finally be able to acknowledge all of the individuals and institutions that helped me along the way.

It is my pride and pleasure to be a faculty member of the Department of Government at the University of Texas. An extraordinary group of colleagues – Dan Brinks, Henry Dietz, Zach Elkins, Ken Greene, Juliet Hooker, Raúl Madrid, and Kurt Weyland – provided invaluable feedback on various parts of the manuscript. In particular, I would like to thank Ken Greene for his insights on the political parties literature, Raúl Madrid for his sound advice and supportive feedback over the years, and Kurt Weyland for reading and commenting on the whole manuscript. A string of talented, dedicated, and good-humored research assistants – Daniel Nogueira Budny, Juliana Estrella, Rodrigo Nunes, Natasha Borges Sugiyama, Jeremy Teigen, and Kristin Wylie – contributed invaluably to the book. I will always be grateful to them. Chairs Gary Freeman and John Higley, together with LLILAS director Bryan Roberts, supported the leaves from teaching that were so crucial to research and writing. I thank the College of Liberal Arts and the Teresa Lozano Long Institute of Latin American Studies at the University of Texas for their financial assistance in this regard. I acknowledge as well the Andrew W. Mellon Foundation for the research trips that it funded.

A year-long residential fellowship at the Kellogg Institute of International Studies at the University of Notre Dame was decisive in getting this project off the ground. I am deeply grateful to Scott Mainwaring for his support in that critical year and for his various contributions since then. Thanks are due also to Michael Coppedge for the many useful suggestions he provided. My enduring friendship with Frances Hagopian, one of the most incisive thinkers I know, helped sustain me during the many years it took to complete this project.

Special recognition goes to Steven Levitsky, whose extensive and intelligent comments enhanced the book. I have also benefited from contact with Timothy Power, whose knowledge and understanding of Brazilian politics knows no rival. I deeply value the professional relationship and personal friendship we have maintained since meeting in Brazil as graduate students in 1989, the year of Lula's first presidential bid. I would also like to acknowledge David Samuels for the impressive work he has done on the Workers' Party and his generosity in sharing it with me. Warm thanks go to David Fleischer, who for years has supplied me with relevant news stories and directed my attention to issues and events in Brazilian politics that would have escaped my attention otherwise. Similarly, I tip my hat to Andrew Stein for his incredible ability to stay on top of current developments in Brazil and the region at large, and I thank him for taking the time to point out relevant news items to me.

Three young talented Brazilian scholars were crucial in helping my research get started: Oswaldo Amaral, Paulo Roberto Figueira Leal, and Celso Roma. I am very appreciative of their generous and patient assistance. Recognition also goes to Leo Avritzer, Barry Ames, Octavio Amorim Neto, Andy Baker, David Collier, Peter Kingstone, Rachel Meneguello, Mala Htun, Gaby Ondetti, Jim McGuire, Ken Roberts, Bill Smith, and Brian Wampler.

I would like to thank editor Lewis Bateman for his interest in the book and for his role in ushering it through to completion.

My debts closer to home are deep, many, and varied. My parents – James and Setsuko Hunter – continue to support my pursuits. Their main contribution in this round involved assuming childcare responsibilities. Anyone who has ever tried to attend a professional conference with two young children in tow knows the value of such help.

My sons, Nikolas and Andreas Weyland, filled my life with joy during the years I wrote this book. Their playfulness and ability to enjoy life as though there were no tomorrow provided relief when energy and enthusiasm lagged. Their miraculous development gave me the fortitude to get back up and resume working.

My debt to Kurt Weyland is without parallel. His sharp theoretical insights, profound knowledge of Brazil, and persistent intellectual questioning helped greatly on the professional front. His loving dedication to our children and ability to deal tirelessly with the endless tasks of managing a household contributed crucially on the home front. With love and gratitude, I dedicate this book to Niko, Andi, and Kurt.

1

Introduction

Understanding the Normalization of the Workers' Party

In 1989, a scruffy bearded figure calling for radical change under the symbol of his party's red star competed in Brazil's first open and direct presidential election in almost thirty years. The candidate was Luiz Inácio Lula da Silva from the *Partido dos Trabalhadores* (PT, or Workers' Party). After a campaign marked by intense political polarization, Lula's narrow defeat to his right-wing competitor Fernando Collor de Mello came as a major relief to conservative sectors of Brazilian society. The specter of a PT-led government prompted the formation of a center-left alliance that would effectively keep the PT in the opposition for years to come. Finally in 2002, after winning progressively greater first-round vote shares in every presidential election since 1989, a more moderate and smartly coiffed Lula led the PT to victory in a presidential campaign that took place in an atmosphere of comparative political stability and consensus. He won reelection by a wide margin in 2006.

Between Lula's first unsuccessful run for the presidency in 1989 and his eventual victory in 2002, the PT became a leading contender at other levels of Brazilian politics as well. Featuring an active legislative delegation that expanded in every successive election, the PT eventually constituted the largest bloc in the lower house of Congress. While its legislators debated issues of national importance, PT mayors won office and governed in an increasing number and array of Brazil's cities. PT-led municipal governments developed a host of innovative social programs – arguably the most prominent being participatory budgeting – that elevated the party's visibility in Brazil as well as abroad. While the PT developed core supporters who were strongly attached to its ideals and part of its unique subculture, it also managed to gain the votes of people who were not PT partisans. By the eve of the party's long-awaited transition from opposition to government, the PT had developed into Latin America's largest, most organized, and arguably most innovative left party.[1]

Part and parcel of this growth trajectory were significant changes in the party and its standard bearers. Over time, the once radical programmatic party – whose impressive rise in Brazil's patronage-oriented political system appeared to defy conventional understandings of Brazilian politics – grew to look more like its catchall or electoral-professional competitors.[2] Rather than continuing to build upon its earlier promise to shape the party system in a more programmatic direction and induce more ethical standards of conduct among the country's notoriously clientelistic and corrupt politicians, the PT adopted many of the strategies and tactics of more conventional Brazilian parties. This shift resulted from the heightened emphasis placed on immediate vote maximization after Brazil's adoption of market reforms and the public's general acceptance of this development rendered the party's socialist project unviable. The goal of vote maximization made the PT more susceptible to the institutional incentives for building electoral and political support in Brazil, incentives that induce parties to undertake measures such as softening their programmatic positions, forging opportunistic alliances, and resorting to patronage.

At the same time, however, the PT's adaptation was incomplete and uneven as a result of historical legacies that hindered change. Although the party instituted visible strategic and tactical adaptations to gain public support, it changed far less on the inside. For example, the PT remained the most disciplined and cohesive party in the political system. Organizational vestiges of its former radicalism and the continued commitment of some within its ranks to a transformative project prevented the PT from undergoing a full accommodation to systemic constraints. On the one hand, the PT's origins and structure created advantages, including a solid base that it could rely on during periods of crisis and transformation,

---

[1] In the Appendix see Tables A.1, A.2, and A.3 on the party's growth at different levels of government.

[2] See Kirchheimer (1966) for a discussion of catchall parties and their characteristics. Kirchheimer defines a catchall party as one that tries to "exchange effectiveness in depth for a wider audience and more immediate electoral success" (1966: 184). The term *electoral-professional* is used by Panebianco (1988: 262–267). It refers less to the social support base that catchall parties obtain and more to the increasing professionalization of party organizations, whereby individuals with specialized knowledge are seen as "more useful to the organization than the traditional party bureaucrats, as the party's gravitational center shifts from the members to the electorate" (1988: 264).

Introduction 3

credibility as an opposition party in the presidential race of 2002, and discipline in passing difficult reforms under the subsequent Lula-led government. On the other hand, such partial adaptation at times left the party in awkward, even messy, in-between positions. Tensions, distortions, and unintended consequences abounded. The party's fund-raising difficulties and its vote-buying practices put these contradictions into stark relief.

In this book I analyze the transformation of the Workers' Party (1989–2009) as a fascinating and complex case of organizational change. My primary goal is to explain why and how the PT moderated its programmatic stances and adopted other aspects of a more catchall profile, thereby widening its electoral appeal. Exceptionally ideological and grassroots oriented, the PT was the kind of party least likely to start behaving in a vote-maximizing way. In other words, a classic institutionalized mass party with a dense organization, the PT was an unlikely candidate for adaptation. As such, it constitutes a least likely case for rational choice analysis. In the end, the PT did adapt and moderate in very crucial ways, as such a framework would predict. The roots of the PT's adaptation lie in the external environment: Brazilian institutions, the structure of electoral competition, and changes in the international economy. They rest also in Lula's leadership role. Whereas complex organizations tend not to adapt quickly, individual leaders (and their top advisors) often respond rationally to external incentives more readily. The PT benefited from having a single virtually irreplaceable leader who enjoyed more societal support than his party. An exceptionally popular figure, Lula both responded appropriately to environmental challenges and used his electability as leverage to demand change within the party. Although there are a few comparable cases of leaders who have used their personal popularity as influence over their parties, such as the Spanish Socialist Party (PSOE) in Spain under Felipe González and the African National Congress (ANC) under Nelson Mandela, this is distinct from most institutionalized left or social democratic parties, at least as they are discussed in the literature.

I also seek to understand why some of the PT's distinctive normative commitments and organizational practices endured in the face of marked adaptations aimed at expanding its vote share, and what consequences their survival had. Insights from historical institutionalism are crucial in this regard. The PT's organizational attributes had a double-edged impact on its adaptive capacity. Even though the party adjusted to the external environment between 1994 and 2002, this successful adaptation would probably not have been possible without the developments that took place in the 1980s. The origins and development of the party organization – which allowed it to build a powerful grassroots network, develop governing experience at the local level, and establish true credibility as a partisan alternative – supported its later transformation. Had the PT adapted too quickly, it might well have gone the way of other failed left-of-center parties, such as the FREPASO (*Frente por un País Solidario*) in Argentina. At the same time, there were negative aspects of the PT's organizational trajectory that historical institutionalism helps to explain. Restrictions on how the party would finance campaigns – most notably a rejection of contributions from big business – led the PT into illegal fundraising schemes in the cities where it governed. Similarly, limitations that party activists placed on the government's ability under Lula to manage executive–legislative relations induced him to resort to buying legislators' votes, resulting in the *mensalão* corruption scandal.

In sum, by combining strategic and historical institutionalist approaches, the book's analysis brings to light the electoral incentives for change, the structural and institutional constraints that molded those incentives, and the historical and organizational legacies that made change more difficult. It reveals that the PT evolved in response to changing environmental conditions but in ways constrained by past trajectories. The party's history conditioned when, how, and to what extent it rose to external challenges.

CONTRIBUTIONS

A Theoretical Interpretation of Institutional Change

In this book I seek to contribute to the larger study of institutional change. Employing rational choice and historical institutionalism, the analysis takes up the call to combine the two approaches in ways that harness their respective strengths and comparative advantages (e.g., Hall and Taylor 1996; Thelen 1999; Weingast 2002; Katznelson and Weingast 2005; Mahoney and Thelen 2010). Despite recognizing that rational choice and historical institutionalist approaches should be integrated, few scholars have actually undertaken this pursuit in a systematic fashion. Aiming to advance this theoretical synthesis, in this book I examine how political and economic contexts create incentive structures that lead to institutional innovation yet within the organizational and normative constraints established by historical legacies. Many of the organizational changes undertaken by the PT leadership are excellent examples of institutional "layering," that is, incremental change that ultimately results in substantial transformation. Emphasizing rather than downplaying the distinctions between strategic and historical institutionalist approaches provides the most analytical leverage on complex outcomes reflecting both adaptation and resistance to change.

By examining the evolution of the PT through explicitly theoretical lines of reasoning, as encouraged by Bates et al. (1998: 10–13), the analysis brings together parsimony and a systematization of detail, one of the key benefits of strategic frameworks, with a sensitivity to context associated with historical institutionalism. Invoking rational choice facilitates explanation of the party's adjustment to external inducements and constraints, whereas referencing historical institutionalism elucidates how historical legacies preserved some of its uniqueness and limited its transformation. Neither approach alone can account for the PT's profile of partial transformation. If an exclusively strategic framework overpredicts change, reliance on historical institutionalism underpredicts it. Moreover, invoking both frameworks shows how the party sometimes found itself caught between opposing logics, thereby illuminating important dysfunctional aspects of its behavior that have puzzled observers heretofore. Indeed, the PT responded to a dense and complex mix of incentives that at times even pulled it in conflicting directions.

Systematically disaggregating the phenomenon of party adaptation, the analysis recognizes the unevenness of organizational change and suggests an expected sequence of transformation: Parties subject to external pressures are likely to first make modifications on matters most directly and immediately relevant for enhancing their standing outside the organization, that is, vis-à-vis voters and competitors (other parties and alliances). Changes in the platforms endorsed and images projected are typically among the first to occur. Parties are slower to proceed on matters that affect internal dynamics, such as relations among party cadres and leaders. Moreover, they may not change at all on norms that were vital to sustaining the organization during its early formation and that bear only indirectly on the party's electoral standing at a later point in time. Whereas a strategic perspective explains shifts on the external front, insights from historical institutionalism shed light on the stickiness typically encountered in the interior of an organization.

A Contribution to the Literature on the Transformation of Left Parties

Comprehending the PT is also consequential for achieving a broader understanding of left parties. The recent electoral success of left parties, movements, and their leaders has led analysts to explore the conditions of their rise, their shifting bases of support, and the determinants of their respective moderation and radicalism once in power (e.g., Petkoff 2005; Castañeda 2006; Cleary 2006; Weyland, Madrid, and Hunter 2010; Levitsky and Roberts forthcoming). As key players in defining the political and economic character of Latin America's recent shift to the left, Lula and the PT are often seen as anchoring the more moderate pole within the region's left turn.

In analyzing the PT as a case of slow but eventually successful adaptation, the book advances general ideas on the conditions under which parties change and on how they change. In this connection, the PT compares favorably within a broader universe of cases in which left parties adapted with different degrees of success under democratic or at least democratizing governments in the region. The *Frente Amplio* (Broad Front) in Uruguay is a good comparison case. Its origins and trajectory parallel those of the PT in many ways, and after several consecutive defeats and eventual moderation it too won power for the first time in 2000. Venezuela's *La Causa R* (LCR) and Peru's *Izquierda Unida* (IU) serve as instructive cases of contrast. Two factors that distinguish the comparatively successful PT and *Frente Amplio* from the LCR and IU are the solidity of their organization and the existence of a single leader who enjoyed both a strong presence within the party and popularity with the electorate. Although the strength of the party organization may have slowed the transformation of the PT and *Frente Amplio* initially, it contributed to their staying power over the long term. The presence of a popular leader with a singular ability to gain societal support served as crucial leverage for change within the party.

A Comprehensive and Updated Account of the PT

While speaking to these larger theoretical themes, in the present analysis I provide a comprehensive empirical treatment of the PT's evolution over the past two decades, a period during which the party changed dramatically. I examine the PT's conduct while it was in the national opposition (1989–2002) and government (2003–2009). I also explore its growth in three different institutional arenas – municipalities, the Congress, and the presidency – and assess the respective influence of each sphere on the party's overall trajectory. Although I give central play to the party's longstanding leader Lula, my emphasis is not on documenting his life story but on determining how he contributed to the PT's transformation and success. While Lula's presidential ambitions reinforced systemic external pressures on the PT to undergo adaptation, his unique appeal to wide-ranging groups in the electorate and persuasive power within the party facilitated the process. My analysis acknowledges the moderating influence of PT mayors and municipal governments but emphasizes the role of exogenous factors – namely, features of Brazilian politics and developments in the global economy – in the adaptations pursued by the national PT leadership.

To date, comprehensive and theoretically informed analyses of the PT's post-1989 evolution at the national level are few and far between.[3] An important exception is Samuels (2004), who in an interesting article-length analysis emphasizes *endogenous* sources of change, especially the flexibility permitted through specific internal rules and the rise of pragmatists following the party's success in mayoral elections. Most of the literature concentrates on specific aspects of the party's story. The lion's share of work is devoted to PT municipal governments and their efforts to implement participatory budgeting schemes, observe practices of transparent government, and institute an array of interesting social programs, such as the *Bolsa Escola* (an income subsidy to poor families conditional on their children's school attendance), micro credit, and family health projects (e.g., Genro and Souza 1997; Abers 2000; Baiocchi 2003, 2005; Nylen 2003; Wampler 2007). Paulo Roberto Figueira Leal (2005) provides a highly focused treatment of the PT in the federal Chamber of Deputies. Other than his account, this critical aspect of the party's evolution has been woefully understudied. The literature also features several biographies of Lula, which chronicle his impressive rise from the depths of poverty to the presidential palace but do not integrate the study of his life with a systematic theoretically informed analysis of the party (e.g., Paraná 2002; Alves 2003; Bourne 2008).

An Optic for Examining Broader Developments in Brazil

Analyzing the rise of the PT – one of the most striking developments in Brazil's postauthoritarian democracy – serves as an interesting optic from which to view vital changes in politics and economy that have unfolded in Brazil during the past two decades. The country's development over this time period crucially affected how the party evolved. Comparing

---

[3] Excellent analyses of the PT in the first decade of its existence are Meneguello (1989) and Keck (1991, 1992). Singer (2001) provides a short analysis of the PT's evolution after 1989 but ends before Lula's victorious presidential campaign of 2002.

Lula's 1989 presidential campaign against Fernando Collor de Mello to the 2002 contest against José Serra is especially instructive in this regard. The 1989 race, the first direct presidential election under Brazil's new democracy, was a highly polarized no-holds-barred competition. The runoff pitted a far-left candidate with strong ties to the autonomous union movement against a right-wing populist with political roots in the recently departed military regime (1964–1985). The military kept a close watch on the campaign. Actors outside the party system, such as the television network *Rede Globo*, interfered to a degree widely considered illegitimate. By contrast, the 2002 contest featured solid candidates from established parties. The fluid free-for-all character of 1989 was gone, which was due in no small part to the consolidation of the party system and enhanced state performance that had taken place during the tenure of President Fernando Henrique Cardoso from 1995 to 2002.

The economic context had also changed dramatically. One of the most closed economies in the developing world in the late 1980s, Brazil had undergone major changes toward globalization and market reform by 2002. Inflation had remained under control since the mid-1990s with the Real Plan. Although Lula benefited from criticizing some of the performance gaps in Brazil's reformed economy (e.g., high rates of unemployment), promoting the PT's previous socialist platform as a matter of principle would have seemed antiquated and unreasonable to most voters in 2002 (Baker 2009). By then, higher levels of political institutionalization, together with a more stable and institutionally consolidated market economy, contributed to pulling the PT and especially Lula into a pattern of centripetal competition. Once Lula assumed the presidency in 2003, these same forces weighed on the PT-led government and caused its policies to be quite moderate. Indeed, the consolidation of structural economic reforms and the growing institutional strength of the state and party system imposed clear limits on the PT's earlier aspirations for far-reaching state-led change.

CHAPTER OVERVIEW

To make sense of these issues, in Chapter 2 I present two frameworks typically used to understand party change – rational choice and historical institutionalism. The model of change used to depict the PT's transformation is that of institutional layering: gradual change that results eventually in significant transformation. The chapter establishes the starting point, which is the PT's distinctiveness prior to the mid-1990s. I focus attention on describing the key characteristics that once made the PT a mass party of the left and distinguished it unequivocally from its catchall or electoral-professional counterparts, analyzing why a policy-seeking rather than a vote-maximizing approach made sense at the time (or at least was not irrational), and providing evidence of the benefits as well as limitations of such an approach.

The chapter then proceeds to portray and analyze the PT as a case of successful party adaptation. It examines the motives for the PT to become less radical and more vote maximizing in the second half of the decade, identifies the adaptations made and their electoral benefits, and discusses the factors that permitted change to occur. It also specifies the dimensions on which adaptation did not take place. The main story that unfolds is that of a radical programmatic party that grew into a less distinctive party over time. That story's most prominent aspects are well told from a strategic perspective, yet there exist important wrinkles that deserve attention. Change occurred much more on some dimensions than on others. Insights from historical institutionalism capture a crucial layer of complexity in the PT's evolution.

Chapters 3, 4, and 5 show that change is context dependent as well as issue specific. Demonstrating that institutional incentives shape political behavior, these chapters trace the PT's development in three distinct arenas while in the national opposition: the Chamber of Deputies, municipal governments, and the presidential contests of 1989, 1994, 1998, and 2002. Evolution along these separate fronts helped shape the party into a highly complex and multifaceted organization. The institutional context of competition and the substantive issues and challenges posed by officeholding are quite different for the three spheres. Important aspects of change and continuity in the PT's profile reflect the party's development around them. The argument that institutional incentives matter – as demonstrated across these chapters – sheds light on why Lula sought increasingly to separate himself from the party's activities in other institutional spheres.

Chapter 3 analyzes how the PT built its reputation as a strong left party by leading the legislative opposition in the federal Chamber of Deputies. The left-leaning programmatic content of the legislation the PT delegation supported, together with the strong and disciplined organization it maintained, became clear in this context. Because the proportional element of electoral design for election to the Chamber of Deputies permitted the party to grow even while it projected a clear left identity, a core goal of the PT's strategizing was to build up the party's legislative delegation and thus stake out its leftist reputation on the national political scene. Key aspects of continuity in the party's alternative identity and organizational uniqueness are rooted in its development within this important body.

Chapter 4 analyzes the role of municipal elections and city government in shaping the PT's development. If leading the legislative opposition positioned the PT to maintain principled stances on key issues of national importance, the institutional requirements of winning mayoral elections and the challenges encountered in governing cities induced the party's mayoral candidates and officeholders toward greater pragmatism. Experiences at this level thus gradually changed the balance of forces within the party as well as its public image and support base. By revealing its ability to compromise and administer – especially in showcase cities such as Porto Alegre – the PT revealed a side of itself not easily discernable from the Chamber, where its radical ideological face remained prominent for a longer period of time. Diversifying its public profile no doubt helped the party win favor among more middle-of-the-road voters. Ultimately, PT governance at the local level became an important face of the party.

Chapter 5 analyzes Lula's pursuit of presidential office in the elections of 1989, 1994, and 1998 and his ultimate victory in 2002. It underscores the decisive role that the quest for presidential office played in moving the PT in a more moderate and catchall direction. It also explains why Lula fell short of victory in his first three bids and was ultimately successful in 2002. Lula and his closest associates are presented as effective strategists behind moves to transform various external pressures into organizational change. In response to these challenges, the PT made a number of important programmatic and organizational modifications designed to broaden its electoral appeal and enhance the influence of moderate factions. Yet there were tensions at every turn; sometimes the vote-maximizing pragmatists lost to the policy-seeking ideologues, and at other times they won only partial victories. Change occurred through a bounded and layered process. Furthermore, a growing disjuncture between the party and its leader emerged as the degree and sources of electoral support for Lula's presidential bids changed more dramatically than those for the party as such. Nonetheless, by the time Lula finally won presidential office in 2002 the PT was a very different organization than it was in 1989.

Chapter 6 examines Lula and the party in national government between 2003 and 2009. Lula's presidential victory brought about an unprecedented development: The leader of a highly organized party with a history of ideological purpose and activism would head Brazil's government. What impact would the PT have on government decisions and processes, and, in turn, how would the experience of governing affect the PT? An analysis of various policy issues and arenas of action suggests that the president frequently found himself caught between a pull to adapt to existing external constraints (economic and institutional in nature) and resistance waged from within the party. The management of executive-legislative relations was where Lula experienced the most difficulty in reconciling these conflicting forces. Whereas the institutional incentives for building legislative support demanded the inclusion of a broad range of parties in the cabinet, significant elements within the PT sought to exclude them. The president ultimately broke the deadlock through legislative vote buying, resulting in the now well-known *mensalão* scandal. This debilitating scandal emerged precisely from the tensions between electoral adjustment and organizational and ideological persistence that the synthetic theoretical framework of this book highlights.

Chapter 6 shows also that if governing presented new constraints then it brought new opportunities as well, most importantly privileged access to federal resources. The provision of concrete benefits made possible through executive officeholding allowed Lula to consolidate an important social base – the poorest and least educated Brazilians – that had responded only weakly to the previous party-based strategy of grassroots mobilization for progressive change. The strong support of this group was crucial in helping Lula win reelection in 2006. However, the PT in the federal Congress benefited far less than the president himself from these social policy provisions, widening the gap between its support base and that of Lula.

Chapter 7, the conclusion, reflects back upon the theoretical issues the book engages and places the study of the PT in comparative perspective. In revisiting the question of what explains the PT's evolution from a radical base–democratic opposition party to a more hierarchical, catchall, and professionalized organization, the chapter underscores the central role of insights from rational choice while noting the additional layer of understanding that historical institutionalism provides. Drawing from both frameworks yields a richer and more nuanced account than either alone can provide. The chapter also returns to the earlier emphasis on the importance of personal leadership and organization as an effective combination for party adaptation. In this connection, it reiterates the importance of appropriate pacing: Overly rapid change may lead to implosion yet change that occurs too slowly creates the risk of stagnation and isolation. The PT struck a good balance. A comparative section asks whether the conditions that explain the successful transformation of the PT apply to other left parties in Latin America. In this connection, it compares the PT and the *Frente Amplio* in Uruguay to the less successful FREPASO in Argentina, LCR in Venezuela, and IU in Peru. The chapter ends by pondering what future directions the PT might take.

2

Strategic Change or Organizational Persistence?

Evolution of the Workers' Party

Events of the late twentieth century put leftist parties in a bind all over Latin America. This was true for Brazil as well. While the international socialist referent lost ground symbolically, economic developments in the very countries where left parties had gained traction forced them into a difficult position. Trade opening, privatization, and the reform and restructuring of the state – backed in considerable measure by key domestic elites, international financial institutions, and public opinion itself – required such parties to adapt in order to survive politically. Successful adaptation generally entails changes in strategy and organization that improve a party's ability to gain and keep electoral office amidst changing environmental challenges. The specific changes required depend on the given context, but in general they involve orienting the party away from the preferences of militants and more toward those of large groups of voters. These changes must find support within the party and the electorate.

To help us understand and assess adaptations within the PT, this chapter presents two broad analytical frameworks – rational choice and historical institutionalism – that offer different insights and perspectives on the issue of change, and it examines several studies on political parties that draw on these frameworks in key ways. Against this backdrop, the chapter examines and analyzes the distinctiveness of the PT as a mass left party prior to the mid-1990s, and it explains how and why it became a more electoral-professional and catchall party in the decade thereafter. Drawing on rational choice and historical institutionalism sheds light on the constellation, sequence, and rate of transformation that occurred.

Adaptation took place sooner and in a more pronounced fashion in some arenas and on some dimensions than it did in others. A strategic perspective helps explain why changes occurred where they did. The PT behaved differently according to the different institutional settings in which it operated. For example, congressional, mayoral, and presidential elections each had their own set of incentives. The specific dynamics that operated in each of these respective arenas caused the party to become heterogeneous and layered. Over time, however, Lula's persistent bid for presidential office came to dominate higher levels of decision making and was responsible for the notable centrist shift of the late 1990s and early 2000s that many Brazilian voters associated with the PT. With respect to the dimensions that underwent modification, those that were immediately visible to the public and that made the most direct impact on the party's electoral appeal – such as the programmatic stances assumed and the images that leading candidates projected – were the first to change.

Evolving at a slower rate or not at all were internal organizational practices that were deeply rooted in the party's history and that bore a less immediate relationship to attracting votes. Historical institutionalism captures this complexity well. The party's transformation was layered, uneven, and incomplete, a situation that created some positive benefits but also important tensions and dysfunctionalities. Whether or not these aspects of change and continuity will continue to coexist is a question taken up in the conclusion.

POLITICAL PARTIES AND THEIR MOTIVATIONS

The central analytical frameworks that the book applies – rational choice and historical institutionalism – have different expectations of the main goals that political parties pursue, the factors that are likely to constrain them, and the behaviors they will tend to adopt. Notwithstanding some points of convergence, they give divergent answers to central questions asked by studies of political party formation and change. These questions include *whether* parties like the PT will remain ideological and policy seeking or whether they will moderate and become vote maximizing and catchall in nature; *under what conditions* such parties shift their goals and undergo strategic adaptations; and *how* they tend to adapt (e.g., in a rapid, punctuated, or more gradual fashion). These differences reflect more general distinctions between rational choice and historical institutionalism.

First, whereas rational choice views human behavior as highly responsive to incentives that exist in the immediate environment, a central tenet of historical institutionalism is that political decisions and behavior cannot be understood in isolation from past experiences. Second, whereas rational choice scholars focus sharply on the instrumental or self-interested aspects of political motivation, historical institutionalists appreciate the enduring influence of norms. Third, rational choice sees good leadership as the capacity to update assessments of the political landscape and reorient an organization's position as quickly and accurately as possible. Leadership is less a matter of cultivating change around hard organizational constraints, as it is for historical institutionalists. For the latter, adept leaders are seen to work "around elements they cannot change while attempting to harness and utilize others in novel ways" (Streeck and Thelen 2005: 19).[1] The broader picture that emerges is that rational choice theory – in affording leaders more autonomy from inherited norms, procedures, and structures – predicts a cleaner and more decisive break with the past (Weingast 2002: 692). By contrast, historical institutionalism tends to dwell on uneasy balances of power and resources, and the dysfunctionality of institutional stickiness. It regards change as more complicated, beset by contradictions, and therefore unlikely to proceed in leaps and bounds but rather in steps or layers (Mahoney and Thelen 2010).

Historical Institutionalist Perspectives

The idea most fundamental to the historical institutionalist perspective concerns the enduring importance of the founding moment of institutions. Articulated originally by Max Weber (1976), this idea has been adopted, elaborated, and modified by a subsequent line of sociologists. For example, the strength of Duverger's belief in the lasting consequences of a party's origins is reflected in this assertion: "It is the whole life of the party which bears the mark of its origin" (1954: xxxv). Focusing on issues of internal organizational power, Panebianco maintains, "the crucial political choices made by its founding fathers, the first struggles for organizational control, and the way in which the organization was formed, will leave an indelible mark. Few aspects of an organization's functioning and current tensions appear comprehensible if not traced to

---

[1] In its strongest articulation, leadership is about overturning or defeating institutionally derived structures (Katznelson 2003).

its formative phase" (1988: xiii). Emphasizing the lasting role played by a party's original following, Lipset and Rokkan contend that even changes in electoral rules are unlikely to alter the nature of established parties. "[P]arties once established develop their own internal structure and build up long-term commitments among core supporters.... [O]nce [a party] has been established and entrenched, it will prove difficult to change its character simply through variations in the conditions of electoral aggregation" (1967: 30).

Discussions about parties that are "externally mobilized," such as the PT, exemplify the historical institutionalist perspective. In Martin Shefter's definition, "Externally mobilized parties are established by leaders who do *not* occupy positions of power in the prevailing regime and who seek to bludgeon their way into the political system by mobilizing and organizing a mass constituency" (1994: 5). Because such parties are led by individuals with strong ideological commitments, externally mobilized parties will not turn readily into catchall parties willing to get ahead by adjusting to the political winds. Nor are they likely to become patronage machines. "The leaders and cadres of an externally mobilized party ... are likely to be committed to an ideology – a vision of society – and once they come to power, they are not going to be willing to fritter away in patronage the authority they now have to remold society, at least not if it was only with great difficulty that they got hold of that authority" (Shefter 1994: 33).

Lacking access to state patronage at the time of their founding, such parties need to rely on other means to gain a following. Able to count only on themselves, they orient their energies toward long-term organization building and the mobilization of an extensive and committed activist base. In this connection, Shefter (1994), Duverger (1954: xxxiv), and others note that parties that come into existence outside of parliamentary channels are more centralized, cohesive, and disciplined than those that arise within the system and that are more exclusively oriented toward electoral activities. They note also that such parties tend to be characterized by a lasting tension between their parliamentary representatives and their internal leaders, for whom the electoral struggle is only one element in a broader quest for influence. In short, the origins of externally mobilized parties generate strong organizations imbued with an ideological policy-seeking cast.

Reinforcing the propensity for continuity over change is the bureaucratic element of the mass organizations created through previous periods of mobilization, widely thought to produce inertia by limiting the strategic flexibility of such parties (Levitsky 2003: 13–15). Another characteristic of such parties is the emphasis placed on quality over quantity in attracting members and elected officials. Born and designed to survive under difficult conditions, externally mobilized parties expect sacrifice and commitment from their affiliates. Activist recruitment entails high barriers, such as stiff financial donations to the party and membership in its associated social networks. Permission to run on the party label is restricted to those with links to core constituencies and who agree to abide by a variety of stipulations designed to select only the most committed. Carried to an extreme, a "bunker" mentality develops among militants in some externally mobilized parties (Greene 2007: 175). The priority given to building up a deeply devoted following may be fruitful initially but limit their expansion later on.

Although analyses informed by historical institutionalism tend to expect externally mobilized parties to resist adaptation, they also recognize that the very survival of any institution depends on exercising some flexibility and adaptability. The framework therefore allows for a certain degree of change. Many historical institutionalists see innovation as most likely to occur in a punctuated fashion in response to exogenous shocks and significant defeats or failures, a vision articulated well by Stephen Krasner (1988). The tendency toward stickiness and persistence means that change is rare. When it comes it is at a breakpoint and in the form of a dramatic breakthrough. A whole line of analysis that examines party and party system formation and change in the context of "critical junctures" can be seen in this light (Mahoney and Villegas 2007: 79–80). In their study of labor incorporation and regime dynamics in Latin America, Collier and Collier (1991) exemplify the notion that the outcomes of critical junctures – points of dramatic and discontinuous change – translate into lasting legacies. Prominent examples of works in American politics that conceive of change in this way include Carmines and Stimson (1989), Baumgartner and Jones (1993), and Burnham (1999).

A variant within the historical institutionalist tradition conceives of institutional change taking place in a more evolutionary or gradual fashion. Adherents to this view hold that even small events and incremental processes of change can produce transformative results over time (Streeck and Thelen 2005).[2] Prominent examples of such analyses include Schickler (2001), Pierson (2000, 2003), Thelen (2003, 2004), and Mahoney and Thelen (2010). Layering is one form of gradual change.

---

[2] Streeck and Thelen outline five modes of gradual but transformative change: displacement, layering, drift, conversion, and exhaustion (2005: 18–30). See also Mahoney and Thelen (2010).

It refers to the introduction of new rules on top of or alongside existing ones (Schickler 2001; Thelen 2003), and it can bring about substantial change if the amendments, additions, or revisions to existing institutions alter their logic (Mahoney and Thelen 2010: 17; Streeck and Thelen 2005: 24).

Regardless of whether change is seen as dramatic, abrupt, and discontinuous or gradual and cumulative, historical analyses stress institutional stickiness, path dependence, and conflict as an obstacle to change more than do strategic frameworks. A party like the PT would be expected to maintain important traces of its former profile, with residues from the past impeding adaptation to a changing external environment with new opportunities and challenges.

Strategic Frameworks

By comparison, rational-actor frameworks tend to regard politicians and their organizations as unequivocally strategic, more or less unified, and therefore likely to adapt rather quickly and markedly to the economic and institutional environments in which they operate. Existing theory about party strategy in the rational choice tradition generally assumes that politicians compete to win. The best-known encapsulation of this instrumental vision is that "election is the goal of those parties now out of power" and "parties formulate policies in order to win elections, rather than win elections in order to formulate policies" (Downs 1957: 11, 28). In this view, neither leaders nor cadres are expected to place restrictions on their parties' expansion in pursuit of other goals.

For rational choice institutionalists, the opportunities and constraints presented by given institutional arrangements (e.g., electoral rules, the system of government, the degree of state centralization) shape in a decisive manner the strategies and actions of political actors whose overriding priority is to win elections (Cox 1997). Institutions are thought to induce preferences. The expectation is therefore that vote-maximizing parties will eventually converge in adopting dominant strategies that conform to institutional incentives. As with strategic analyses that focus on economic pressures as a catalyst of change and a homogenizing force over time, the assumption of rational choice institutionalism is that the group of primary concern around which parties orient themselves is the electorate, not party militants or members of the party apparatus.

Beyond Downs and Cox, leading proponents of the view that parties are rational and efficient include Wright (1971), Epstein (1986), and

Schlesinger (1991). Emphasizing the competitive struggle in the political marketplace and viewing political leaders as entrepreneurs, they reflect the Americanist tradition of viewing parties as responsive primarily to the electorate and largely ignoring or subordinating issues of program and organization (Wright 1971: 35). Following logically from their utilitarian view of parties, party organization is shaped by political ambition and the quest for electoral success (Schlesinger 1991: 33–46). Because the primary consideration is the appeal of candidates to voters, not organizational service and loyalty, a party's politicians can easily be recruited from outside the party organization.

Although the strongest articulation of such views rests in the Americanist literature, strategic perspectives go well beyond it. In his classic piece on Western European parties in the aftermath of World War II, Kirchheimer (1966) agrees that most parties eventually seek to capture as large a share of the electoral market as they can and are willing and presumably able to dilute their ideological platforms for this purpose. In their seminal study on the trade-offs faced by Western European social democratic parties in trying to expand beyond their original working-class constituencies, Przeworski and Sprague (1986) view the structure of electoral competition as the main obstacle to the realization of socialism. Also addressing the transformation of European social democracy, Wilson (1994) focuses on the role of leadership in whether parties respond effectively to external incentives yet relegates to distinctly secondary status the organizational context in which leaders make their decisions.

In summary, if rational choice suggests that most parties experience a strong pull toward vote maximization and that they tend to respond in a fairly uniform fashion to similar external pressures and systemic incentives, then historical institutionalism predicts greater variability: Even parties that undergo some strategic modification will continue to bear important traces of their past. Rather than succumbing to the homogenizing effects of a competitive logic of interests, parties will continue to be highly influenced by the conditions surrounding their formation, the paths and sequences they pursued earlier in time, and inherited organizational legacies. Despite modifications, important aspects of a party's original profile will still be recognizable. When adaptation occurs, it will probably be halting, uneven, and replete with intraorganizational tension. Groups that cling to the past will resist those seeking renovation. Often a generational divide exists; those who joined earlier and under less favorable conditions harbor a "bunker" mentality that is far less pronounced among those who joined later and under more open conditions.

Studies that Integrate Strategic with Historical Analysis

Although many of the leading studies in the literature on political parties stress either the determining role of political ambition and electoral contexts in party adaptation or the effects of internal organization in impeding change, some important studies integrate strategic and organizational perspectives. In so doing they recognize the complexity of party change. For example, Herbert Kitschelt (1994) sees electoral defeat in the wake of changing social structures as a key force behind the reorientation of social democratic party strategies in Europe, yet he appreciates that organizational structures affect their adaptive capacity. In a historical institutionalist vein he notes, "Most likely, these changes do not amount to a wholesale replacement of existing arrangements but an incremental adjustment that blends existing routines with new operating procedures" (1994: 217). Indeed, mass bureaucratic social democratic parties were slow to adapt in Western Europe.

Writing on Peronism in Argentina, Steven Levitsky (2001) recognizes the unevenness of party adaptation in observing that traditional Peronism and its organizational structure remained largely intact at the provincial level despite the striking market-oriented turn of the national leadership. Although the PJ (Justicialist Party) is conventionally viewed as having been transformed from above in the 1990s, in fact its provincial organizations became neither neoliberal nor much subject to the influence of President Carlos Menem. Continuity within the party's provincial branches helps explain the rapid erosion of Menem's influence within the party after he left office in 1999.

Writing on Mexico in the 1980s and 1990s, Kenneth Greene (2007) examines the failure of opposition parties to present a more formidable challenge to the dominant PRI (Institutional Revolutionary Party). Constrained by their origins, the PAN (National Action Party) and the PRD (Party of the Democratic Revolution) did not broaden their appeal as much as one might expect in light of increasing dissatisfaction with the PRI after the 1982 economic crisis. Both were "niche parties" whose early joiners had created protective structures that limited them from reaching out to new voters once opportunities for expansion arose. Yet despite these structures, presidential ambition, extraparty political support, and the independent economic base of Vicente Fox led him to circumvent the PAN and ultimately defeat decades of PRI dominance.

This study of the PT follows in the tradition of works that combine strategic and historical analysis. While emphasizing the former's ability to explain the very notable adaptations that the PT made, it also problematizes theoretically the issue of partial adaptation, whereby parties undergo changes in some arenas and on some dimensions more than others. The analysis takes as a point of departure the external forces (economic and institutional) that motivated the PT to adapt, noting also how differential institutional arenas unleashed varying electoral incentives. At the same time it pays central attention to the internal commitments and structures that both facilitated and impeded change. Systematically disaggregating the phenomenon of party adaptation, the analysis recognizes the unevenness of change according to external versus internal considerations and suggests an expected sequence of adaptation: Parties subject to strong exogenous pressures are likely to first make modifications on matters immediately relevant for enhancing their electoral appeal, such as softening their most radical policy stances and images, listening more to voters via opinion polls, marketing the images of their leaders, and forging broader alliances. They are slower to proceed on matters of internal dynamics and organization, such as changing the rules to diminish the weight of the party bureaucracy and instituting new requirements and expectations for assuming membership and political office.[3] Finally, they may not change at all on norms that were vital to sustaining the organization during its early formation and that do not immediately affect the party's electoral standing at a later point in time. Whereas a strategic perspective explains shifts of the first type, that is, on the external front, insights from historical institutionalism shed light on the stickiness encountered on the internal front.

PLACING THE PT IN THEORETICAL CONTEXT

The PT is an interesting case to analyze for these debates because it began as a highly ideological party and resisted the adoption of vote-maximizing measures for quite some time. Its organizational characteristics – high barriers to recruitment and affiliation, low leadership autonomy, and burdensome rules of decision making – militated against strategic flexibility. Based on these factors, the PT was an unlikely case for significant transformation. At the same time, the PT developed in a political system that contained strong institutional incentives for normalization and in

---

[3] This accords with the observation by Michael Coppedge (2001) that "the nature of individual party organizations – centralization, discipline, cohesion, recruitment, mobilization, socialization, financing – seems to change very slowly, if at all."

an economic context that promoted convergence. Would organizational variables, which suggested resistance to change, or environmental factors, which predicted adaptation, prevail in influencing the direction of things to come?

Institutional Legacies of the PT

The PT's origins conform well to Shefter's conception of an externally mobilized party. Formed in 1980 by a heterogeneous grassroots coalition of labor organizers, Christian-base communities, and leftist intellectuals, the PT struggled hard from outside the official political system against the military dictatorship of 1964–1985 in its waning years. Working against the odds of opposition party formation during the time, activists went to great lengths to have the party officially registered and recognized. Growing out of a labor movement whose organizers risked life and limb to challenge Brazil's system of corporatist regulations in the late 1970s, the PT went on to help found a landless movement that eventually became the largest and best organized of its kind in Latin America, the MST (*Movimento dos Trabalhadores Rurais Sem Terra*, or Movement of Landless Rural Workers).[4] In 1984 it also helped to mobilize masses of citizens in favor of direct presidential elections to usher in the country's new democracy. Indeed, the PT is often described as the only Brazilian party to have truly formed through societal mobilization and not elite politics (Mainwaring 1999: 100).

The PT's organizational structure is that of a mass bureaucratic party. Combining the goal of widespread membership participation with the strong organization and authority necessary to ensure the party's initial survival and growth, the PT established a centralized organization of party committees and structures that reached down from the national to state and local levels.[5] Decisions of the national organization would take precedence over those of local and state units. Having to consult with and gain the approval of the party bureaucracy (most importantly, the

---

[4] See Ondetti (2008).
[5] Each municipality has its members elect a Municipal Directory, which in turn chooses the Municipal Executive Committee. Parallel processes take place on the state and national levels. Municipal level delegates elect state delegates, who in turn elect delegates to the national meeting. Each state is allowed to send at least one delegate to the national meeting, and more depending on the number of active party members in that state. Those delegates elect the eighty-four-member National Directorate, which in turn elects the twenty-eight-member National Executive Committee.

National Directorate and the National Executive Committee), all candidates (including several-time presidential candidate Lula) and elected officials enjoyed limited autonomy on matters that affected the direction of the party in a central way. Deliberation was encouraged but ultimately the rules of democratic centralism were expected to hold.

From the outset, the expected obligations of members filtered out all but the truly committed. To maintain a considerable degree of ideological coherence, the PT required candidates to sign a "Commitment to PT Principles," which included the notion that parliamentary mandates belonged to the party and not to individuals.[6] To maintain linkages with civil society, it stipulated that candidates should have a history of involvement in union activities or social movements.[7] To further ensure a connection to the PT's grassroots origins, candidates were required to garner a certain level of support at relevant state and local party meetings. If they won, the expectation was that they give to the party a substantial portion of their monthly salary, as much as 30 percent in the case of federal legislators.[8] Effectively keeping outsiders from running on the party ticket, such hurdles were nonexistent in the catchall parties. As Mainwaring writes, "[t]he catch-all parties are generally oblivious to the ideological predilections of individuals who want to use the label. They accept a broad range of candidates without making ideological or organizational demands" (1999: 148). Although instrumental in building up a dedicated core following in the early life of the party, these provisions could be predicted to hinder the PT's ability to innovate and undergo adaptation later on. At the very least, it is not difficult to imagine that the same individuals willing to make the sacrifices just described would have strong reservations about making the adjustments necessary to appeal to a wider audience, and vice versa, that those willing to undertake pragmatic adaptations would not want to be hemmed in by such stringent organizational rules and demands.

---

[6] This pledge prohibited aspiring candidates from ever using the uniquely Brazilian provision of the *candidato nato* (birthright candidate), which allowed an incumbent deputy an automatic slot on the party list at reelection time (without the party's approval).
[7] A document approved at the second national meeting of the party in 1982 also specifies that candidates were required to fulfill at least one of the following criteria: participation in the labor movement, activism in a grassroots movement associated with the party, or involvement in the founding of the party. See Partido dos Trabalhadores (1998b: 133).
[8] In 2002, the maximum contribution required from top politicians dropped to 20 percent of their monthly salary. See Partido dos Trabalhadores (2003: 22). The maximum required for other parties is 3 percent.

Institutional Aspects of Brazil's Political System

The PT would develop in the broader context of a political system with strong pressures to erode its organizational distinctiveness. What features characterize the institutional context of competition in Brazil, and what predictions about rational party strategies can be derived from them? In general, the country's politicians face a landscape of high party system fragmentation, low partisan identification, and strong orientations toward personalism and pork barrel, characteristics that have received ample treatment in the literature on political parties in Brazil (Mainwaring 1999; Ames 2001). The open-list feature of the system of proportional representation for lower house elections, which weakens parties as collective organizations, exacerbates these characteristics.[9] Whereas the element of electoral design for election to the Chamber of Deputies permitted the party to grow in that arena under a clear left profile, the need to capture an electoral majority to win the presidency and mayoral office in large municipalities unleashed strong incentives toward moderation. This was especially the case because Brazil's political system as a whole strongly encourages the pursuit of executive over legislative office (Samuels 2003; Amorim Neto 2005). Carrying extensive prerogatives, the presidency is by far the most coveted position (Shugart and Carey 1992: 155; Mainwaring 1997). The strong quest for presidential office came to dominate decision making within the PT and influence the programs and images the party assumed.

Winning Brazil's presidency requires a candidate to capture a majority of votes in a direct popular election, at least in a runoff. The same holds true for gubernatorial races and (since 1992) mayoral contests in municipalities with more than 200,000 voters. In general, the majority requirement puts at greatest disadvantage those candidates furthest from the political center, thereby providing an incentive for parties to undergo a centrist shift, especially in the second round.[10] The special challenge facing candidates for executive office is to meet this high threshold of support in a system of such pronounced party fragmentation and fluidity.

---

[9] Other factors thought to contribute to party fragmentation include runoff elections, low barriers for party registration, and easy access to radio and television advertising (Geddes and Ribeiro Neto 1992).

[10] There is a clear trend in the region away from plurality and toward runoff systems, with reduced thresholds in some instances (Payne, Zovatto, and Mateo Díaz 2007: 23). Lanzaro (2010) argues that the establishment of a majority runoff in Uruguay in 1996 was intended to induce the radical left to moderate.

Given the low rates of partisan identification and the shallow ideological roots of parties in society, presidential candidates have few constituencies on which they can consistently rely. Especially in combination with weak parties, the majoritarian feature of presidential elections suggests a dominant strategy for parties whose foremost goal is vote seeking. Such parties will (1) adhere to watered down mainstream messages rather than promote ideological programs; (2) pursue electoral alliances across the political spectrum; (3) put forth candidates with widespread personal appeal, hiring consultants to better market them; (4) closely track and conform to trends in public opinion, often with the help of professional pollsters; and (5) base political campaigns on the projection of slick images and the distribution of material goods rather than on substantive ideas and platforms, a strategy that requires ample financing. In short, faced with the institutional constraints just described, vote-maximizing parties can be expected to moderate their policy positions and adopt other aspects of a catchall or electoral-professional strategy. How the PT moved in this direction while preserving some of its core organizational features is taken up in the next section.

POLICY SEEKING AND DIFFERENCE UNTIL THE MID-1990S

Long resisting the pull of these institutional incentives, the PT initially pursued a radical leftist program and concentrated on building a strong organization. Even the most pragmatic elements within the party – the *Articulação* faction linked to Lula and his fellow trade unionists – rejected vote maximization and adaptation to the incentives of the political environment as the PT's catchall competitors understood them. In fact, Lula cautioned repeatedly, "[w]e must not let electoral concerns take over the party's agenda" (Machado and Vannuchi 1991: 6, author's translation). He insisted that electoral losses were not necessarily political defeats if the PT managed to get its name out and promote the party's programs.

The PT developed a highly distinctive organizational and programmatic profile in the initial years of its existence. Notwithstanding some signs of moderation on the programmatic front between the early and late 1980s, this profile was maintained more or less intact until the mid-1990s. Strictly enforced organizational rules governed wide-ranging aspects of the conduct of party members, bureaucrats, and elected officials. Members made financial sacrifices to the party and engaged in long-term organization building. Drawing on the labor and financial sacrifices of activists, there was a strong mobilizational aspect to campaigns. In line with these developments, the party experienced a steady growth of a partisan following independent of Lula's personal popularity (Carreirão and Kinzo 2004; Samuels 2006a). Party cadres played a crucial role in influencing party programs, alliance policy, and candidate selection. They engaged in extensive consultations with the party's elected officials and sometimes blocked their preferences. The party orientation of the PT's elected officials – reflected, for example, in the high rates of cohesion, discipline, and loyalty displayed by its legislative delegation – was without parallel (Mainwaring and Pérez-Liñán 1998; Melo 2000; Souza 2004; Hagopian 2005; Leal 2005; Roma 2005). Indeed, *petistas* (PT activists) remained true to their organization at a time when legislators from other parties defied the directives of their leaders, engaged in rampant party switching, and forged coalitions in line with shifting political calculations. The media highlighted these opportunistic practices and their deleterious effects on governability and citizen well-being, giving the PT a perfect way to separate itself from the crowd.

The PT distinguished itself in programmatic terms by its insistent promotion of state-led development and management (couched in terms of socialism, albeit ambiguously defined) and redistributive reforms, such as agrarian reform. The emerging discussion of economic restructuring saw the party assume a leading role in opposing trade liberalization, privatization, deregulation, labor "flexibilization," and measures to institute greater fiscal efficiency in the social sectors. The PT adopted pro-labor, anti-foreign-capital positions in the Constituent Assembly (1987–1988), called for socialism in Lula's 1989 and 1994 presidential bids (even proposing a complete nationalization of the financial sector in 1989), fiercely opposed President Fernando Collor's pursuit of market reforms (1990–1992), and rejected many of the "neoliberal" reform proposals ultimately implemented under the first government of President Cardoso (1995–1998). Efforts to promote citizen participation and government transparency through schemes like participatory budgeting, and attempts to combat clientelism and corruption, contributed further to the PT's unique programmatic profile during a time when the twin maladies of clientelism and corruption drew heated public attention through numerous high-profile scandals. While the party sought zealously to expose and hold guilty parties accountable in national corruption scandals, PT policies at the municipal level aimed to make governmental decision making more transparent to the public (Avritzer and Navarro 2002; Baiocchi 2005; Wampler 2004). In short, for most of its existence in the opposition, the PT met unequivocally the key criteria to be considered a left party. In the words of Herbert Kitschelt (1989: 2), parties that are left wing in the socialist tradition "affirm solidarity and equality and reject the primacy of markets and allocative efficiency as the final arbiters of social development and justice." Like the ecology parties of Western Europe, however, this focus may be combined with "calling for a society in which individual autonomy and citizen participation in public affairs have high priority" (Kitschelt 1989).

As part of its desire to keep a strong identity, protect itself from outside influences, and maintain programmatic coherence, the PT also observed a restricted alliance policy. Until the mid-1990s, including in the 1989 and 1994 presidential elections, it joined exclusively with parties on the left. This differentiated the PT not only from major parties on the right, such as the PFL (Party of the Liberal Front), but also from its main center-left competitor, the PSDB (Party of Brazilian Social Democracy), and leftist rival, the PDT (Democratic Labor Party).

Understanding the PT's Distinctiveness

Why did party leaders initially follow a policy seeking approach, manifested most visibly in the special niche of statist economics and party-oriented politics that they carved out and defended? Why did they advocate raising public consciousness and promoting the party's label and programs instead of conforming to preexisting public opinion, making strategic alliances with nonleft parties, and turning toward patronage? No doubt these were individuals with strong ideological commitments, motivated enough to have defied the military regime but a few years earlier. All indications are that most *petistas* believed firmly in the developmental and redistributive task of the state and opposed vehemently the clientelistic and personalistic orientation of Brazilian politics. There were also conditions present that made the strategy seem minimally viable. In other words, there was a certain compatibility between remaining true to the party's historic goals and organization and thinking that such an approach had a reasonable foundation on which to bear fruit. What made *petistas* think that radical change would be possible to enact in Brazil, a new democracy that was dominated by the civilian heirs of the military regime and that was born precisely when socialism was faltering internationally?

A Belief in the Viability of Socialism

Party leaders did not immediately regard the fall of socialism in Eastern Europe as signaling the end of their transformative project. They were not altogether daunted by the international developments of the late 1980s, in part because the PT's socialist aspirations had never followed the Soviet model anyway. A focus on the many advantages Brazil enjoyed with respect to an inward-looking development strategy – a large population, diverse resource endowment, and a well-developed state sector – helped sustain such hopes. State-led development had experienced considerable successes in Brazil. For example, many public enterprises had been engines of modernization, growth, and even social mobility. Lula noted publicly that capitalism had not addressed the misery that existed in the country and that the PT's historic role would be to construct a "socialismo brasileiro" based on the specific structural advantages Brazil enjoyed (Mendes 2004: 29). The exceedingly poor macroeconomic performance of 1987 to 1993 and the precarious governability that accompanied it created an atmosphere of volatility that seemed to leave the door open for a major reorientation of economic policy. In this period, average gross domestic product or GDP growth was less than zero and inflation was out of control, averaging 1,300 percent annually from 1987 to 1992 and spiking to nearly 2,500 percent in 1993 (Power forthcoming).

A Quest for Political Transformation

Party leaders wanted voters to follow their lead rather than having the PT follow voters and their preexisting preferences. They also had faith in the intrinsic appeal that their redistributive platform would have in a country of record socioeconomic inequality. Their hope was to impart the PT's message and outlook to the poor (Sampaio 1989), who by virtue of sheer numbers exert a greater impact on electoral results than do their more economically privileged counterparts. Although aware that the party's core support base rested with organized interests, intellectuals, and progressive middle-class urbanites in the industrial states of the South and Southeast, the leadership hoped that the uncompromising advocacy of equity-enhancing structural reforms would eventually pry other voters away from patronage-wielding politicians and help the party advance into poorer regions of the country.

Similarly, they saw the loose attachment of citizens to other parties, a sign of weak institutionalization in the party system, as a condition that would help them gather support for their radical program. Far less than half of the electorate expressed a preference for any party in 1989. Among the large group of voters with only a primary school education, that number was closer to 30 percent (Carreirão and Kinzo 2004: 141). Brazil's dense civil society promised to facilitate the PT's goal of collective

Strategic Change or Organizational Persistence?

empowerment.[11] Party militants viewed their links to preexisting organizational networks as a way to reach large numbers of people. Groups that the social movements of the 1960s and 1970s had mobilized, such as Christian-base communities, trade unions, and urban neighborhood organizations, held particular potential in this regard. Party leaders hoped that such organized networks would give the PT a reliable support base.[12] In this connection, PT leader José Dirceu asserted that "[w]e are confident of eventual victory because the PT is a party with a history, militance, and a popular base" (author's translation).[13]

The PT leadership was obviously aware that garnering a majority of votes to win the presidency on a radical platform would be a tall order. Yet politics in Brazil was still quite fluid in the late 1980s and early 1990s, reinforcing the party's "anything is possible" outlook. Party volatility and other signs of weak institutionalization abounded amidst a broader climate of social mobilization. Party strategists regarded Lula's strong showing against Fernando Collor in the 1989 presidential contest as evidence that it was possible to capture executive power by promising Brazilian voters far-reaching change. In that runoff, Lula secured 47 percent of all valid votes. Only subsequently did they attribute Lula's performance to circumstances particular to that campaign, namely the fact that Brazilian voters faced two polar alternatives and many who would not have ordinarily been drawn to Lula found themselves hard pressed to endorse his populist right-wing competitor, who was a son of the military regime.[14] Considering that Lula's first-round vote share was only 17.2 percent, his core support was quite low.

The Benefits of Differentiation

One important consequence of the PT's policy-seeking stage was that it built a cadre of committed activists, a process no doubt enhanced by its

---

[11] Brazilian society is considered relatively well organized (Encarnación 2003): Rates of church affiliation are comparatively high (Hagopian 2008; McDonough, Shin, and Moisés 1998), trade union membership has remained steadier than in other countries that have undergone market reform (Roberts forthcoming), and neighborhood organizations abound in a cross-section of the country's cities.

[12] Many of the insights in this paragraph come from an author interview with Paulo Vannuchi, a founding member of the party and Special Minister of Human Rights under the Lula government. This interview took place in Brasília on August 17, 2006.

[13] "Confiança na vitória," *Jornal do Brasil*, August 29, 1997.

[14] This was reported to me in an author interview with Luis Gushiken in Brasília on August 14, 2006. Gushiken was president of the PT from 1988 to 1990 and served several terms as PT deputy.

distinctiveness. Surveys of specific groups conducted around the 1989 and 1994 elections, such as Catholics linked to Christian-base communities,[15] union affiliates (especially those from the labor confederation closely associated with the PT),[16] and members of the landless movement[17] reveal overwhelming support for Lula in these years. A poll conducted just before the 1994 presidential election shows that 88 percent of those expressing a partisan preference for the PT intended to vote for Lula. That they supported Lula strongly over Cardoso even in an election that the latter was able to sweep – as a result of the wildly successful stabilization plan (*Plano Real*) he had devised as finance minister – testifies powerfully to their loyalty. It is highly doubtful that a more "watered down" PT could have consolidated such a following.

What impact did the PT's distinctive status have outside of this core following of militants? At the very least, it helped make the PT a household name and gave Brazilians a sense of what the party stood for. A survey conducted in February of 1994 shows that more people expressed a familiarity with Lula than with any other contemporary politician, including Fernando Henrique Cardoso.[18] The same survey put forth a list of parties and for each party asked respondents to say whether they favored it, opposed it, or had no basis for an opinion. The PT elicited the clearest opinions (positive and negative) second only to the PMDB (Party of the Brazilian Democratic Movement). The PT's emphasis on social equity resonated among people who were not necessarily *petistas* but who reported voting for the party in 1989 and 1994. In one survey, respondents who expressed a vote intention for the PT in the 1989 presidential election ranked as their highest motivation Lula's commitment to social goals, such as bettering the lives of workers and the poor (Carreirão 2002: 89). A similar pattern shows up for the 1994 election. Lula voters attached higher salience to issues like hunger and unemployment than did supporters of other candidates (Almeida 1996: 192–193) and noted "Lula's concern for socio-economic problems" as one of the principal reasons for selecting him (Carreirão 2002: 130).

From these perspectives, the PT's left strategy during the 1980s and early 1990s was not irrational. Indeed, there was a "logic of difference"

---

[15] Pierucci and Prandi (1995) compare Catholics organized into base communities with those who were not. Support for Lula and the PT among the former in the 1994 presidential election was nearly universal. Unorganized Catholics showed an average propensity to vote for Lula.
[16] Datafolha poll, no. 00730, August 1997.
[17] Datafolha poll, no. 00806, February 1997.
[18] IBOPE poll, no. 339, February 1994.

(Keck 1991). The political and economic environment was fluid and uncertain. The economy was weak and the party system was highly unstable. In such a context, the optimal vote-seeking strategy was unclear. The PT also benefited in important ways from a left strategy. It built strong organizational networks and established itself as a distinctive brand. It made steady albeit slow electoral progress in legislative and municipal politics by unifying behind clear alternative positions on major economic and political cleavages and restricting its alliances to within the left. By forgoing a more meteoric political ascendance, the party managed to retain a core identity and not be sucked into the corrupting whirlpool of Brazilian politics. Some observers even went so far as to argue that the PT was inducing other parties to become more programmatic, especially with regard to the state–market dimension (e.g., Rosas and Zechmeister 2000).

Factors Motivating Change

A systematic set of factors that became especially pronounced in the second half of the 1990s motivated the PT to place ever greater emphasis on vote seeking and become more like other Brazilian parties. The timing and deliberate nature of the PT's ideological moderation and adoption of other catchall behaviors conform to a strategic understanding of change. It was specific contextual and historical factors that modified the party's preferences and shifted its behavior. An especially serious reassessment occurred in the wake of Lula's loss to Cardoso in the 1994 presidential election. If party leaders had previously interpreted key economic and political factors as making possible a socialist transformation of society, by the mid-1990s they recognized and slowly accepted the hard constraints imposed by the international political economy and by Brazil's political institutions. With the decision to jettison their project of far-reaching change and abide by the institutional parameters of competition for election to the presidency and other majoritarian offices, the party shifted its programmatic positions and adopted other features of parties within the electoral-professional model, such as political marketing and image making. Meanwhile, most core organizational features of the PT remained intact.

Economic Limitations to Socialist Transformation

If the PT had not advanced further when socialism was still seen as a viable alternative and significant fluidity–volatility existed in the electoral system, party leaders were forced to admit even greater challenges by the second half of the 1990s. Brazil's adoption of market reform was a crucial external factor that motivated the party to change course. The party's radical program, which included proposals to nationalize leading industries and launch a major land reform, had placed the PT on the far left end of the political spectrum and distribution of voter preferences. By the mid-1990s, however, the *Articulação* leadership observed that important segments of the citizenry favored key aspects of market reform, rendering a far-left position untenable electorally.

Surveys showed public opinion to be especially favorable toward free trade. Over two-thirds of Brazilians persistently supported free trade in the fifteen-year period following the initiation of Collor's trade liberalization. That Brazil was extremely closed to consumer-goods imports throughout the era of ISI (Import Substitution Industrialization), widely understood to have elevated prices and lowered quality, shaped public opinion positively toward reversing this situation (Baker 2009: 211–214, 224–225). Similarly, a large majority favored foreign investment. Polls suggested that most Brazilians associated foreign direct investment with visible consumer benefits and comparatively well-paying jobs (Baker 2009: 214–215, 226). Moreover, they cited foreign firms as better managed than their domestic counterparts (Lafer and Lottenberg 1992: 72–73; Nóbrega 1992: 33–34). As for privatization, support reached higher levels in Brazil than in many other Latin American countries, although it was always lower than for free trade and foreign investment (Baker 2003, 2009). In the mid-1990s, a majority of the population supported sell-offs in sectors deemed nonessential to citizens' basic welfare or to national sovereignty.

Cementing the PT's decision to conform to (rather than try to change) public opinion on market reform was the recognition that actually *reversing* the liberalizations begun by Fernando Collor and furthered by Fernando Henrique Cardoso would be too costly and controversial, too distant from the average Brazilian's preference.[19] Thus, as one member of Lula's inner circle emphasized, it was not abstract deliberations about the demise of international socialism that convinced party leaders to shift course. Instead, the fact that economic restructuring was already well underway and had generated positive effects on public opinion, which was recognized and digested only with time, led pragmatic leaders to set

---

[19] "Falta auto-estima," *Veja*, August 12, 1998.

aside the PT's historic project and replace social transformation with the pursuit of power.[20]

Even after the new market model faltered in the late 1990s, manifested in anemic growth, unemployment, and financial crisis, roughly two-thirds of all Brazilians agreed with the view that only with a market economy could Brazil become a developed country (Latinobarómetro 2005). Moreover, specific events spoke volumes about public opinion in general on such issues. For example, citizens were outraged when PT Governor of Rio Grande do Sul Olívio Dutra (1999–2002) drove such a hard bargain with Ford Motor Company that its executives decided against installing a multimillion-dollar plant in the state. The loss of Ford's investment and the media play that surrounded it, which focused on foregone employment opportunities for state residents, was a political disaster for Dutra and no doubt a setback for the PT's reputation as well (Nelson 2003: 293–294).

Political Limitations to Radical Transformation

Although a strategy of differentiation had helped the PT consolidate a core following, there were downsides to this course, especially if the party wanted to win the presidency in the foreseeable future. Party leaders were forced to recognize that consciousness raising and organization building would be much slower processes than they had imagined. Poverty and inequality, however egregious, did not translate readily into support for the party. The electorate was fragmented and not very ideological.[21] Most voters in the higher income and education brackets did not lean strongly to the left. Furthermore, those at the lower ends – who by virtue of compulsory voting would turn out in numbers roughly proportional to their large population size – appeared even less open to the PT's partisan project and more concerned with acquiring concrete material benefits sooner rather than later.

A sequence of electoral defeats fueled discussions of the limitations entailed in the party's radicalism, especially in majoritarian races

---

[20] Author interview with Luis Gushiken.
[21] According to the World Values Survey, only 30 percent of all respondents placed themselves on the left in 1991 and 27 percent did so in 1997. In the latter year, a full 50 percent placed themselves on the right. Using data from the Latinobarómetro 2002, Colomer (2005: 21) shows that 32 percent of all respondents placed themselves on the left in 2002 and 39 percent placed themselves on the right. A full 29 percent placed themselves exactly in the center.

(Almeida 1996: 44). In fact, the poorest and least educated sectors of society voted decisively *against* Lula and for the conservative populist Fernando Collor in 1989 (Singer 1990), leading pragmatists to conclude that there were firm limits to a party-based strategy of grassroots mobilization aimed at progressive macrosocietal change. In 1994, the evaporation of Lula's early lead over Fernando Henrique Cardoso with the success of the inflation-reducing *Plano Real* suggested that the PT's promises to combat deep structural causes of poverty and inequality (e.g., unequal land distribution) were much less attractive to poor voters than immediate albeit limited improvements (Meneguello 1995). In another majoritarian context – gubernatorial races – the party did extremely poorly. For example, of the nineteen PT candidates who competed in the 1994 gubernatorial races, only nine managed to win more than 10 percent of all valid votes and only three (all from the party's moderate wing) made it to the second round. Even when it came to the best opportunity possible for the election of radicals – contests decided by proportional representation to fill federal Chamber seats from the industrial states of the South and Southeast – it was those PT politicians with moderate profiles who tended to get elected.[22] Pragmatists argued that if radicalism hurt the party in this context, it was especially unrealistic to expect the PT to prevail in majoritarian races involving higher concentrations of conservative voters. Clearly, they argued, an electorally driven PT needed to be more attuned to the preferences of the electorate and to attract more support from demographic groups that leaned systematically toward more conservative options: the least educated and poorest segments of the population, residents of small towns and rural areas, the elderly, and women.

Improved governance also set serious limits on a strategy aimed at radical change. The reduction of inflation and the overall stabilization of the economy under Cardoso, accompanied by an institutional strengthening of the state, made it difficult to launch a frontal attack on the administration and come out ahead.[23] The decisive first-round reelection that Cardoso won in 1998 reinforced this conclusion. Enhanced governability –

---

[22] Author interviews with two key actors from opposing sides of the moderate–radical divide – José Genoino and Valter Pomar – confirmed the importance of electoral defeats in the party's decision to moderate. Genoino was president of the PT from 2002 to 2005 and was elected to the Chamber on the PT ticket several times. Pomar has been a long-standing party militant and high-ranking cadre. The interview with Genoino took place in São Paulo on August 8, 2006. I interviewed Pomar in São Paulo on August 3, 2006. See also "Baixos Teores de Radicalismo," *IstoÉ*, November 2, 1994, and "Bancada quer tomar dos radicais commando do PT," *Jornal de Brasília*, October 19, 1994.

[23] For a discussion of how improvements in the Brazilian economy resonated with the public, see Armijo, Faucher, and Dembinska (2006).

reflected in factors ranging from lower levels of ministerial turnover,[24] a decline in corruption, and a downward trend in party system volatility[25] – suggested a state and party system undergoing consolidation. The convergence of better economic performance and better governance precluded the possibility of the successful rise of political outsiders promising sweeping change.

The perception of new opportunities presented by the landscape of competition reinforced the rationale for a gradual move toward the center by the mid-1990s. Before then, spatial dynamics had constrained the party's room for maneuver. The social-democratic character of the PSDB – a party full of experienced high-profile politicians and reputable technocrats – made it difficult for the PT to present itself and compete successfully on center-left terms.[26] However, after 1993 the PSDB (the party's main opponent at the national level) moved to the right (Power 1998). Its advocacy of market reform and the alliance it struck with the conservative PFL marked the start of this rightward drift. Governing Brazil for the next eight years would reinforce the PSDB's moderation and adoption of clientelistic tactics. In addition, especially because the lack of serious competition to its left meant that undertaking a centrist move would not exact a cost as far as retaining left voters, the newly available space in the center left presented itself as an invitation with the PT's name on it. Together with the recognized limitations of staying on the far left, spatial dynamics and the possibility of success that these opened up lured the PT onto a more mainstream course. This would render the PT much more susceptible to the institutional pressures and incentives for building electoral support in Brazil.

To the extent the economic and electoral environment shaped the incentives for party leaders to undertake adaptive strategies and tactics, other factors affected their ability to institute these changes. Lula's role

---

[24] Many indicators suggested growing state institutionalization. Key among them was lower ministerial turnover. Most notably, whereas Brazil had thirteen finance ministers between 1985 and 1994, Cardoso had the same minister of finance (Pedro Malan) during his entire tenure in office (1995–2002). Similarly, whereas there were nine ministers of education between 1985 and 1994, Cardoso kept the same minister (Paulo Renato Souza) during his eight years in office.

[25] See Panizza (2000: 515) for a discussion of how political competition became more structured over the 1990s, and Power (forthcoming) for figures on the decline of electoral volatility after 1994.

[26] Paraphrasing one PT senator, "Competing against credible centrist opponents put us in a difficult situation. We preferred polarized races in which we faced an openly right-wing competitor." Author interview with Ana Julia Carepa, former PT senator and former PT governor of Pará. The interview took place in Brasília on August 12, 2003.

in advocating change and facilitating adaptation was crucial. Notwithstanding the PT's institutionalization and mass structures, it had a single leader who was and remains more popular than the party. Without this, it seems improbable that the PT would have adapted so successfully. The source of Lula's influence lay in the widely held conviction among *petistas* that Lula was the only figure in the party who could conceivably win the presidency as a result of a unique ability to bridge the organized sectors of the developed South and the informal poor in the Northeast and other outlying areas. Lula's historic status as a labor leader who emerged in the ABC district of São Paulo and opposed the military regime in its last years gave him clout with the former. At the same time, his humble Northeastern origins endowed him with an ability to relate to common people from that region. Moreover, as a founding member and long-standing leader within the PT, Lula had the authority to convince a wide range of party militants that he could win presidential office if only they would go along with the measures he advocated for change. These factors would prove to be a winning combination.[27]

The plurality of groups constituting the PT lent itself to some diversity of opinion, openness to new ideas, and shifting factional control. As Kitschelt observes, "electoral defeats have a greater impact on changes of party strategy if the party has been open to ideological pluralism already at an earlier point of time" (1994: 222). Also affording the PT a degree of flexibility was the fact that it was never formally beholden to organized labor in the same way that some socialist parties are. Notwithstanding considerable overlap among union leaders, party activists, and party politicians, the PT did not depend on labor economically. Nor did labor enjoy a privileged place in the party's decision-making structures.

RESPONDING TO EXTERNAL INCENTIVES AND INTERNAL EXIGENCIES: STRATEGIC ADAPTATION AND PATH DEPENDENCE

A shift toward vote seeking compelled the leadership to negotiate changes in the PT's strategy in line with the constraints and inducements already discussed here (Almeida 1997; Dulci 1997). Although Lula and his closest allies in the party underwent a major rethinking in the mid-1990s, they did not institute transformations all at once. Instead, change followed

---

[27] Felipe González is an interesting parallel of someone who drew on his popularity among the electorate and within the party to gain acceptance for measures that encountered strong internal opposition. See Share (1999: 105–107) for an interesting discussion of the role of the political leadership of Felipe González in guiding the adaptation of the Spanish Socialist Workers' Party (PSOE).

a model of layering. The nature of change within the PT suggests that the firmer and more entrenched the organization, the less change takes the form of "wholesale replacement" and the more it takes the form of layering. Innovation was negotiated, with many alterations secured via addition, that is, by placing new elements on top of or alongside established ones instead of displacing them altogether. It was not a clean and quick break but rather a process full of tensions and contradictions. In the end, the PT did reorient first and markedly on measures that concerned its relations with the public, namely those most directly and obviously linked to expanding its vote share. Bearing out the expectations of a strategic perspective, it moved to the center programmatically, toned down its militant image, hired political pollsters and marketing agents, fielded candidates high on personal appeal, and made opportunistic alliances with other parties.

At the same time, pragmatic leaders who pursued adaptation did not always bring the party fully in line with systemic incentives. The PT retained its historic uniqueness with respect to core internal practices, for example, making sure that candidates aspiring to run under the PT label had some link to the party's grassroots base, expecting high discipline and loyalty of its legislators, requiring that officeholders make sizable donations to the party, and retaining the considerable influence of party cadres and not just elected officials in party decisions. These not only lay at the heart of the party's externally mobilized origins but also bore a less immediate relationship to expanding its vote share. Several concerned building up and maintaining the organization from the inside by means of the sacrifices of affiliates while protecting it from the incursions of outsiders with unclear loyalties. Others maintained the standing of well-established groups within the organization, preventing their displacement by those in search of change. Thus, although the pursuit of votes did cause the PT to become more catchall in character, its transformation was incomplete. The party's efforts to adapt to external pressures bear out a strategic understanding of politics. Some of the gaps in its adaptation reflect the influence of historical legacies. This mixed picture calls for integrating insights from rational choice institutionalism with ideas from historical institutionalism.

Aspects of Adaptation and Normalization

Programmatic Adaptation. In a major programmatic shift, the party publicly acknowledged the benefits of having Brazil conform to international market trends. This occurred first with Lula's third run for the presidency in 1998. The trend was accentuated in a striking fashion in the 2002 campaign. Beyond omitting the word *socialism* from the party's electoral program, a notable sign of moderation was the promise to adhere to Brazil's existing agreements with the International Monetary Fund (IMF), widely seen as the ultimate enforcer of global capitalism. Retaining some "product differentiation," the party continued to underscore its commitment to poverty reduction and equity enhancement yet through policies well within the existing system. These included job creation, substantial increases in the minimum wage, and a minimum income provision. These and related measures were less ideologically charged and would deliver immediate tangible gains to less privileged segments of the electorate. No doubt the party's ideological moderation brought it closer to the center of the distribution of popular preferences.

Political Marketing. Another practice the PT adopted after 1994 was to engage professional consultants and publicists who would track public opinion through polling and focus groups and then help the party adjust to their findings. This represented a break with the party's historical aspiration to *lead* rather than to *follow* the masses. Introducing the use of media experts rather than relying entirely on party officials follows a core criterion of Panebianco's "electoral-professional" party (1988: 264). In a departure from the previous eschewing of such practices – in favor of building support for the substance of the PT's ideals and programs – party strategists had come to advocate taking account of voters' views, especially regarding the party itself.[28] In this connection, they hired an analyst known to be sympathetic to the PT away from one of Brazil's major commercial polling firms. That individual's initial charge was to soften resistance within the party to the very idea of tracking and conforming to public opinion.[29] Moreover, a survey research unit affiliated with the party was created.[30] The adoption of political marketing went hand in hand with the increasing use of survey opinion research. An outstanding case of this involved the hiring of Brazil's best-known and most expensive publicist, Duda Mendonça, to run Lula's 2002 campaign.

---

[28] An excellent article on the PT's adaptation to the findings of survey research is "Pesquisas fazem PT adaptar discursos," *Folha de São Paulo*, October 9, 2000.

[29] Author interview with Gustavo Venturi, pollster and PT adviser, in São Paulo on August 9, 2006.

[30] The special purpose of this *Fundação Perseu Abramo*-affiliated unit was to tap deep currents in societal sentiments, not to follow more daily fluctuations in public opinion, which the party judged to be covered adequately by private polling firms.

Accepting the fact that most voters lacked strong ideological moorings, campaign strategists focused ever more on candidate attributes and media images. In line with the concept of layering, making institutional provision for opinion polling was added as a strategy. Nothing was done to prevent PT activists from continuing to try to change the hearts and minds of Brazilians.

Broadening Alliances. Similarly, the leadership began to consider alliance partners that it would have rejected out of hand earlier.[31] The unavailability of the PSDB – a natural partner from an ideological standpoint yet the PT's archrival politically – made coalition building particularly difficult. Lula and his closest associates engaged in insistent efforts to convince militants of the mathematical odds against winning majoritarian races – most importantly the presidency but also gubernatorial and mayoral contests – without loosening the party's restrictive alliance policy. It was evident by 1998 that the PT was broadening the alliances it forged in gubernatorial races. Greater pragmatism on this dimension was also manifest in many mayoral races by the second half of the 1990s. The starkest concession to pragmatism occurred in 2002, when the PT allied with the small right-wing Liberal Party (PL) in the presidential race. With similar calculations in mind, the PT sought support from a large faction of the PMDB, arguably the most opportunistic of Brazilian parties. Notably, this was an additive change: Rather than dropping its long-standing alliances with left parties, the PT extended its allies to include parties on the right.

REMAINING DISTINCTIVENESS

Despite notable adaptations, path dependence was ever apparent. On core organizational characteristics, the PT remained quite distinctive even after moderating ideologically and instituting other changes in the period leading up to Lula's 2002 presidential victory. Reflecting the historical institutionalist perspective that behavior is bounded by norms and practices embedded in the past, the PT continued to give ample decision-making influence to members of the party bureaucracy – especially those on the National Directorate and Executive Committee. It persisted in scrutinizing individuals before allowing them to run under the PT label and held

---

[31] See "PT reelege José Dirceu e abre para alianças," *Gazeta Mercantil*, September 1, 1997; and "Partido começa a discutir alianças," *Jornal do Brasil*, September 13, 1999.

them to strict standards of conduct if and when they assumed office. The party thus maintained its reputation for having the highest rates of cohesion, discipline, and loyalty of any political party in the system. PT legislators manifested the highest levels of agreement with one another over a host of issues (Roma 2005). The rate at which they voted together and in line with the leadership's directives was without parallel (Souza 2004). Distinct from other parties, hardly any legislators migrated into the PT. Outward migration was also minimal. The requirement that PT politicians make sizable financial donations to the party remained intact. In short, even though the leadership made pragmatic changes with an eye toward boosting the *organization's* vote share, as *individuals* PT politicians did not act with the blatant self-interest that characterizes many of their counterparts from other Brazilian parties.

Notably, the one organizational change of significance that occurred between the party's reorientation in the mid-1990s and Lula's presidential victory in 2002 was designed to consolidate the internal power of the group responsible for spearheading the PT's adjustments to rising environmental challenges and constant institutional incentives. Because organizational power stems in part from the rules governing internal competition, it stands to reason that attempts to secure political control might well induce organizational modifications (Panebianco 1988: 244; Harmel and Janda 1994: 282). In 2001, years after the first visible outward modifications were made to shape the party in a catchall direction, the PT reformed its statute and instituted direct membership elections for the National Directorate and for party president (Partido dos Trabalhadores 2001b). Party members would also directly elect the presidents of state and municipal directorates. This change is known as the PED or *Processo de Eleições Diretas* (Process of Direct Elections). Before then, delegates to the annual national convention (themselves chosen within the party apparatus in Brazil's various states) chose the party president and the National Directorate. By increasing the weight of average party members over figures more closely associated with the party bureaucracy (where radical factions remained entrenched), the change was intended to favor party moderates who backed Lula. Similarly, the new statute made possible the holding of internal plebiscites, a measure that permits the party leadership to circumvent organized factions and appeal directly to the rank and file.[32]

---

[32] Hoping to further reduce factional conflict, the reform also extended the term of office for the party president and other leaders from two to three years.

Strategic Change or Organizational Persistence? 41

Evidently, reformist factions within the PT felt the need to undergird their control of the party with the organizational innovation of direct membership elections. Without securing their influence, the ability to change the external face of the PT was at risk. That organizational change occurred on a dimension central to the selection of party leaders – the gateway between the party's internal organization and the outside world – is not surprising. Whether and when it would occur on a dimension further removed from the external face of the party is less clear. Nonetheless, the PED reform does suggest that, at some key points, external pressures create incentives for internal organizational change.

PARTIAL ADAPTATION: CAUGHT BETWEEN THE SYSTEM AND THE PARTY'S PAST

The preceding discussion suggests that the institutional incongruence that layering can produce may lead to a coexistence between the "fringe and core" as envisioned by Schickler (2001). This coexistence can be fruitful, as it was in some key respects for the PT. The norms of loyalty, cohesion, and discipline – together with the organizational structures that promoted their persistence – allowed the party to keep its activist following, weather hard times, and undergo important programmatic transformations while nonetheless retaining a distinctive identity. At the same time, however, efforts to continue former norms and practices on issues more directly related to winning office created serious sources of tension and dysfunctionality. In other words, the coexistence produced by layering was an uneasy one when it came to such issues.

An important example of problems caused by the party's incomplete transformation concerns its fundraising efforts. The PT had always struggled in a system where political campaigns, financed disproportionately from corporate contributions, are among the most expensive in the world. Legal allowances for businesses to contribute directly to candidates and at exceedingly high rates (up to 2 percent of their gross yearly income) favor conservative political elites with ties to the private sector. Candidates receive free television and radio time – in proportion to their party's representation in the lower house of Congress – yet they face large expenses for the production of these advertisements, for additional promotional materials like flyers and posters, and for food and drinks and other handouts at events designed to drum up support (Samuels 2001).

Corporate support is thought to be especially decisive in presidential campaigns. Monetary restrictions had hampered the effectiveness of

Lula's previous campaigns in crucial ways, such as limiting his ability to travel and even to pay campaign workers. Furthermore, the shift toward vote maximization turned the PT's limited resources into an even greater obstacle than when party building was the overriding priority and mobilizational strategies and membership fees rather than catchall tactics were relied upon. Although the PT's image and aspirations had shifted by the second half of the 1990s, its more radical past posed an obstacle to its new ambitions by limiting any contributions it could expect from the private sector.

Compared with other leading parties, the PT not only received less money from donations overall but a far smaller percentage of it came from corporations.[33] Its more mainstream counterparts, especially those in government, enjoyed access to *legal* campaign finance through their ties to the private sector. On the "supply" side, large businesses were understandably reluctant to finance a party that had for most of its existence called for significant economic redistribution. On the "demand" side, leading members of the PT's left wing actively rejected the Lula faction's desire to cultivate the business class. Fearing that business interests could co-opt and pervert the party's decisions over major economic issues and orientations, they even launched a campaign to prevent PT mayors and governors from accepting *legal* donations from major companies, going so far as to force two PT governors to return such donations they had received from construction firms in their states.[34]

To make up for these shortfalls the party developed an *illegal* centrally organized fund-raising network with smaller businesses in cities where it governed, a secret that was well guarded for years. PT mayors extracted kickbacks from private and public firms seeking municipal contracts (most prominently in garbage collection, transportation, and cleaning services) and then diverted these forced contributions into a secret campaign slush fund, the *caixa dois* (or "second till"). The party also engaged in shady deals with local bingo and lottery operations. Key actors within the PT have since underscored the special constraints the

---

[33] Cardoso's declared contributions in the 1994 campaign were U.S. $41,366,843, whereas Lula's were $1,741,401. The numbers for 1998 were $37,088,337 and $1,933,129, respectively (Samuels 2001: 31). In 1994, PT candidates (for various offices) each raised only about 10 percent of the amount from business that candidates from nonleftist parties raised. They did only slightly better in 1998 (Samuels 2001: 39).

[34] See "Diretório do DF decide devolver dinheiro," *Estado de São Paulo*, November 30, 1994. My interview with Paulo Vannuchi confirmed the left wing's reservations about the party's developing closer relations with big business.

party faced and how it tried to overcome them through such clandestine exchanges. The brother of a former PT mayor murdered in connection with a *caixa dois* deal gone awry (Celso Daniel of Santo André) testified that his brother regarded the scheme as a "necessary evil, the PT being denied the donations from big business available to its political opponents."[35] The conventional interpretation that PT corruption signals the party's complete sellout and its convergence with other parties fails to appreciate the distinctiveness of these activities. Path dependence, a key notion within historical institutionalism, forced the PT's reliance on such tawdry operations as the only available alternative to typical (and mostly legal) corporate contributions. The highly centralized organization of the *caixa dois* network run by the PT bears the mark of the party and its history. Although other parties have engaged in such "off-the-books" schemes in municipalities, they have generally done so in a decentralized fashion. Isolated groups, not the party per se, have been implicated. Another important and distinguishing characteristic of PT malfeasance is that those involved seem to have engaged in misconduct for the sake of the party and its growth rather than for their own personal enrichment.

In short, while initial appearances might suggest that the PT became just like any catchall Brazilian party after the mid-1990s, important details suggest otherwise. The PT's financing scheme (and subsequent scandal) suggests that the party found itself caught between the incentives of Brazil's political system and its own historical commitments. It wanted to compete in the mainstream political game but was not entirely willing or able to play by its rules. This contradiction ultimately and all too ironically took a toll on the party's image as the standard bearer of ethics in politics.

Thus, will the PT's increasing movement in a catchall direction induce a more thoroughgoing internal organizational realignment? In other words, will change, which started on the external front, proceed increasingly toward the internal front, making the PT look even more like other Brazilian parties? Will the tensions engendered by layering and incomplete transformation persist, or will the new institutional layer that gains a dynamic and support base of its own eventually displace the previous structure (Streeck and Thelen 2005: 23)? This question will be taken up anew in the book's conclusion.

---

[35] "How a Murder is Reviving Brazil's Furor over Corruption," *Financial Times*, March 28, 2006.

CONCLUSION

This chapter began by presenting and comparing two important analytical frameworks for understanding issues of continuity and change in political parties. It contrasted strategic and historical institutionalist perspectives, paying special attention to the former's emphasis on the speed and ease with which organizations respond to external incentives in their immediate environment, and the latter's concern with the importance of enduring norms, obligations, and historical legacies in constraining decision making even amidst such pressures. Prominent examples of studies that recognize the influence of both sets of pressures were also examined.

The chapter then asked which approach better explains the PT's trajectory over the past two decades. Is its profile more a reflection of the conditions under which it was founded, or a response to its changing external environment? What can be learned of broader relevance from the PT's evolution? The party's complex profile can be systematically understood in terms of both founding and changing conditions, thereby bearing out historical institutionalist as well as strategic perspectives. Adaptation took place first on dimensions affecting relations between the party and the *external* public, specifically those most directly related to efforts to expand the PT's support base (e.g., its public image and electoral tactics). By contrast, continuity prevailed on the *internal* front (e.g., decision-making procedures, norms and rules concerning the obligations of candidates and officeholders, relations between the leadership and militants). Indeed, environmental pressures are likely to make the first and most significant impact on a party's external face, proceeding only over time and with far greater difficulty to its internal core.

The next three chapters flesh out in greater detail how specific institutional environments shaped the PT over time. Beyond the broad economic and political changes that informed the party's trajectory were factors specific to various institutional arenas in which the PT competed and played a role. For example, vying for the presidency had a different logic than winning and holding office in the Chamber of Deputies. Governing a municipality involved yet a different set of imperatives. Reinforcing the hybrid character of the party that resulted from the tension and interplay between broad economic change and organizational stickiness was the variety of factors militating in favor and against adaptation in these various spheres.

3

Opposition Politics

The PT in the Chamber of Deputies

The present chapter analyzes the key role that leading the legislative opposition until 2002 played in building and reinforcing the PT's development and reputation as a strong left party with a mass bureaucratic profile.[1] This institutional arena, less subject to strong pressures to adapt than its mayoral and presidential counterparts, was conducive to promoting the party's left programmatic leanings and its strong and disciplined organization. Key aspects of continuity in the party's distinctive identity and organizational uniqueness are rooted in its development within this body of government.[2] Institutional rules governing election to the lower house of Congress, together with the logic of the PT's opposition role, supported the retention of a strategy aimed at furthering the party's distinctive profile and long-term growth. Like many other parties that develop over a long period in national-level opposition, the PT grew in organizational strength (Panebianco 1988: 69). The most prominent changes within the PT were enacted vis-à-vis other institutional arenas. However, rather than replacing important elements of continuity that existed in the legislative sphere, they emerged and developed alongside them. This led to the coexistence of discrepant policies embraced by the party and hybrid images it projected for many years.

---

[1] See Panebianco (1988: 264) for a description of this ideal type, as compared to its electoral-professional counterpart.
[2] Given the relatively small number of Senate seats held by the PT until recently, it is more relevant to analyze the PT in the lower house of Congress. In 1990 there was one PT senator, in 1994 there were five, in 1998 there were eight, in 2002 there were fourteen, and in 2006 there were twelve.

PROFILE OF THE PT IN THE CHAMBER OF DEPUTIES

Trajectory of Growth

Voting for the PT in the legislature is generally understood to be the best indicator of support for the party organization and its ideals. Votes for PT candidates seeking executive offices (mayor, governor, or president) may well involve less partisan considerations. This is not only because candidate personality matters more in such races but also because the majority requirement forces broader alliances to be made. The PT delegation in the Chamber of Deputies grew slowly but steadily from 1986 to 2002. Every election represented an advance upon the previous one. The PT captured 3.3 percent of all Chamber seats in 1986, 7.0 percent in 1990, 9.6 percent in 1994, 11.3 percent in 1998, and 17.7 percent in 2002,[3] which eventually made it the largest party in Brazil's highly fragmented lower house.[4] The delegation's growth is more impressive when one takes into account the numerous systemic factors working against it. For example, deputies are helped by having a governor of the same party in office to distribute patronage (Samuels 2003), but most PT deputies have not enjoyed this benefit because the party has never managed to elect many governors.[5] Another disadvantage is lower house malapportionment and the favor it gives to rural states and, by implication, conservative politicians (Snyder and Samuels 2001).

Chart 3.1 shows the growth in aggregate support for the PT in the Chamber of Deputies along with shifts in its regional distribution over time. In earlier years the delegation was highly skewed toward the more developed regions of the country. Although deputies from the Southeast

---

[3] These seats corresponded to winning a vote share of 6.9 percent in 1986, 10.2 percent in 1990, 13.1 percent in 1994, 13.2 percent in 1998, and 18.4 percent in 2002.

[4] The fragmentation of Brazil's legislature is a long-standing phenomenon. For example, when Cardoso took office in 1995, none of the eighteen parties in the Chamber held more than 21 percent of the seats.

[5] Winning gubernatorial victories has been a historical weakness of the PT. Across the country's twenty-seven states (including Brasília, the Federal District) the party had only two governors in 1994, three in 1998, three in 2002, and five in 2006. One reason for the difficulty lies in the demographics of most states: Gathering an absolute majority of votes requires winning candidates to be able to carry many municipalities of under 20,000 voters. In addition, such a high threshold for election favors parties open to forging alliances with large parties of the center and center right, not something the PT tended to do historically.

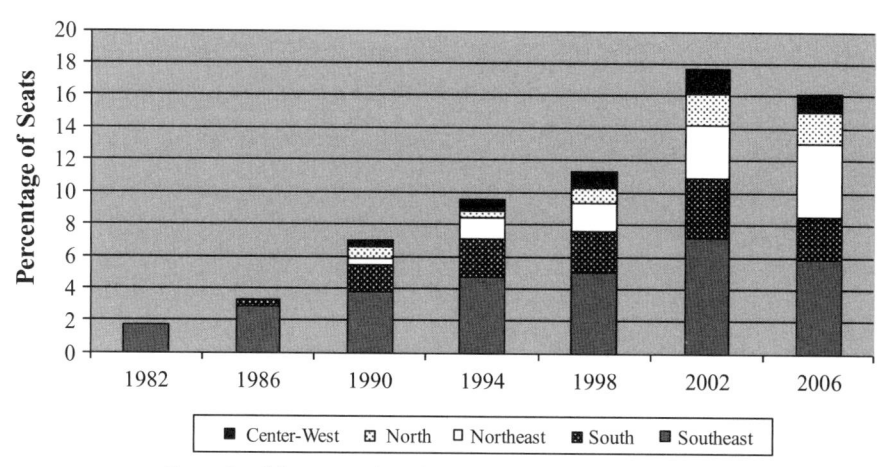

CHART 3.1. Growth of the PT in the Chamber of Deputies, 1982–2006. (*Sources:* Nicolau, Jairo. *Banco de Dados Eleitorais do Brasil (1982–2006)*; *Tribunal Superior Eleitoral.*)

and South have continued to predominate numerically, other regions have gained in representation over time.[6]

As the PT expanded, it came to assume a leading role within a growing parliamentary left. Whereas the left comprised barely one-fifth of the Chamber in 1990, it made up about one-third in 2002. After 1994, when the PT surpassed in size the PDT's delegation in the Chamber of Deputies, it became the dominant force within the expanded left bloc (see Table 3.1). That same year the PDT's longtime leader, Leonel Brizola, agreed to serve as Lula's vice presidential running mate, a stark statement that the PT had arrived to lead the left mantle.

Programmatic and Organizational Dimensions of the PT Delegation

The PT distinguished itself in both programmatic and organizational terms. Programmatically, the party held economic policy positions

[6] The spread of the PT's legislative vote mirrors the distribution of party identifiers by region. For example, in 1996, of those who reported a partisan identification with the PT, 69 percent resided in the Southeast and South (combined) vs. 31 from the three other regions. By contrast, partisanship with the main party of the right, the PFL, was rooted in Brazil's less developed regions: 73.8 percent of those who professed a partisan attachment to the PFL came from the Northeast, North, and Center-West vs. 26.2 percent from the South and Southeast (Mainwaring et al. 1999: 40).

TABLE 3.1. *Ideological Blocs in the Chamber of Deputies: 1982–2006*

Bloc	1982	1986	1990	1994	1998	2002	2006
Chamber of Deputies (%)							
Right	49.1	33.4	42.2	38.9	35.7	33.3	29.2
Center	44.5	56.9	36.7	39.0	41.5	33.3	34.7
Left	6.5	9.6	19.9	21.6	22.1	32.3	36.1
PT share (%)							
Left	26.1	34.3	35.1	44.4	51.2	54.7	45.0

Note: Coppedge (1997) informs these categorizations of left, right, and center.
Sources: Nicolau, Jairo. *Banco de Dados Eleitorais do Brasil (1982–2006)*; *Tribunal Superior Eleitoral*.

considerably to the left of all other major parties. Organizationally, it was the most disciplined and cohesive party on Brazil's political landscape. Together, these two dimensions gave the PT a clear and identifiable niche in a party system replete with weak, fragmented, and patronage-oriented entities. Notwithstanding some softening on the programmatic front over time, the PT delegation maintained this niche during its time in the opposition.

The Party's Unique Economic Policy Orientation. The crux of the debate dominating the legislative arena in the 1990s concerned whether the market or the state would be the primary agent of economic development and management. By the late 1980s, problems of debt, inefficient public enterprises, and other statist maladies had put on the table the issues of trade opening, privatization, and fiscal reform in Brazil, which remained among the most closed of the major economies in the developing world. Whereas President Fernando Collor took important steps to open trade in the early 1990s, President Cardoso (1995–2002) put forth a sustained effort to institute other market-oriented reforms thereafter. In the wake of the *Plano Real*, Cardoso sought to keep inflation under control, observe fiscal austerity at all levels of government, and increase domestic savings. Central to his agenda were the privatization and regulation of state monopolies together with structural reforms in the social security and fiscal systems.

The emerging focus on economic liberalization contradicted the PT's ideologically inspired vision of using the state to develop the economy and to redistribute Brazil's substantial wealth. Legislative surveys attest to this orientation. For example, a 1987 survey by Leôncio Martins Rodrigues asked deputies what economic system they preferred for Brazil: (1) a "pure" market economy; (2) a "social democratic" economy with an equal distribution of responsibilities between the state and private sector; (3) a "moderate socialist" system with an active state but some private enterprise; or (4) a "radical socialist" or command economy. Of the sixteen PT deputies surveyed, ten (nearly two-thirds of the delegation) supported "radical socialism," six (slightly over one-third) supported "moderate socialism," and none chose either the "social democratic" or "pure market" options (Rodrigues 1987). A 1997 readministration of the survey by Timothy J. Power found that the PT remained strikingly less pro-market than other major parties, notwithstanding a move away from the far left, which was indicated by the fact that no one selected "radical socialism." Not a single PT respondent selected "pure market," one-fourth of the delegation chose "moderate socialism," and three-fourths selected "social democracy" (Mainwaring, Meneguello, and Power 1999: 19). Surveys designed and administered by IDESP (*Instituto de Estudos Econômicos, Sociais, e Políticos de São Paulo*) reflect similar reservations about the market.[7]

The PT's legislative behavior mirrored the views revealed in surveys. Amidst calls for the diminution of trade barriers, privatization of the economy, and reform of the state, the PT delegation continued to advocate a state-centric model of economic development. The antimarket positions it assumed in the debates of the Constituent Assembly (1987–1988), together with its rejection of President Collor's market reform program (1990–1992), left no doubt about the party's economic orientation. The delegation went on to launch its most sustained and strident opposition against "neoliberalism" with the reforms pursued by President Cardoso. In contrast to the strong support of the PSDB and PFL for the market reform program, PT deputies rejected the major legislative projects of the Cardoso era, most prominently social security and tax reforms, privatization bills, minimum wage laws, and the fiscal responsibility law. A study of ten roll-call votes on key issues of neoliberal reform in President

---

[7] Deputies were asked if they agreed completely, somewhat, or not at all with whether the state should act only in essential areas (e.g., security, education, justice) and leave the rest to the private sector. No PT deputy agreed completely in either 1991 or 1995: 87 percent (in 1991) and 81 percent (in 1995) did not agree at all, and 13 percent (in 1991) and 19 percent (in 1995) percent agreed only somewhat. Although opinion did soften somewhat over the four years, the PT remained an outlier on Brazil's political landscape. By 1995 deputies from center-left parties like the PSDB and PDT were far more likely than their PT counterparts to hold liberal economic views. See Almeida and Moya (1997) for details on how other parties responded to these same questions.

Cardoso's first term (1995–1998) documents this nearly total opposition (Power 1998: 60–61).

The PT's Distinctive Political and Organizational Orientation. Another crucial aspect distinguishing the PT was its political organization. In a country known for having weak political parties, the PT stood out as uniquely well organized and unified. This was the case despite serious internal debates among the party's various factions. Notable were the exceedingly high rates of cohesion, discipline, and loyalty displayed by the legislative delegation. PT representatives manifested among the highest levels of agreement with one another over a host of substantive issues (Roma 2005). Moreover, they voted together at rates without parallel for a major Brazilian party (Mainwaring and Pérez-Liñán 1998; Figueiredo and Limongi 1999: 112; Nicolau 2000; Souza 2004). In a political system marked by rampant party switching, PT deputies remained within the party to an extraordinary degree. Leaving the PT for another party was almost unheard of (Melo 2000; Nicolau 2000). On average, 30 percent of all deputies switched parties at least once in the period between 1985 and 1999. By comparison, only 5.6 percent of PT deputies migrated out of the party during these same years (Melo 2000). Even some other parties on the left, for example, the PDT and PSB (Brazilian Socialist Party), had much higher rates of switching.[8] By the same token, only on the rarest of occasions did a deputy from another party switch into the PT.

Comparisons with Other Parties. Reference to how other major parties lined up on these same dimensions lends greater perspective to the unique niche occupied by the PT delegation.

The PFL constituted an obvious point of distinction for the PT. By the mid-1990s, the PFL and PT had emerged as the main forces on opposing sides of the political spectrum, with the decline of the PPB (Brazilian Progressive Party) on the right[9] and the PDT on the center left. The PFL delegation strongly supported the market reform agendas of Presidents Collor and Cardoso. A party dominated by old-time notables and individuals from the business world, its representatives also displayed a pronounced tendency to identify themselves as economic liberals.[10] The

---

[8] The figures for the PDT and PSB are 31.1 percent and 26.7 percent, respectively.
[9] The PPB was a successor to the official party of the military regime.
[10] In 1987, when few politicians reported an affiliation with economic liberalism, 62 percent of PFL deputies did so (Rodrigues 1987), a figure that rose to 70 percent in 1997

only party ranking higher than the PFL in behavioral and subjective indicators of economic liberalism was the much smaller and more ideological PPB (Rodrigues 2002: 66–68).

Whereas adherence to economic liberalism gave the PFL a programmatic pillar of cohesion and identity, other aspects conformed to a more traditional political profile.[11] The conduct of PFL deputies with respect to the electorate, within the legislature, and toward the executive revealed a political machine aptly described as a *partido de sustentação*, a "support party" or "collection of clients whose patron is the president but who are patrons themselves in their states, regions, and municipalities" (Power 2000: 184). The PFL generally backed the government of the day and received resources in return. Legislative surveys show a pronounced tendency among PFL deputies to regard engagement in patronage-oriented rather than program-oriented activities as the most appropriate role for congressional representatives (Hagopian 2005).

The PSDB has been aptly described as the "principal force of the modernizing center" (Power and Zucco 2009). Like the PT, its members tended toward programmatic politics but came to differ strikingly on the substantive economic positions they embraced. Seasoned yet socially committed politicians who broke away from the PMDB in 1988, PSDB deputies supported statist positions in the late 1980s but by 1993 had begun to advocate market reforms.[12] Reforms pursued under the successive administrations of Fernando Henrique Cardoso consolidated the party's pro-market profile. The percentage of PSDB representatives who professed a liberal affiliation doubled between 1987 and 1997, rising from 31 to 60 percent (Power 1998: 58).

The PSDB (whose members are informally called *tucanos*) ranked comparatively highly among Brazilian parties in terms of the programmatic cohesion it displayed throughout the 1990s (Hagopian 2005: 21;

(Power 1998: 58). The PFL's internal diversity should also be recognized. Alongside the ideological liberals who imbue the party with its pro-market profile exist those whose lifeblood is pork and patronage. The ideological liberals – embodied in individuals like Jorge Bornhausen – tend to come from the party's southern wing. The clientelists – whose best-known representative was Antônio Carlos Magalhães – typically hail from the Northeast. See Cantanhêde (2001: 60–63) on the "two PFLs."

[11] Hagopian (2005: 21) discusses some exceptions to this profile, such as the relatively high rate of voting discipline displayed by PFL deputies.

[12] The PSDB's voting record in the Constituent Assembly debates would merit putting it somewhere between the PT and the PFL but arguably closer to the former in these years. The rise of economic liberals within the party and coalitional building efforts surrounding the 1994 presidential election contributed crucially to this reorientation.

Roma 2005: 114–115). This was true even though a number of legislators joined the party opportunistically during the Cardoso government. Whereas the PT was radical and activist in nature, the PSDB was reformist and technocratic in orientation. PSDB deputies tended to come from the ranks of urban-based business and the professional and intellectual classes (Rodrigues 2002; 68–71). Actions taken by the PSDB leading up to the 1994 election – namely forging an electoral alliance with the barons of the PFL – muddied the party's principled image. In its struggle to overcome notable disadvantages against the more mainstream party, the PT launched a vociferous public campaign against these measures. The hope was to give itself an exclusive claim to principled politics.[13]

The PDT tended to share the PT's statist orientation yet differed strikingly in its political style. Being a champion of economic nationalism gave the PDT a "moderately leftist" cast (Ames 2001: xiii), but the party eluded simple classification on a left–right scale as a result of the personal prominence and populist style of its leader Leonel Brizola. One observer describes the PDT as reflecting "a contradictory mix of economically progressive platforms, 'family and country' discourses, and an allegiance to a few notable politicians" (Baiocchi 2005: 13). Brizola built the party's following in the states of Rio de Janeiro and Rio Grande do Sul, where its support remained concentrated. On key dimensions, such as party loyalty, the PDT lacked a programmatic or party-oriented profile. PDT deputies switched parties at high rates and moved across the political spectrum when they did. The PT stood out as being less personalistic, better organized, and more national in its reach than the PDT.

The PMDB and PTB (Brazilian Labor Party) were classic catchall parties, from which the PT distinguished itself readily. The broad-based PMDB was arguably the most opportunistic and internally diverse of Brazilian parties. Although it began on the center left of the political spectrum, it became more catchall in orientation upon losing many social democrats to the PSDB in 1988. Often divided between government and opposition supporters, PMDB members were notorious for switching in and out of the party according to what served them best at the time. As a result of the large size of its delegation and the "flexibility" of its members' programmatic commitments, the PMDB was often sought out as a governing ally. Similar to the PMDB although smaller and somewhat more conservative was the PTB.

---

[13] See Roma (2006) for an excellent comparison of the PT and PSDB.

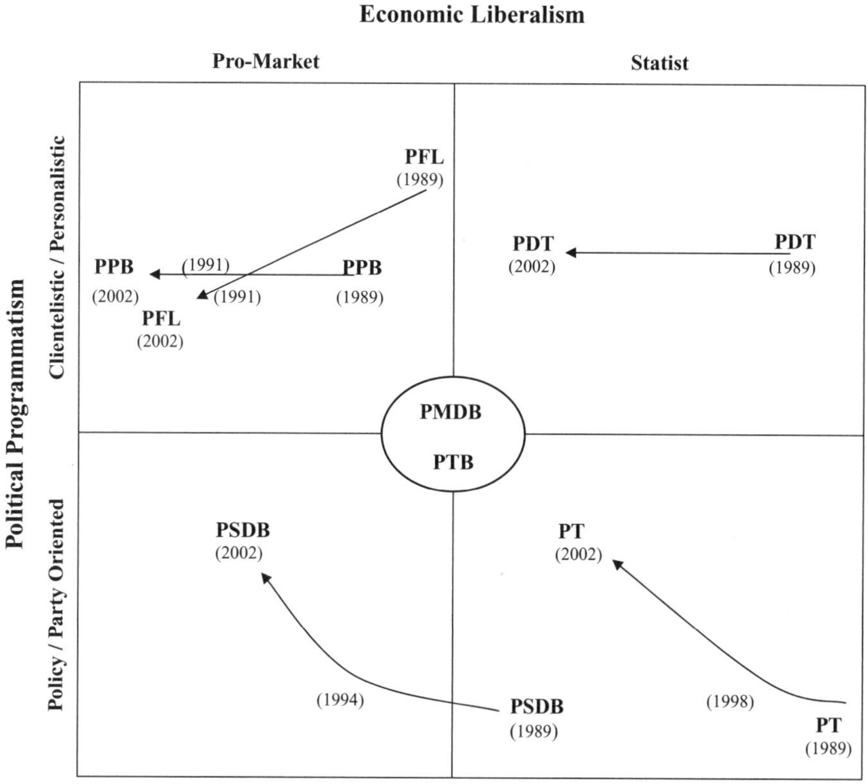

Opposition Politics

Economic Liberalism

FIGURE 3.1. Brazil's political landscape, 1989–2002. (*Source: World Politics* 59, No. 3, April 2007: 440–475, Johns Hopkins University Press; reprinted with permission.)

Figure 3.1 places the PT in comparative perspective.

Demographic Characteristics of the PT Delegation

Demographic characteristics also distinguished PT deputies from counterparts in other parties.[14] The PT delegation contains simultaneously the highest percentage of people with graduate degrees and of individuals who have never completed high school (Rodrigues 2002: 101,

---

[14] Although Rodrigues' study analyzes the specific group of deputies elected in October 1998 for the fifty-first legislative term, he notes that the social composition of the various parties has remained quite stable over time with the slight exception of a diminution of PT politicians from working-class and labor backgrounds (Rodrigues 2002: 79).

79).[15] University professors are numerous in the first group. Former factory workers and rural laborers account largely for the second. The PT also displays a highly skewed distribution between former public school teachers and people from the business world. Although the number of teachers and business people is inversely related in most parties (with the concentration of teachers being highest in left parties), this pattern is the most pronounced in the PT.[16] On the whole, PT deputies are of modest financial means, ranking the lowest of all deputies in personal assets (Rodrigues 2002: 85).

The gender breakdown among its deputies further distinguishes the party (Macaulay 2003a, 2003b). Compared with other major parties, the PT has consistently run a higher percentage of women candidates on its lists for election to the Chamber of Deputies. Moreover, its record in having women elected exceeds that of other parties. For example, women comprised 14, 8.5, and 15.4 percent of all PT deputies elected in 1994, 1998, and 2002, compared with a combined average for all other major parties of 6.2, 5.7, and 8.2 in these same years, thus giving the PT roughly twice the percentage of women in its ranks (Macaulay 2003b: 7–9).[17]

The preponderance of deputies from urban backgrounds further sets the PT apart. Compared with deputies from the major center and right-wing parties, PT deputies are markedly urban in origin. For example, 28 and 35 percent of PT deputies elected in 1994 and 1998 came from the capital cities of their states compared with 8 and 7 percent for the PMDB delegation and 6 and 13 percent for the PFL delegation. Similarly, almost 60 percent of PT deputies lived in one of Brazil's 100 largest cities at the time of these elections, compared with roughly 15 percent for the PMDB and the PFL. PSDB deputies are more urban in background than their PMDB and PFL counterparts but not as uniformly so as PT deputies (Carvalho 2003: 156–161). It is cause for special celebration when a PT candidate with strong rural roots and associations is elected.[18]

---

[15] Other parties, such as the PSDB, have a wealth of deputies with graduate degrees but virtually no one with less than a completed high school education.

[16] For example, in the fifty-first legislative term (1999–2002), 33.9 percent of PT deputies were former primary and secondary school teachers whereas only 3.4 percent had backgrounds in business (Rodrigues 2002). On the opposite end of the ideological spectrum, 6.7 percent of deputies from the PPB and 9.6 from the PFL had backgrounds in education compared with the 68.4 and 60.9 percent who came from the business world.

[17] Macaulay (2003b: 8) attributes the success of female candidates in the PT largely to their grassroots leadership.

[18] This comes from an interview with Athos Pereira in his role as Chief of Staff, Leadership of the PT in the Chamber of Deputies. The interview took place in Brasília on August 1, 2003.

A related feature distinguishing the PT delegation is the spatial distribution of its constituents. The most typical pattern of PT candidates is to concentrate votes in distinct locales (mainly large urban centers) and to share these areas with candidates of other parties (Ames 2001: 81; Souza 2004: 31). Labor leaders and heads of social movements tend to have such geographically concentrated followings (Ames 2001: 73). For example, 61 and 58 percent of all PT deputies elected in 1994 and 1998 displayed this profile compared with only 14 and 16 percent of the PMDB and 15 and 25 percent of the PFL delegations (Carvalho 2003: 122).[19] The clientelistic pattern of a scattered-dominant vote base, whereby a deputy gathers votes across a state but dominates in given areas, is virtually nonexistent for the PT but common to the large catchall parties of the center and right. Almost no PT deputies (4 percent in 1994 and 0 percent in 1998) displayed this pattern compared with 49 and 55 percent of the PFL delegation and 52 and 33 percent of the PMDB delegations (Carvalho 2003: 123).[20]

GROWTH WITH RADICALISM: CONTRIBUTIONS TO CONTINUITY

Historic Norms and Practices in the Context
of Proportional Representation

What allowed the PT delegation to grow and simultaneously retain its determined programmatic focus and cohesive organization in a political system notorious for its program- and party-weakening incentives, namely the open-list aspect of the system to elect deputies to the lower house of Congress (Mainwaring 1999; Ames 2001)? Institutional norms, practices, and procedures central to the PT's past contributed crucially to sustaining the party's transformative programmatic project and keeping its internal organization intact. Even when party leaders moderated the PT's program and image, they maintained its distinctive organizational characteristics of cohesion, loyalty, and discipline.

Before I elaborate on this discussion, it must be understood that an institutional precondition of the party's growth in the Chamber of Deputies was an electoral design characterized by proportional

---

[19] The Brazilian average in these years was 29 percent and 31 percent, respectively.
[20] Some PT deputies – 24 percent in 1994 and 16 percent in 1998 – were elected on the basis of more territorially diffuse support (scattered and nondominant). This situation describes typically middle-class individuals who represented the PT's programmatic values and were not former union leaders, social movement activists, or former mayors. See Carvalho (2003) for additional details.

representation (with low thresholds for representation) in districts of high magnitude (entire states themselves).[21] Meeting required thresholds of representation while projecting a strong left identity would have been far less likely under a plurality arrangement or even a proportional representation system with smaller districts. The relative ease of entry into a key decision-making body that treated national issues of ideological significance made increasing the party's legislative delegation a core strategic goal.[22] Bearing out institutionalist logic, there were several occasions in which the party's candidates for majoritarian posts performed poorly while *petistas* fielded for deputy positions fared quite well. For example, in 1990, the PT more than doubled its delegation in the Chamber (going from sixteen to thirty-five seats) despite the poor performance of its candidates for gubernatorial and senatorial seats.[23] Beyond opening up growth possibilities for the party overall, the proportional representation element of electoral design for deputy races permitted the election of some candidates from the party's far left wing, who in turn reinforced the party's opposition profile and energized its base. True to the present day, many of the most radical PT politicians have made their home in the Chamber.[24]

Adding a twist to the institutional context for the PT's growth was the open-list aspect of the system. A well-documented pathology of Brazil's open-list system is that politicians end up competing against members of their own party, dispensing pork and making personalistic appeals to gain an extra edge (Mainwaring 1999; Ames 2001). The inability of parties to impose an order on candidate lists is generally thought to reduce their control over candidates.[25] How the PT managed to keep its legislative delegation so programmatically cohesive and party oriented in a system

---

[21] Between 1985 and 1995, there was no national threshold stipulated. For the changing rules on this issue see Mainwaring (1999: 128–131).

[22] Author interview with PT Deputy José Eduardo Cardozo in Brasília on August 14, 2003. See also "PT jogo o futuro no congresso," *Estado de São Paulo*, January 7, 1990.

[23] "PT cresce e também suas 'tendencias,' "*Correio Braziliense*, October 21, 1990.

[24] For example, PT politicians from the extreme left that held positions within the Chamber include Vladimir Palmeira, João Batista Oliveira de Araújo (Babá), and Luciana Genro. In addition, led by Adão Pretto (PT-RS), the *Movimento dos Trabalhadores Rurais Sem Terra* (MST) had several deputies representing the landless throughout the 1990s. It is hard to imagine such figures capturing an electoral majority or even the plurality required of executive positions.

[25] The sum of all votes for a party's list of candidates determines the number of deputies elected from that party, but precisely which candidates are elected is determined by the number of votes each individual candidate receives.

where candidates face strong incentives to adopt individualist strategies and message-weakening behaviors is a question that deserves attention.

Understanding how the PT managed to retain its collective partisan identity in the context of the open list begins with the rigorous requirements that party founders established regarding the conduct of PT politicians. These requirements effectively filtered out those individuals who were not highly committed to the party and its ideals.[26] For example, having to donate 30 percent of one's salary to the party was among the many sacrifices that PT deputies were expected to make. Similarly, knowing that they would have to vote en bloc or be suspended or expelled outright from the party – a stipulation the leadership exercised on a number of high-profile occasions – no doubt reduced the ranks of those who might waver.[27] The establishment of these and related rules made sense for a party that struggled from the outside to gain a foothold in Brazil's political system. The expectations set in motion and reinforced over time helped self-select for the most committed individuals, thereby buffering the PT from the party-weakening effects that the open list tended to exert otherwise.

The requirement that candidates for legislative office be nominated by the party's base (*núcleos* or local organizations) winnowed the field. Anyone with a background outside of the party's collective culture and vision was unlikely to be chosen. Early in the party's history, strong preference was given to the most active militants who had participated in social movements and party-building activities (Sader and Silverstein 1991: 80). Nominees also underwent a process of scrutiny and approval by the party leadership before they could run for office. For those who served out terms in the Chamber, party control was reinforced by the PT's refusal to go along with the uniquely Brazilian provision of the *candidato nato*, which allowed incumbent deputies an automatic slot on the party list at reelection time.[28]

---

[26] This section draws on Samuels (1999: 506–512).
[27] One high-profile case of the PT's demanding allegiance concerned whether the party should support the presidential candidacy of Tancredo Neves against Paulo Maluf in the Electoral College after the 1984 campaign for direct elections had failed. The hard-line stance the leadership assumed was to boycott the Electoral College altogether on the grounds of opposing a pacted transition. The pragmatic position assumed by three PT deputies was that Tancredo would be preferable to Maluf. The three resigned upon threat of expulsion (Keck 1992: 219–223).
[28] See Mainwaring (1999: 255) for a discussion of the *candidato nato* provision, which was abolished in 2002.

The marked dependence of PT candidates on the party for the resources to run effective campaigns tightened the link between the two. The financial shortages typical of *petista* campaigns rendered aspirants for deputy especially reliant on the party's organizational resources, structure, and broader message. PT candidates were not only the least favored in terms of campaign donations (Samuels 1999: 497) but also typically the least able to rely on their own (modest) personal finances (Rodrigues 2002: 85). Moreover, most could not draw on the clientelistic networks that candidates from other parties had developed. The heavy dependence of PT candidates on the party to compensate for these shortfalls made individualist campaign strategies much less likely for these candidates than they were for candidates from other parties.

Given these circumstances, it made sense for the PT to cultivate votes for the party label rather than for individual candidates, a provision that is permitted in Brazil but rarely in other candidate-centric systems. In races far and wide the PT promoted "13," the number assigned to the party in the ballot system.[29] Courses to encourage candidates to achieve a certain unity in their slogans and discourse constituted another aspect of this collective emphasis (Carvalho 2006: 84). The party label emphasis translated into lower campaign costs and allowed the PT to elect candidates with a lower number of total votes (Samuels 2001; Souza 2004: 15).[30] Simplifying the staggering array of choices available to voters was no doubt an important factor in the PT's legislative growth trajectory. In 1990, 43 percent of all votes for the PT were in the form of votes for the party label. Although the percentage of party label votes declined throughout the 1990s, the PT remained the party with the largest percentage of votes cast for the party label instead of individual candidates (see Chart 3.2).

Legislative surveys confirm the perception by PT deputies of the party's centrality to their election. When asked about the relative contribution to their electoral success of the party versus their individual qualities and efforts, 42.5 percent of the 1999–2002 PT delegation listed "the party" as the dominant influence; 17 percent saw their own personal efforts

---

[29] "Sem nomes representativos, PT via incentivar voto na legenda," *Folha de São Paulo*, June 30, 1990.
[30] Powerful testimony to the strength of PT efforts to cultivate party label votes is a poll in which 93.08 percent of all respondents were able to associate the number 13 with either the PT (77.13) or Lula (15.95 percent), whereas less than 1 percent could correctly link any other party to the corresponding number on the list (Centro de Estudos de Opinião Pública 2002a).

Opposition Politics

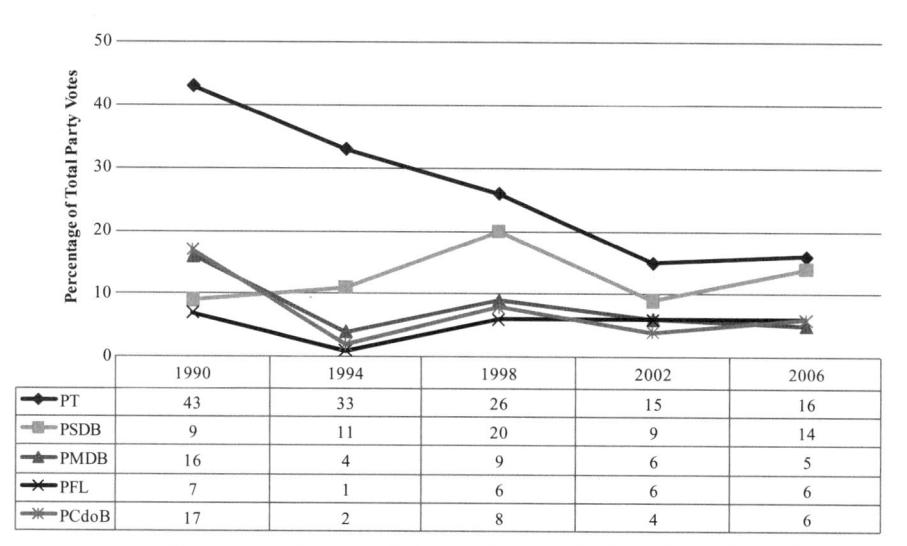

	1990	1994	1998	2002	2006
PT	43	33	26	15	16
PSDB	9	11	20	9	14
PMDB	16	4	9	6	5
PFL	7	1	6	6	6
PCdoB	17	2	8	4	6

CHART 3.2. Percentage of party label votes for principal parties in lower house elections, 1990–2006. (*Sources:* Nicolau, Jairo. *Banco de Dados Eleitorais do Brasil (1982–2006); Tribunal Superior Eleitoral.*)

as central; and 40.5 percent saw the two as roughly equal in importance (Leal 2005: 77).[31] Another study of the 1999–2002 Chamber of Deputies confirms the PT's distinctiveness in this regard (Carvalho 2003: 172–173).[32] Furthermore, when asked to predict what would happen to their political careers if they shifted to another party, 83 percent of all PT deputies thought they would suffer seriously versus only 26, 31, 50, and 17 percent of deputies from the PSDB, PFL, PPB, and PMDB, respectively (Carvalho 2003: 174).

Viewing the party as a crucial source of their mandate, PT deputies voiced a strong sense of accountability to it. In a survey that asked PT deputies to rank their allegiance to the party, the voters, and their individual conscience or social movements, the most common first choice was by far "the party" (Leal 2005: 73).[33] A survey of deputies from all parties found that those from the PT expressed the greatest willingness to support the party program and label over their individual interests and the districts they represented (Hagopian 2005: 44). In line with their

---

[31] Paulo Roberto Figueira Leal managed to survey over 80 percent of the PT delegation from the 1999–2002 legislative term.
[32] A survey reported by Carvalho (2006: 89) lends additional evidence for this perception.
[33] Note that 61.7 percent chose "the party," 12.7 percent said "the voters," 14.8 marked "individual conscience," and 14.8 said "social movements."

commitment to the party program, PT deputies reported spending the highest percentage of their time on "policy analysis" instead of activities like "attending to lobbies or requests from individuals" (Hagopian 2005: 46). In this connection, more so than many other Brazilian parties, the PT encourages its deputies to develop special expertise in certain legislative areas, such as agrarian reform, taxation, social security, human rights, and labor issues (Carvalho 2006: 83).[34]

In sum, the legacy of struggle to break into Brazil's political system and the institutional practices that this history generated effectively allowed the party to avoid the typically fragmenting effects of Brazil's open-list arrangement. In this way, it could take full advantage of the proportional element of the electoral system, building up its legislative delegation while endorsing left programs and maintaining a cohesive and disciplined organization. In the context of an electoral framework of proportional representation, the tight links that history had forged between PT politicians and their party allowed the delegation to remain distinctive on both programmatic and organizational grounds.

The Party's Opposition Role

The strong opposition role the PT played also helped build its unique profile and catapult it to public prominence. As long as the PT was in the opposition, as it was before 2003, it had the privilege of criticizing the government and presenting itself as an alternative to the current direction of policy. Less accountable than the governing coalition for national-level policy results, this was the advantage of nonincumbency. For the most part, the PT also remained more radical in the legislature than in municipal office. Unencumbered by the daily challenges and responsibilities that fell to their counterparts in municipal government, PT deputies on the sidelines of power focused on ideologically charged debates concerning major topics like land distribution, social security reform, and the restructuring of the Brazilian economy. Unlike Lula, who grew more moderate with each successive bid for the presidency, they did not need to appeal to an electoral majority. Instead, they positioned themselves for when issues

---

[34] Notably, however, PT deputies rarely sought research assistance from the services provided by the Chamber of Deputies, preferring instead to have their own staff gather information and elaborate bills themselves. An author interview in Brasília on August 11, 2003 with Ricardo José Pereira Rodrigues, director of this service, and an examination of the research requests by Chamber politicians over a period of several years reveals this somewhat hermetic tendency.

Opposition Politics   61

would break their way, which they eventually did. By the 2002 election, the political cycle and electorate favored change. Several developments in the second term of President Cardoso – most importantly, the devaluation of Brazil's currency in 1999, the growth of unemployment and erosion of real wages, and blackouts in major cities caused by energy shortages that were blamed on the Cardoso government's privatization policies – had hurt his popular approval and that of his party, the PSDB. Since the rebirth of Brazil's democracy in 1985 until 2003, the PT was the only major party that had not been in the government. The party's role as the standard bearer of the opposition ultimately contributed to consolidating and expanding the size of the PT delegation as well as to placing Lula in the presidency.

OPPOSITION POLITICS AND ITS SUBSTANCE

What were the substantive issues over which the PT made its mark? How did PT deputies go about resisting government policy and what were the political repercussions of the opposition strategy they pursued? The PT played out its opposition role over politics as well as economics. The delegation's most highly pitched battles on the political front concerned the unscrupulous and corrupt behavior of the country's political class. As I describe in the subsequent text, PT legislators played an important role in the impeachment of President Collor in 1992, followed by actions to expose malfeasance and punish wrongdoing among Chamber politicians. The crux of the economic struggle took place over government efforts to place Brazil on a firmer fiscal footing and restructure the economy in market-conforming ways. In the following paragraphs I examine the PT delegation's resistance to the privatization of state enterprises, the reform of Brazil's pension system, and restrictions on minimum wage hikes.

The PT and Politics

On the political front, the PT delegation engaged in activities that reinforced its image as being above "politics as usual." Alongside activities carried out in municipal politics, PT legislators worked to expose and hold guilty parties accountable in corruption scandals at the national level. The most visible of these involved the party's role on the parliamentary investigatory committee (*Comissão Parlamentar de Inquérito* or CPI) that led ultimately to President Collor's impeachment in 1992. The PT also took an active role in the CPI surrounding a major congressional scandal involving members of the budgetary committee in 1993. Together, the two episodes helped cement the image of the PT as the party of ethical government.

The congressional fact-finding committee that led ultimately to President Collor's removal was instituted in May 1992 to verify the accusation that one of the president's associates was operating an extortion scheme with his knowledge. For its size in the Congress, the PT managed to garner a disproportionately large share of seats on the committee. Although it had only thirty-five deputies and one senator at the time, it obtained one seat for a member with full rights and responsibilities and one seat for a *suplente* (a substitute member). These were granted to the PT for the leading role it assumed in having the CPI installed, a process that began with collecting signatures among opposition deputies (Kada 2003: 53). The committee members most highlighted by the media were those from the PT. Information they unearthed forced the CPI to first conduct a thorough investigation into allegations against the president and later to transfer to the media the information gathered (Kada 2003: 39–40, 50). The subsequent media storm provoked enormous public demonstrations against the Collor government, the largest since Brazilians had taken to the streets in 1984 for the direct elections (*diretas já*) campaign for president. Huge crowds – made up disproportionately of middle-class Brazilians – wore black to protest Collor's appeal for the population to support him by wearing yellow and green. The public reaction was so strong that it became virtually impossible for Collor's dwindling circle of allies to keep backing him. In the end, both the Chamber and the Senate voted overwhelmingly against the president's continuation in office.[35]

The PT also took an active role in the CPI surrounding the congressional budgetary scandal of 1993. In a scheme that operated from the late 1980s until 1992, deputies submitted budgetary amendments for the construction of public works in their states, which their allies on the budget committee approved. The firms, which received contracts through a process of rigged bidding, made huge profits and paid large kickbacks to the deputies, who in turn laundered the money. The PT, along with the PSDB, was one of only two major parties not implicated in the scandal.[36] Investigation, much less prosecution, was an uphill battle given the range of

---

[35] The Chamber decided by a vote of 441 to 38 (with 23 absentees and 1 abstention) to impeach Collor. The Senate voted 76 to 3 against him.

[36] See Ames (2001: 56) for a list of the ringleaders implicated in the scandal and their associated parties.

deputies involved and the fact that most members of the CPI were judging their own in an institution where impunity and mutual protection were long-established norms.[37] Two prominent PT legislators, Senator Eduardo Suplicy and Deputy Aloizio Mercadante, were members of the CPI. Suplicy played a key role in raising the signatures necessary to have the CPI formed.[38] Mercadante, together with PT deputy Chico Vigilante, pushed hard to gain approval for opening the bank accounts and tax returns of the suspected legislators.[39] PT deputy José Genoino leaned on fellow legislators to pressure committee members to take more vigorous action.[40] The National Directorate of the PT threatened to mobilize citizens on the streets if the accused were absolved.[41] In the end, most of those charged either resigned or lost their political rights. That they suffered consequences for their malfeasance was no doubt cause for celebration among Brazilians who wished to see officials held accountable.

PT Opposition to Economic Reform

Privatization. Opposing the efforts of Brazil's market reformers to privatize state enterprises was a key challenge the PT bloc assumed. Although state-led development had enjoyed decades of considerable success, by the time Fernando Collor took office in 1990 it was apparent that many of the country's publicly owned companies were inefficient. Telephone, electricity, and mail services had long begun to deteriorate. The state's capacity to invest in these sectors fell in the 1980s, causing further decline. The telephone system (*Telebrás*) operated below the Latin American average (Kingstone 2003a: 25–26). In an overall context of market reform, underperforming state companies became targets for privatization. The privatization wave began in 1990 with the establishment by President Collor of a list of firms to be privatized. The process of selling off state companies or opening them to some private capital gained momentum with the election of Cardoso in 1994. Privatization was made harder by the 1988 Constitution, which protected sectors deemed strategic to the economy, including all public utilities and mining. Change could not be achieved through executive decree but required the high threshold of

---

[37] "A terra treme," *Veja*, October 27, 1993.
[38] "Congresso decide abrir a CPI do Orçamento," *Jornal do Brasil*, October 19, 1993.
[39] "Deputado quer quebrar sigilo," *Jornal do Brasil*, October 16, 1993; "CPI se empenha em proteger parlamentares," *Jornal do Brasil*, October 27, 1993.
[40] "Até onde vai a CPI," *Veja*, December 15, 1993.
[41] "PT pedirá nas ruas punição de corruptos," *Jornal do Brasil*, October 25, 1993.

congressional approval necessary for constitutional amendments. In the end, however, and over strident PT resistance, a significant portion of the economy's public sector was transferred into private hands.[42]

The PT delegation led the battle against privatization, organizing other left-wing parties such as the PDT, PSB, PCdoB, and PPS on its side.[43] The ideological argument its members advanced was that the Brazilian state would be more likely to defend national interests than would private shareholders, especially foreigners. They contended that successful enterprises like *Petrobrás* and the iron ore giant *Companhia Vale do Rio Doce* positioned Brazil to compete well in an increasingly globalized market, that public utility firms served the poor by charging lower prices for services than would privatized companies, and that profitable state-owned enterprises that relied on the country's rich natural resource base could apply revenues toward social spending.[44] The labor confederation CUT (*Central Única dos Trabalhadores* or Unified Workers' Confederation) and associated PT deputies also had interest-based grounds for opposing the sale of public firms. Because privatization elsewhere had led to large-scale layoffs, the CUT feared the loss of constitutionally guaranteed job stability and the growth of unemployment (Kingstone 2004: 27). At least fifteen of the thirty-six individuals who comprised the PT delegation in the early 1990s had an electoral support base rooted in public sector unions.[45] Heading this group were deputies Paulo Paim from Rio Grande do Sul and Maria Laura from the Federal District. With few exceptions, the PT delegation opposed privatization outright rather than debated the details of the government's proposals or defined a realistic alternative position with the assistance and expertise of the congressional research staff.[46]

---

[42] Between 1991 and 2001, sixty-eight state-owned enterprises were privatized, including almost all steel, chemical, petrochemical and fertilizer companies, the largest mining corporation, the rail system, and several electricity enterprises. The entire telecommunications sector was auctioned between 1998 and 2001. Important privatizations also occurred at the state level.

[43] As I mentioned in earlier text, the PSB is the Brazilian Socialist Party or *Partido Socialista Brasileiro*. The PCdoB is the *Partido Comunista do Brasil* or Communist Party of Brazil. The PPS is the *Partido Popular Socialista* or Popular Socialist Party.

[44] Editorials by PT legislators to this effect include "Por que dizer não à doação da Vale?," *Folha de São Paulo*, April 22, 1997; and "Privatização das teles e o atendimento social," *Folha de São Paulo*, May 30, 1997.

[45] "Radicais do PT vão pressionar candidato," *Folha de São Paulo*, May 16, 1994.

[46] "O PT é a mula-sem-cabeça," *Folha de São Paulo*, May 4, 1994; "PT quer suspender votação de lei das teles," *Folha de São Paulo*, June 13, 1997. See also Kingstone (2003a: 31).

Party and labor opposition manifested itself in a variety of ways. Whereas PT deputies used legislative action, the CUT and associated unions engaged in more direct tactics, such as strikes, protests, and court challenges. PT deputies sought first to prevent the congressional voting process from occurring.[47] When this proved impossible, the PT-led bloc voted solidly against the various bills and amendments that opened the public sector to private investment. It was greatly outnumbered in most of these episodes.[48] Even after the legal framework for various privatizations had been approved, PT legislators presented bills in a desperate attempt to impede the process from actually taking place.[49]

The most highly pitched battles occurred after the privatization program was approved. Left-wing parties and unions belonging to the CUT engaged in direct protests and made court appeals to block privatization from being realized. Protestors tried to break up nearly every important auction through street rallies near the stock market building where the sales took place (Almeida 2004: 65–66). The sell-off of some enterprises was more controversial than others. For example, the CUT brought out more than 70,000 people to oppose the privatization of the *Companhia Vale do Rio Doce*.[50] Oil workers went on strike for thirty-one days in May 1995, continuing even after the labor court ruled the stoppage illegal.

The unions often combined a strategy of strikes with court injunctions (*liminares*) to suspend privatizations from occurring. PT deputies were generally at their side. Lacking sufficient strength to carry the day in the legislature, they pursued their goal through a "judicialization of politics" (Oliveira 2005; Taylor 2008). In 1991, opposition parties and unions appealed in vain to the Supreme Court to revoke the National Divestiture Program issued under President Collor. Thereafter, the PT and its union

---

[47] For example, Jacques Wagner, Milton Temer, and Walter Pinheiro went to the *Supremo Tribunal Federal* to suspend the vote about telecoms scheduled for the following week. "PT quer suspender votação de lei das teles," *Folha de São Paulo*, June 13, 1997.

[48] For example, over 70 percent of all those present voted to break the state's monopoly in telecommunications. A support bloc of similar proportions endorsed allowing private shareholders into partnership with public capital in the ownership and management of the oil firm *Petrobrás*. For further details, see Câmara dos Deputados, Secretaria Geral da Mesa, Lista de Votantes por Partido, Proposition PEC 3/95 and Proposition PEC 6/95, Sessions of May 24, 1995 and June 7, 1995.

[49] "Projeto dá ao Congresso poder de vetar privatizações," *Folha de São Paulo*, August 30, 1996.

[50] "CUT realiza protesto no ABC contra a privatização," *Folha de São Paulo*, May 2, 1997.

allies filed countless injunctions to suspend the auctions of firms (Oliveira 2005: 569–571). Attempted repeatedly at the state and national levels, the tactic ultimately proved unsuccessful.[51]

Notably, the strong resistance shown by PT legislators did not obtain for their counterparts in executive positions. Because privatization provided cities and states the same financial incentives it offered the federal government, PT mayors and governors could not afford to adopt the perspective of opposition politics. Wanting to unload costly and inefficient public enterprises from municipal and state budgets, they took issue with the PT delegation's categorical stance against privatization.[52] For example, Antônio Palocci, mayor of Ribeirão Preto from 1993 to 1996 and later minister of finance in the first Lula government, proceeded to open the local telephone and sewage company to private capital.[53] Similarly, PT Governor Vitor Buaiz (1995–1998) oversaw the privatization of the poorly performing public electricity company in the state of Espírito Santo.[54] He did so over the objections of the national party, the PT delegation in the state legislature, and the CUT. The ensuing conflict between Governor Buaiz and forces within the party and union movement was fierce and ugly, leading Buaiz to leave the PT immediately after finishing out his term.[55] Even those from the party's ideological center – including

---

[51] "Liminar suspende "privatização" do Banerj," *Folha de São Paulo*, February 2, 1996; "Venda do Meridional vai á Justiça," *Folha de São Paulo*, April 3, 1996; "Justiça suspende leilão de ferrovia no Paraná," *Folha de São Paulo*, December 5, 1996; "CAE do Senado derruba proposta do PT que daria ao Senado poder para impedir a venda da estatal," *Folha de São Paulo*, November 27, 1996; and "Oposição usa STF para barrar governistas," *Folha de São Paulo*, November 16, 1997.

[52] Furthermore, PT executives, especially governors, did not feel they could afford to join in a frontal political opposition against President Cardoso because they would need to be in his good graces for resource reasons. Even had there not been specific reasons for pursuing privatization, most states depended heavily on the federal government for transfers and debt rollovers. Only the largest states, such as São Paulo, Rio de Janeiro, and Minas Gerais, were generating sufficient revenues to avoid being cowed into submission by the federal government's control of finances (Kingstone 2004). For an article on the dual and sometimes conflicting identities of the party, see "Dupla identidade," *Veja*, May 3, 1995.

[53] "Palocci defende nova relação com iniciativa privada," *Folha de São Paulo*, November 4, 1996; "Parceria com empresas é lema da situação no PT," *Folha de São Paulo*, July 15, 1997. See also "Erundina faz defesa de privatizações," *Folha de São Paulo*, June 15, 1996.

[54] In the first cohort to break through the difficult gubernatorial barrier, Buaiz was one of only two PT governors at the time. The other was Cristovam Buarque from the Distrito Federal.

[55] See "Petistas admitem aliança com Maluf," *Folha de São Paulo*, November 14, 1996 and "PT busca uma saída para crise com Buaiz," *Folha de São Paulo*, November 25, 1996.

José Dirceu – criticized him sharply. The contrast between the positions held by its governing executives and opposition legislators underscored the importance of institutional context in shaping political interests and actions even for a party as cohesive programmatically as the PT.

Pension Reform. The PT also made its mark opposing the pension reform efforts of President Cardoso. Brazil's pension system suffered from its exorbitantly expensive as well as highly inequitable character.[56] Large numbers of people, especially the poor in the informal sector, had access to neither the public nor the private regime. Beneficiaries in both systems could retire based on time of service: men after thirty years and women after twenty-five.[57] Those who retired under the time-of-service provision – at an average age of 54.9 for men and 53.3 for women – generally maintained or even exceeded their full pay (Madrid 2003: 141). Full pension eligibility for those who retired at the standard age (sixty-five for men and sixty for women) rested on only five years of contributions. The most privileged were public servants, who paid out little for comparatively high benefits.[58] Organized labor was also relatively well protected by the system. The 1988 constitution enshrined a number of benefits that increased the already high cost of the system. Constitutionally secured benefits could be changed only by means of constitutional amendment, which required the support of three-fifths of the Chamber of Deputies and Senate in two consecutive sessions of each body. This high threshold was required for many of the Cardoso era reforms.[59]

The overarching goal of the Cardoso reform effort was to limit benefits among the most privileged and to expand contributions by requiring people to work longer and pay more into the system. Central aspects of the initial proposal included imposing a minimum age requirement on people who wanted to retire based on time of service, and modifying the time-of-service provision by a stipulation of years of *contribution*. The

---

[56] When Cardoso initiated the reform process, the pension system covered only 18 percent of the poorest two quintiles compared to the 80 percent with at least some university education (IDB 1998: 149, as reported in Baker 2009). As of 1999, the General Social Welfare Regime (*Regime Geral de Previdência Social*) covered only 39.9 percent of the eligible working population (Kingstone 2003b: 225). That same year the social security deficit was estimated at US $10 billion (Kingstone 2003b: 221).

[57] Some privileged categories – journalists, university professors, and pilots – could retire with even less time of service.

[58] That system spent on roughly 3 million retirees almost as much as the general social security regime paid its 18 million beneficiaries (Weyland 2006: 93–94).

[59] This would be difficult because the three parties that formed the core of Cardoso's electoral alliance (the PSDB, PFL, and PTB) did not even enjoy a majority in Congress.

bill also sought to extract continued contributions from comparatively affluent individuals who were already retired and to trim privileged pension schemes for various groups, such as university professors, journalists, the judiciary, and the military.[60]

The PT, together with other left parties and the CUT, fiercely opposed the reform effort from the outset. Especially intent on protecting the public system, which covered several groups within the PT's core constituency, PT deputies depicted the reform proposal as motivated by neoliberal ideas and the international financial community against the "acquired social rights" and interests of the Brazilian people ("*o povo brasileiro*") and vulnerable seniors ("*velinhos*"). Furthermore, they maintained that the central problem lay in the high degree of fraud and corruption in the system, and that attacking those fronts would go a long way toward increasing the system's solvency. Although studies showed that it was mainly middle-class people who took advantage of the time-of-service provision (Nassif 2002: 576), party legislators maintained that minimum age and contribution requirements disadvantaged the poor, who often start working early in life but lack proof of contributions. This was part of a larger assertion that the proposed reform did little to change the regressive character of the pension system. The PT insisted also that any prospective changes obtain only for those coming into the system henceforth.

Putting up such strong resistance was part and parcel of the PT's opposition strategy. Public sector employees, an important component of the PT's base, did have a privileged place in the existing system. It is noteworthy that even the CUT expressed willingness to go along with some provisions the PT delegation opposed (Melo 2002: 126, 138; Madrid 2003: 153). Similarly, the party's National Directorate and most within its congressional delegation rejected a proposal that had been formulated in 1993 by a fellow *petista* mainly because central figures in the Cardoso government found it appealing.[61] At times it seemed that the

---

[60] See Melo (2002) and Madrid (2003) for details.
[61] The deputy was Eduardo Jorge from the moderate *Democracia Radical* faction. *Democracia Radical* supported Eduardo Jorge's proposal. José Genoino, a member of that faction, spoke vocally in its favor. The National Directorate demanded that *Democracia Radical* drop its support for Eduardo Jorge's plan and align itself publicly with the party's position. On internal PT controversy over the text elaborated by Eduardo Jorge, see "Comissão acata emenda sobre Previdência," *Folha de São Paulo*, January 6, 1995 and "PT intima ala de Genoino por causa das reformas," *Folha de São Paulo*, April 26, 1995. For a defense by Eduardo Jorge, see "Seguridade social e solidariedade," *Folha de São Paulo*, April 7, 1995.

PT delegation sought an opposition platform more than a reasonable reform. In fact, only one PT deputy requested help from the *Consultoria Legislativa* (Parliamentary Assistance Office) to develop an alternative to the proposal formulated by the Cardoso government (Kingstone 2003b: 234). In addition, in 2003 the Lula administration instituted measures that the PT had combated fiercely while in the opposition. That Lula took this action after years of resistance suggests the important role that the specific institutional context played in shaping the PT's position in the debate.

After nearly four years of struggle, in 1998 the Cardoso government approved a change (Constitutional Amendment 20), albeit one greatly watered down from the original proposal. Due in no small part to obstructionism by the PT-led bloc in the Chamber, the government was unable to reduce appreciably the pension levels for higher-salaried civil servants, institute a minimum retirement age for private-sector workers, or secure immediate enactment of the changes it did achieve so that financial savings could start accruing sooner rather than later.[62] The standard age of retirement remained the same (sixty-five for men and sixty for women) even in the absence of being able to prove one's contribution to the pension system. Nevertheless, for the early retirement of civil servants, the amendment did impose a minimum age requirement (sixty for men and fifty-five for women) and demand proof of contributions (for at least thirty-five years in the case of men and thirty for women). Privileged pension schemes were eliminated for some groups but not others.[63] In the end, the PT bloc in the Chamber voted uniformly against the passage of the constitutional amendment.[64] Some deputies from parties comprising the government coalition (especially the PMDB and PPB) defected and joined them. Little did anyone imagine that Lula would tackle the issue of pension reform upon assuming the presidency but a few years later.

---

[62] The only part of the Cardoso reform with an immediate effect on public employees was a provision by which then-current employees of the state would have to add 20 percent of their remaining time as contributors to receive full benefits.

[63] Privileges were reduced for university professors, the judiciary, and legislators but not for the military or primary and secondary school teachers. Because of the small numbers of people involved, the elimination of special regimes represented a symbolic victory more than a significant financial savings.

[64] Among 461 votes, the final vote in the Chamber was 318 for the bill, 136 against, with 7 abstentions. All forty-eight PT deputies voted against it, as did the nine members of the PCdoB. From the PDT all but two of twenty-four voted "no." All but one of the twelve members of the PSB voted against the bill as well. Some of the votes against the proposal represented defectors from the large PMDB and PPB delegations.

Defining the Minimum Wage. The minimum wage provided another battleground for the PT. Even though advocacy of a higher minimum wage was not as ideologically charged as many of the structural reforms the PT promoted, it was compatible with the pro-poor focus of the party. The level of the minimum wage exerts a strong influence on the welfare of lower-class families. One PT deputy in particular – Paulo Paim from Rio Grande do Sul (1987–2002) – built a reputation for pressuring the government to institute larger wage hikes. Speaking on behalf of the PT delegation and the CUT, he took issue with the government's annual assessment of the purchasing power entailed in the existing minimum wage, arguing that it had eroded more than the government admitted. He also rejected the government's claim that larger salary hikes were impossible because of the negative impact they would have on inflation and unemployment levels and because of the deficits they would cause as a result of the automatic linkage between the minimum wage and pensions.[65] Paim argued that squeezing the minimum wage was not the answer to problems in the pension system and that the government should decrease fraud in the system and increase the number of contributors by providing more jobs.

The dynamic that played out over the course of the Cardoso presidency involved the spearheading of efforts by the PT (together with the CUT) to raise the minimum wage, to which the government initially responded by maintaining that the proposed values would destabilize the economy and later by instituting an increase higher than what it wanted but lower than the value advocated by the PT-led bloc. Notably, the PT often had a disproportionate presence on the Chamber committee that formulated the initial proposal (the *Comissão do Trabalho da Câmara*).[66] Some members of the governing coalition – excluding those from the PSDB and PFL – voted with the opposition.[67] At one point the government conceded the

---

[65] Articles that discuss the highlights of the minimum wage debate in 1996 include the following: "Leia a íntegra da medida," *Folha de São Paulo*, January 5, 1996; "Mínimo deverá subir entre 12 e 13%," *Folha de São Paulo*, April 30, 1996; "Trabalhador vaia reajuste de 12% no D.F," *Folha de São Paulo*, May 2, 1996; "Não há razão," diz Paiva, *Folha de São Paulo*, May 8, 1996; and "FHC veta tramitação de projeto que eleva mínimo," *Folha de São Paulo*, May 8, 1996.

[66] The year 1994 marked the start of a series of concerted attempts made by the PT on the minimum wage. Paulo Paim headed the committee, *Comissão do Trabalho da Câmara* (Labor Committee in the Chamber), which with seven PT deputies (of twenty) was disproportionately weighted toward the PT. There was one deputy each from PSDB, PCdoB, PTB, and PDT; two from PSTU; four from PMDB; and three from PPR.

[67] See "Governo já tem maioria para aprovar MP," *Folha de São Paulo*, April 19, 1994 and "Comissão da Câmara aprova correção mensal de salário," *Folha de São Paulo*, October 20, 1994.

wage level advocated by the PT but only on the condition that prospective recipients of the hike increase their contributions to the pension system. The PT tried unsuccessfully to delink the wage and contribution issue such that hikes could occur irrespective of adjustments in the social security system. In the end, the real variation upward in the minimum wage was estimated at 6.7 percent on average per year from 1995 to 1998 and 2.4 percent on average per year from 1999 to 2002 (Giambiagi 2006: 28).[68]

Complementing the attention that the PT delegation gave to the minimum wage issue throughout the 1990s was a discussion led by PT Senator Eduardo Suplicy about guaranteed minimum income programs. He introduced the issue in April 1991 with a bill to provide all citizens with an income deemed adequate to fulfill basic needs. Whereas the minimum wage issue spoke most directly to the formal sector work force, a core PT constituency, the idea of a minimum income (*renda mínima*) cast the net broader to include more marginalized citizens (Suplicy 2002). Although it was not carried out as originally conceived (as a universal program with no conditions attached), Suplicy's proposal gained partial enactment in programs that did materialize eventually, such as the *Bolsa Escola* (School Stipend), implemented initially at the subnational level and later federalized by the Cardoso government, and the *Bolsa Família* (Family Stipend or BF), which took off under the Lula government. Notably, however, some of the most obstructionist PT deputies were reluctant to endorse Suplicy's efforts in part because they had drawn the positive attention of President Cardoso.[69]

THE PT DELEGATION'S PUBLIC IMAGE

Although few Brazilians followed the details of the aforementioned debates, the positions the delegation adopted in the Congress marked it in the public's mind as being the principal opponent of Brazil's postauthoritarian governments. How did the PT's opposition role affect the party's public image? No doubt many Brazilians regarded the party's delegation as obstructionist and unreasonable. Yet other important factors mitigated this perception in the specific areas just detailed and in the general image projected by the delegation.

---

[68] The minimum wage was increased incrementally each year, from R $112 in 1996 to R $120 in 1997, R $130 in 1998, R $136 in 1999, R $151 in 2000 and eventually to R $180 in 2001. For a list of the value of the minimum wage from 1940 to the present, see Histórico do Salário Mínimo (accessed via http://www.portalbrasil.net/salariominimo.htm).

[69] Author interview with PT Senator Eduardo Suplicy, Brasília, August 5, 2003.

Understanding public reaction to the PT's antiprivatization stance rests on distinguishing between an initial phase when Brazilians were comparatively open to privatization and a later phase when they became more aware of its drawbacks and limitations. By the early 1990s, deteriorating services and widespread accounts of inefficiency, patronage, and corruption in state companies generated positive sentiments toward selling off portions of the public sector. Opinion polls reflected the public's dissatisfaction with key services (Nóbrega 1992) and propensity to think that privatization would improve quality and price levels (Manzetti 1999: 181–2).[70] This was especially evident in certain sectors, such as telephone service (Kingstone 2003a: 35). As long as Brazilians saw matters in this light, it was easy to portray the PT as backward and defensive in its orientation. Moreover, the attention paid to preserving the jobs of unionized state workers lent itself to the criticism that the PT–CUT alliance was defending narrow interests at the expense of collective well-being.[71]

Over time privatization yielded some impressive results but also showed serious limitations. For example, the performance of private firms in public utilities, which often resulted in job losses and sometimes in higher fees for inferior services, did not convince Brazilians that privatization was a superior alternative. In May 2001 the Cardoso government was forced to issue a warning that the country's electrical energy supply faced significant shortfalls. To stop blackouts from occurring it imposed stiff rationing requirements on both residential and commercial customers, imposed fines on violators, and demanded a significant reduction in street lighting, no small matter in a country of such high crime. Similarly, by 2002 a crisis in the telecommunications sector had emerged. A number of firms had left the country and existing operators demanded relief from the government (Kingstone 2004: 47–48). Opinion polls reflect the public's growing skepticism over time. Surveys from the Instituto Brasileiro de Opinião Pública e Estatística (IBOPE) conducted in 1990, 1992, 1995, and 1998 show a decline in support for

---

[70] Of respondents, 45 percent predicted that quality would improve and 39 percent expected that price levels would decrease with privatization. The second most common answer (31 and 31 percent) was to expect no significant change. Only 11 and 17 percent expected quality and price to worsen.

[71] This occurred with the thirty-one-day strike conducted by oil workers in May of 1995, which shut down production and led to shortages of several products, including gas for cooking. The striking workers came off as privileged elites protecting their job status at the expense of others, including the poor. Public opinion turned sharply against the unions and their leftist allies, a situation that President Cardoso used to build momentum for reform.

privatization between 1995 and 1998 (Garcia and Gastaldi 2007: 23).[72] Latinobarómetro data reveal a further rise in discontent between 1998 and 2002 (Checchi, Florio, and Carrera 2005: 28).[73] Respondents cited price rises and increased unemployment as the two most serious disadvantages entailed in the sell-offs (Garcia and Gastaldi 2007: 26). By 2001 a clear plurality of Brazilians called for President Cardoso and his successor to terminate the privatization program (Brazil Focus, September 21, 2001). Given that the 2002 election occurred amidst such deepening dissatisfaction, the PT may ultimately have benefited from its opposition strategy and associated identity on this key issue.

In the battle over pension reform, although well informed citizens had every reason to doubt the PT's defense of the existing system as financially feasible and protective of society's most vulnerable members, large numbers of people did not appear to comprehend the workings of the system or even appreciate the basic fact that most of the benefits proposed for trimming were not ones they enjoyed in the first place. This striking lack of understanding helped the opposition come off more positively than it might have otherwise. When surveyed in 1996, 70 percent of respondents admitted to not understanding the pension debate even though they recognized its importance and were inclined to believe that the reform would hurt most people. Large majorities opposed the government and sided with the opposition (Kingstone 2003b: 232–233).

The PT's advocacy of a higher minimum wage was a winning platform with large numbers of voters. Not responsible for government budgets, the PT delegation could push for sizeable hikes and build a reputation for siding with the working poor. On more than one occasion the leader of the PSDB in the Chamber, José Aníbal, accused the PT of irresponsibly playing to the fans because it was indisputable that the proposed increases would generate economic distortions.[74] Once in 1996 President Cardoso called a special meeting of leaders of the governing parties to ask for special urgency in tabling the PT's proposal to increase the minimum

---

[72] Whereas only 24 percent, 27 percent, and 34 percent claimed to be against privatization in 1990, 1992, and 1995, respectively, this number rose to 51 percent in the 1998 IBOPE survey.
[73] One question asked at both times was this: "The privatization of state companies has been beneficial to the country: Do you strongly disagree, somewhat disagree, are uncertain, somewhat agree, strongly agree? In 1998 only 8.82 percent said that they strongly disagreed with the statement, compared with 38.22 in 2002.
[74] "Câmara eleva mínimo a R $100, FHC vetará," *Folha de São Paulo*, January 19, 1995; "Mínimo leva Aníbal a atacar Paim," *Folha de São Paulo*, April 5, 1995.

wage by 80 percent. Notably, not wanting to be outdone by the PT, other parties – even the PFL – eventually felt pressured to defend higher wage hikes.⁷⁵ Reinforcing the banner the PT delegation raised in the Chamber, Lula began promising to double the minimum wage if elected president.⁷⁶

Above and beyond the specific policies the party endorsed was the overall image the delegation projected. Although for many Brazilians the PT behaved in too strident and intransigent a fashion, few could doubt the dedication and commitment of its deputies. Indeed, they earned a positive reputation for diligence and integrity amidst a political class sorely lacking in such traits. Various media outlets enhanced public awareness of the PT's conduct as a serious programmatic party. In a country where citizens have an exceedingly low opinion of political parties and of Congress as a whole, news reports of PT legislators being a cut above the norm no doubt helped the party.⁷⁷

An important source in this regard was the *Olho no Congresso* or Congress Watch, a special supplement published annually by the well-regarded newspaper *Folha de São Paulo*. Detailing the performance of federal deputies and senators, the Congress Watch consistently identified PT deputies as being among the most active legislators.⁷⁸ Year after year the opposition PT earned high marks in an overall rating based on committee assignments, submission of policy proposals, speaking time on the floor, and attendance in sessions. One of the report's most widely advertised sections concerns legislators' attendance records, a subject that typically generates considerable public disgust. The opposition PT scored exceedingly well in this regard, frequently making it onto the list of

---

75 "Aumento do salário mínimo também gera disputa," *Folha de São Paulo*, January 26, 1998.
76 "Proposta de dobra mínimo divide frente," *Folha de São Paulo*, July 2, 1998; "Lula divulga pacote contra a crise," *Folha de São Paulo*, October 1, 1998; "Petistas defendem indexação salarial," *Folha de São Paulo*, March 18, 1999. Behind closed doors, PT economist Guido Mantega told the party leadership that such a position was unrealistic and unadvisable should Lula actually win. In a similar vein, the PT governors made it discreetly known to party leaders that they did not have the conditions to possibly concede salary adjustments on that order to public employees in their states.
77 As reported in Turner and Martz (1997: 68–69), Latinobarómetro surveys conducted in the mid-1990s reveal that Brazilians expressed the least confidence in political parties and the Congress when asked to rank order a list of basic institutions, which included the military, trade unions, the church, the police, the judiciary, the press, television producers, and big business.
78 In 2001, the *Olho no Congresso* rated the PT as having the single most active congressional delegation of all parties. The pool of comparison was parties with more than forty deputies and senators (the PFL, PMDB, PSDB, PT, and PPB). See "Avaliação revela quem mais atuou," *Folha de São Paulo*, March 22, 2001, Especial-2.

"10 best attending deputies and senators."[79] The legislators flagged for their chronic absenteeism tended to be from catchall parties in Northeastern states. When pressed, they justified their poor records on the grounds of attending to constituent demands back home. By comparison, the emphasis that PT deputies placed on shaping national policies made Brasília a priority location.[80]

Another source, the *Departamento Intersindical de Assessoria Parlamentar* or Inter-Union Department of Parliamentary Assistance, produces a yearly study of the 100 most influential figures in the Congress (Chamber and Senate). Despite being a union-based lobby, the Inter-Union Department enjoys a reputation for informative and impartial legislative analysis. *Os Cabeças do Congresso Nacional* (Leading Figures of the National Congress) classifies parliamentarians into proposal drafters, negotiators, debaters, and public opinion leaders. In the 1990s the two parties that figured most prominently among the 100 figures selected were the PT and PSDB, the leading opposition party and the principal party of government.[81] The number of PT deputies who appeared on the list greatly exceeded the relative size of the party's Chamber delegation.[82]

SUBTLE SHIFTS TOWARD MODERATION

Notwithstanding the party's strident and uncompromising public views, there was more change underway than met the eye. The PT's comparatively unified opposition profile masked important differences within the delegation. Beneath the surface were voices calling for moderation and modernization. Deputies like José Genoino, Eduardo Jorge, Paulo Delgado, and Aloizio Mercadante urged fellow party members to create an alternative to neoliberalism rather than to simply obstruct change.[83]

---

[79] See, for example, "Os Deputados Mais Assíduos," *Folha de São Paulo*, January 14, 1996, Especial-4. For the Senate, see "Os 10 mais assiduos do Senado," *Folha de São Paulo*, February 5, 1998, Especial-4. Eduardo Suplicy and José Eduardo Dutra represented two out of six senators with the best attendance records. See also "Os mais assíduos na Câmara e no Senado," *Folha de São Paulo*, January 30, 1997, Especial-4.

[80] "Ausentes culpam as 'bases eleitorais,'" *Folha de São Paulo*, January 14, 1996, Especial-5.

[81] See "Os 'Cabeças' do Congresso Nacional: Uma pesquisa sobre os 100 parlamentares mais influentes no Poder Legislativo," *Departamento Intersindical de Assessoria Parlamentar* (various years).

[82] Carvalho (2006: 84) shows the breakdown by party of the deputies chosen for the "Cabeças do Congresso Nacional" list from 1994 to 2006.

[83] "Morte de um quase partido moderno," *Folha de São Paulo*, February 20, 1994; "A desmedida do governo," *Folha de São Paulo*, May 24, 1996.

More specifically, they discussed the need to revise aspects of the 1988 constitution that were progressive but excessively constraining and fiscally unviable in nature. Contradicting the party's categorical opposition to privatization, José Genoino, Jacques Wagner, and other moderates called for a more nuanced stance that accepted private initiative in certain areas as long as the state maintained regulatory power (Manzetti 1999: 39). Such views led these individuals and their allies into conflict with more radical PT deputies as well as members of the party directorate.[84]

Instrumental electoral calculations as well as genuine ideational shifts motivated moderation in the PT delegation. It became increasingly clear that candidates with moderate profiles tended to get elected over their more radical counterparts. This was true even in races to fill lower-house seats from the developed industrial states, the context most suitable for the election of radicals.[85] For example, of the forty deputies elected in 1994, only four were from the extreme left.[86] In 1998, moderates like José Genoino, Aloizio Mercadante, Telma de Souza, and Antônio Palocci won by large margins in São Paulo. At the same time, more left-leaning figures like Luiz Eduardo Greenhalgh (who provided legal council for the MST) and Ivan Valente (who left the PT for the Party for Socialism and Liberty in 2005) did not win reelection.[87]

Authentic shifts in the attitudes held by members of the PT delegation were also apparent. For example, José Genoino stepped forth and advocated change in an interesting and compelling 1997 essay in which he cautioned the party against remaining mired in a strategy of pure negation and opposition directed against the *"fantasma"* of neoliberalism. Concerned that the party risked appearing excessively wrapped up in the rhetoric of its social movement base, he pointed out that aspirations to govern demanded the development of clearer and more realistic ideas about directing the state and running the economy. Genoino pointed out that global transformations, such as economic integration, new technology, and the end of the Cold War, required a redefinition in the role of the state: How would the PT revise its views on these and related questions?[88]

Evidently, other PT deputies followed Genoino's lead in questioning the delegation's approach. Studies of ideological patterns among

---

[84] "PT recua e desiste de punir deputados," *Folha de São Paulo*, 15 May, 1995.
[85] "Baixo Teores de Radicalismo," *IstoÉ*, November 2, 1994.
[86] "Bancada quer tomar dos radicais commando do PT," *Jornal de Brasília*, October 19, 1994.
[87] "Eleição fortalece o group moderado e muda perfil do PT," *O Globo*, October 10, 1998.
[88] "Os dilemmas do PT para 98," *Folha de São Paulo*, January 1, 1997.

legislative parties in Brazil document the movement of many PT deputies from the left to the center left. In a series of surveys administered in 1990, 1993, 1997, 2001, and 2005, federal legislators were asked to place legislators from other major political parties on a scale of 1–10, with 1 being furthest left and 10 being furthest right. There was a slight but nonetheless discernable shift in perceptions of the PT over time. Rated as 1.51 in 1990, the PT was assigned a score of 2.27 in 2001. The biggest leap occurred between 2001 and 2005, when it was placed at 3.94 (Power 2008). Studies that combine the ideological self-placement of legislators with the perceptions of those from other parties document a similar pattern (Power and Zucco 2009).

CONCLUSION

The PT was and remained at its most radical and distinctive in the legislative arena, notwithstanding subtle signs of adaptation that occurred in the Chamber over the 1990s. In this decade, the delegation remained programmatic in its approach and highly disciplined in its organization and voting record. Its members were unwilling to purchase a more dramatic electoral ascendance by making a sharp turn toward pragmatism. They resisted the temptation to hitch themselves to stars that might have ascended more rapidly yet also stood at risk of burning out. This allowed the PT to consolidate grassroots support and build a strong organization over time.

One of the important implications of this opposition role was that the PT was well poised to capitalize on the misfortunes of the PSDB and its allies when the economic and political winds shifted against the Cardoso government in the late 1990s – with exchange rate crises, a devaluation, high unemployment, stagnant real wages, and electricity failures that were blamed on Cardoso's privatization policies. The context of Lula's winning 2002 campaign was one of considerable dissatisfaction with the status quo in the country (Meneguello 2005). Although Lula moderated his discourse to attain a long-sought presidential victory, his remained the voice of an opposition that had managed to create strong roots in society and was widely perceived as an alternative to the status quo. The PT's conduct in the Chamber was decisive in contributing to this foundation of Lula's eventual victory.

If the opposition role that the party played in the Congress allowed the PT to represent a truly alternative ideological option, its role in municipal government provided a counterbalance. A second track upon which the

PT evolved was that of executive positions in local government, which encouraged and induced the party toward pragmatism. Thus, in local government the PT would complement the image it had carved out as a protest party in the legislative arena. Endorsing a softer or at least more workable version of its views would build upon the PT's reputation and ultimately yield electoral returns, as many candidates – most prominently Lula himself – would see.

4

The PT in Municipal Government

The Pragmatic Face of the Party

In this chapter I analyze the role of mayoral elections and local governmental officeholding in shaping the PT's development. Invoking principles from rational choice, I seek to understand how the PT adapted and learned from its experience in municipal government. If leading the legislative opposition positioned the PT to maintain far-left stances on issues of national importance, the institutional requirements of winning mayoral elections and the array of challenges and responsibilities involved in governing cities motivated the party's mayoral candidates and officeholders to enact changes that reflected greater moderation and pragmatism. Rational choice institutionalism would expect that the institutional context of mayoral elections and municipal government would induce such changes.

However, combining the role of governing cities with the PT's transformative political project and maintaining smooth relations with local party adherents often proved problematic, especially in the beginning. Adaptation took place only after considerable internal conflict. Historical institutionalism sheds light on the tensions that preceded and surrounded the process of adaptation. This was summed up well by a leading PT figure: "The major problem, when we analyze the role of our mayors and governors, lies in how to combine the governing of cities and states with the national political struggle" (Dirceu 1999: 19, author's translation). Many of the fiercest battles fought within the party concerned contradictions stemming from the simultaneous opposition and governing roles played by the party. Similarly, tensions arose between party officials at the local and national levels and the mayors themselves. The former were highly committed to having the PT's municipal administrations reflect the party's historical project. The latter struggled against hard economic and political constraints to address collective problems and needs that arose in the daily governing of cities. Among some activists, ideology was tempered by the reasoning that a solid record in municipal governments could serve as a stepping-stone to the presidency. Notably, however, in line with what historical institutionalism would predict, internal resistance to adopting measures to conform to changing times and circumstances was strongest in cities where the party was founded and where activist networks were strongly entrenched (e.g., São Bernardo do Campo, Santo André, and other municipalities of the ABC district of São Paulo).[1]

How these various forces came together and evolved over time is the subject of this chapter. Whereas internal disputes took a toll on the governing and reelection records of many early PT municipal administrations, demonstrating a capacity to govern helped expand the PT's electoral base and positioned it – at least temporarily – as an alternative to the government at the national level. The changing orientation of PT mayors over time reflects this dual recognition, bearing out the expectations of a rational choice institutionalist framework. The party learned from its mistakes and successes and seemed to accept a certain separation between the long-term ideological project of the PT at the national level and the more immediate and concrete challenges facing its mayors.

Thus in the end the PT demonstrated a real adaptive capacity. There was centralized learning from the initial mistakes made in municipal government, followed by the encouragement, from above, of a decentralized process of policy innovation. The development of signature programs such as participatory budgeting and the *Bolsa Escola* (School Stipend) reflected a commitment to honoring and furthering the party's basic values of participation, transparency, and redistribution yet within the confines of the extant political and economic order. Despite the heterogeneity of municipalities governed by the PT, there were core experiences and programs that contributed to forming a distinctive PT image – the *modo petista de governar* – at the local level. Popular participation, an "inversion" of investment priorities toward the poor, and greater transparency in government constituted the principles that characterized the "PT mode of governing."

[1] "PT de resultados," *Istoé*, October 14, 1992.

THE PT IN CITY HALLS ACROSS BRAZIL

Similar to its upward trajectory in other electoral arenas, the PT increased the number of mayoralties it governed over time. As in the Chamber of Deputies, its initial strength lay in the South and Southeast regions. Early PT administrations were found disproportionately in the country's larger cities. Over time the party extended its reach into small towns and interior regions. In 1988, the PT elected thirty-six mayors, up from the one it held in 1985 (Fortaleza) and the two it had won in 1982 (Diadema and Santa Quitéria do Maranhão). Besides winning three state capitals – São Paulo, Porto Alegre, and Vitória – the PT carried six middle-sized industrial cities in the state of São Paulo, three smaller industrial cities in Minas Gerais, and many smaller towns throughout the country. When the thirty-six new mayors assumed office in 1989, approximately 10 percent of all Brazilians came to live under a PT administration (Bittar 1992: 9). In 1992, the party increased the number of city halls it governed to fifty-four. Its victories included the capital cities of Porto Alegre, Belo Horizonte, Rio Branco, and Goiânia. In 1996 the PT won 115 municipalities, sustaining itself in power in Porto Alegre and gaining Belém, the capital city of the northern state of Pará. The year 2000 was a big year, with the party sweeping 187 city halls, placing roughly 18 percent of Brazil's citizens under PT government (Baiocchi 2003: 13). The party was reelected in Porto Alegre and Belém, regained São Paulo after losing it in 1992, and won several other capital cities. By 2001 the PT could claim to have governed in a broad array of cities ranging in size and nature from the highly industrialized megalopolis of São Paulo to small rural towns in the interior of the country. After winning the presidency in 2002, the number of PT-run municipal governments leapt to 411 in 2005. That election placed the PT in government in nine (of twenty-six) capital cities.[2] Like all parties that have held national executive office, the PT increased its electoral following in small towns in rural regions. That trend continued in the 2008 elections (see Charts 4.1 and 4.2).

These increases in the number of PT mayoralties did not occur casually or in the absence of a favorable institutional context. In 1988 the party created the National Secretariat for Institutional Issues (*Secretaria Nacional de Assuntos Institucionais*), one of whose principal charges

---

[2] These were Belo Horizonte, Porto Velho, Rio Branco, Macapá, Palmas, Fortaleza, Recife, Aracajú, and Vitória.

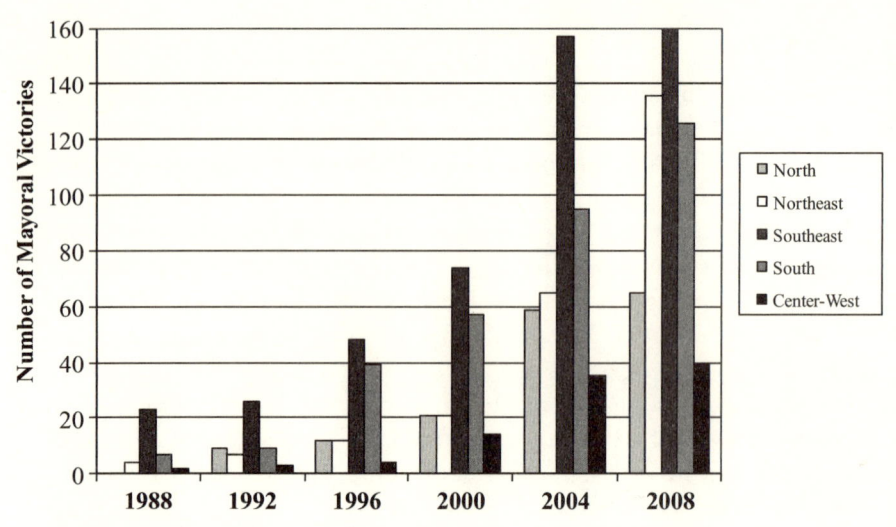

CHART 4.1. Mayoral PT wins by region, 1988–2008. (*Source: Tribunal Superior Eleitoral.*)

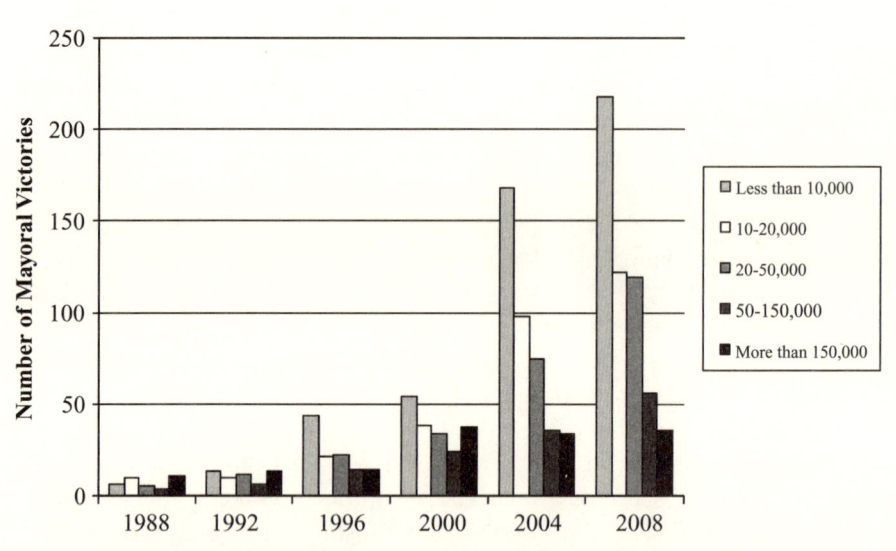

CHART 4.2. Mayoral PT wins by city size, 1988–2008. (*Sources: Tribunal Superior Eleitoral, Instituto Brasileiro de Geografia e Estatistica.*)

was to coordinate plans to win local-level contests and help elected PT mayors oversee innovative and successful governments.³ This kind of systematic and centralized strategy designed to expand the party's network at the local level was almost unheard of in the major catchall parties, which in many cases were mere collections of regional machines (Bittar 1992). An important part of the discussion involved formulating key principles that PT municipal governments should strive to promote: redistribution, popular participation, transparency, the democratization of the state, and the creation of a less elitist and more popular political culture. Indeed, despite the heterogeneity of Brazil's municipalities, the party aspired toward some level of uniformity among its municipal governments.

The broad institutional context for enacting innovative local-level policies was rendered more favorable by the 1988 Constitution, which "made Brazil one of the most decentralized countries in the world in terms of the distribution of its fiscal resources and political power" (Souza 1996: 529). The reforms it enshrined were responsible for both increasing the transfers to municipalities and enhancing local government powers of taxation and revenue collection, thereby loosening the constraints that the federal and state governments could exert on opposition mayors (Abers 2000: 28). Stated well by one analyst, "Brazil's decentralization created the institutional openings for actors with ties to civil society and social movements to carry out progressive experiments" (Baiocchi 2005: 8). Leftist municipal governments in other Latin American contexts (e.g., the *Izquierda Unida* in Peru) encountered greater difficulty, given their lack of power and resources in highly centralized and resource poor states (Roberts 1998: 247). Besides gaining political and fiscal autonomy from higher levels of government, Brazil's municipalities were given more responsibility for major aspects of social service delivery. The Constitution recognized that cities would be the main administrative unit responsible for health, education, and transportation services. It also established legal provisions for participatory mechanisms in the development of social programs, such as citizen councils. By allowing for innovation, decentralization helped the PT build up political support while in the national political opposition.⁴

---

³ "PT cria instituto para dar assessoria aos prefeitos eleitos pelo partido," *Folha de São Paulo*, November 5, 1988.
⁴ Clearly, however, certain municipalities were better positioned than others to make use of these provisions. Most of the country's more than 5,000 municipalities have struggled to generate their own income, remaining highly dependent on transfers from higher levels of government (Souza 1997: 103). Similarly, because there are shortages of experienced professional staff, many have been exceedingly challenged by their new administrative

What kinds of policy innovations distinguished local PT governments? A programmatic consensus emerged in the mid- to late 1980s around the goals of "inverting priorities," redistributing wealth, enhancing popular participation, and promoting transparency in government affairs, which in turn formed the basis of signature programs the PT developed.[5] The inversion of priorities refers to shaping public policy to favor the poor: enhancing the quality and availability of public education, health, transportation, and low-income housing. The inversion would be accomplished by requiring more affluent sectors to pay higher taxes and improving tax collection overall.[6]

The PT's commitment to popular participation was best exemplified by the implementation of participatory budgeting schemes in the municipalities it governed. The first major experience of participatory budgeting began in 1989 under the PT administration in Porto Alegre, a city governed by a succession of PT mayors from 1989 to 2004.[7] Participatory budgeting spread to dozens of other cities after its emergence in Porto Alegre.[8] By the mid-1990s such programs had become standard – albeit

responsibilities. Places like Porto Alegre and São Paulo – where the PT was able to gain traction early on – are favored by rules privileging the kinds of property taxes that can be raised by large, rich cities, such as building and urban land taxes. These municipalities have the financial leeway to enact policies directed toward poorer neighborhoods without unduly hurting other more privileged interests. They also benefit from being able to draw on a larger pool of personnel with relevant administrative and professional experience.

[5] Bittar (1992) and Magalhães, Barreto, and Trevas (1999) capture well the principles that the PT tried to achieve in its programs and policies.

[6] For example, the mayoral administration of Luiza Erundina (1989–1992) in São Paulo increased social spending nearly ten percentage points above what it had been in the previous fifteen years. An increase in the direct tax on property, the *Imposto Predial e Territorial Urbano*, and improved tax collection in general funded this hike (Macaulay 1996: 222). By publishing lists of tax evaders, ending previous amnesties, and making property taxes more progressive, Porto Alegre mayor Olívio Dutra (1989–1992) used tax reforms to raise more money for new socially minded investments (Goldfrank 2003: 37). Marta Suplicy, the PT mayor of São Paulo elected in 2000, also used progressive taxation on urban properties and land toward social ends (Couto 2003: 86). Similarly, Mayor Edmilson Rodrigues increased city revenues in Belém by instituting a new *Imposto Predial e Territorial Urbano* based on an updated geographic survey (Guidry and Petit 2003: 69).

[7] These were Olívio Dutra (1989–1992), Tarso Genro (1993–1996), Raul Pont (1997–2000), Tarso Genro (2001–2002), and João Verle (2002–2004).

[8] The Porto Alegre model has been the subject of much reflection (e.g., Fedozzi 1997; Genro and Souza 1997; Santos 1998; Abers 2000; Nylen 2003; Baiocchi 2005; Goldfrank and Schneider 2006; Wampler 2007). The city allocates a comparatively large portion of the budget for participatory decision making and mobilizes far more participants than elsewhere. Since implementing participatory budgeting, Porto Alegre has seen appreciable improvements in areas such as housing, sewage, street paving, health care, and transportation (Goldfrank 2007: 160).

with enormous variations – in PT governed municipalities.⁹ Participatory budgeting refers to a process whereby ordinary citizens decide how to allocate a portion of the municipal budget. By having citizens establish annual investment priorities in public assemblies, the PT hoped to fulfill a wide range of goals: strengthen its connections with civil society, stimulate participation by its actual and potential voter base, promote outcomes that favored the interests of poorer residents, create a more democratic political culture, circumvent legislative opposition, provide an alternative to clientelism as a means of resource distribution, help participants identify and advance collective interests, and even tame the demands of the most highly organized interests (e.g., unions) by mobilizing others less privileged.¹⁰

Participatory budgeting was but one step in the PT's broader effort to promote the principles of transparency and accountability. Forcing open bidding for municipal contracts, firing "phantom" employees, and doing away with secret voting in municipal chambers were among other actions for which PT officials became known. Two figures who later assumed important national legislative positions, Eduardo Suplicy and José Eduardo Cardozo, spearheaded important anticorruption efforts while serving in the municipal chamber of São Paulo. Suplicy launched investigations and pressed corruption charges successfully against numerous former officials, including four past presidents of the council. By insisting on open voting, Cardozo sought to make council members more accountable for their actions. These and related actions gained positive media attention.

The *Bolsa Escola* (School Stipend) is another program closely identified with PT governance at the local level. A conditional cash transfer program, the core idea behind the *Bolsa* is to increase school attendance among children of impoverished families by providing their parents (more specifically their mothers) with an economic incentive to keep them in school. For a low-income family, forgoing the informal child labor that consistent schooling entails represents an opportunity cost on top of the more direct costs of schooling, such as supplies, transportation, and

---

⁹ By 2004, all PT governments in municipalities with at least 100,000 residents had adopted participatory budgeting. Most PT governments in smaller cities had done so as well (Wampler 2007: 25–26). Many non-PT administrations eventually adopted the model, albeit across a range of commitment levels.

¹⁰ These goals have been achieved with varying degrees of success. Examining a range of cases, Wampler (2007) presents a systematic and even-handed treatment of participatory budgeting. Among the key factors associated with the positive experiences are strong mayoral support, cordial mayoral–legislative relations, and a solid financial base.

uniforms. In most municipalities, receipt of the monthly stipend depended on undergoing a "means test" and showing regular school attendance of one's children. PT governor Cristovam Buarque, who assumed office in the Federal District in 1995, drew widespread attention and acclaim to the *Bolsa Escola* (Aguiar and Araújo 2002). In 2001 the Cardoso government enacted a federal version of the program (Sugiyama 2007: 102–103). Core features of the *Bolsa Escola* made their way eventually into the *Bolsa Família*, a larger, more unified and better-funded program enacted by the Lula government.

FACTORS INDUCING MODERATION

If decentralizing reforms increased the opportunities available to PT-led administrations, a parallel set of constraints worked to reduce the degree of radicalism exercised by PT mayors. The requirements for election and the challenges of governing were key among these.

Electoral Requirements

Winning a mayor's race entails securing a higher threshold of support than does election to the Chamber of Deputies. This is especially true for larger municipalities. From 1992 onward, gaining mayoral office in a municipality with more than 200,000 voters has rested on receiving an absolute majority of valid votes (not counting blank or null ballots) – at least in a runoff race.[11] Sixty-eight cities in 2004 were required to have second-round elections in the event that no candidate received an absolute majority of the valid vote in the first round.[12] Smaller municipalities require a plurality, which is still more than necessary to secure a seat in proportional races for the lower house of Congress. These high thresholds, together with the nonideological or centrist composition of a large portion of the Brazilian electorate, favor candidates willing and able to make appeals across the political spectrum. Recognition of this reality also influences whom the party leadership nominates to run in the first place. Over time, top party leaders came to believe that moderates were both more likely to win mayoral elections and oversee the most

---

[11] "Mais municípios podem ter segundo turno nesta eleição," *Jornal do Brasil*, October 1, 1996.
[12] Only three capital cities have fewer than 200,000 voters: Rio Branco (Acre), Boa Vista (Roraima), and Palmas (Tocantins). These numbers from the *Tribunal Superior Eleitoral* are reported by David Fleischer in *Brazil Focus*, January 12–18, 2008.

successful administrations. With few exceptions, considerations of electoral and governing viability favored the selection of candidates with moderate profiles.

Nevertheless, the process of choosing a single nominee has often stirred up conflict. Unlike the selection of the large number of candidates to compete in Chamber races, several bitter battles have been fought over the nomination of mayoral candidates. The selection of Luiza Erundina as the PT candidate for the 1988 mayoral election in São Paulo represented a case in point.[13] The candidacy for that race was disputed between Luiza Erundina and Plínio de Arruda Sampaio. Closely identified with popular movements on the periphery of the city, Erundina represented the militant face of the party. Plínio Sampaio, a more middle-class figure, enjoyed the support of the majority of party leaders and the majority faction, the *Articulação*. The decision was ultimately made by a primary election, in which Erundina won 56 percent of the vote. Against the leadership, the party's base opted for the more militant social worker with the "face of the PT" (Singer 1996: 18–20).[14] In general, however, the evolution has been toward mayoral candidates who promise to appeal to a wide range of voters and navigate their way as smoothly as possible through complicated issues and interests once in power.

Governing Responsibilities

The challenges of executive office pushed most elected PT mayors toward greater pragmatism. The responsibilities of governing provided impulses for change within the party. Being held accountable to a broader electorate as opposed to merely criticizing the government in the legislature generated incentives to come up with workable solutions to a wide variety of municipal problems. Once in office, PT mayors discovered that the pressures to compromise and negotiate with a broad range of groups, including private business, were considerable. For example, city transportation has been a vexing issue for many mayors, who have found themselves caught between unions of transportation workers that bargain for higher wages, citizens who resist price hikes, and bus

---

[13] Primaries for executive candidates have been held when consensus within the party leadership has proven elusive. In general, however, the party tries to avoid them.

[14] More recently, in 2004, a serious conflict broke out over whether to allow Luizianne Lins to run on the PT ticket for mayor of Fortaleza, which she eventually succeeded in doing. In both episodes, considerations of electoral and governing viability caused the Lula faction to side against the candidate who eventually emerged.

companies – private and public – that demand more money to operate satisfactorily. It grew apparent that the more radical PT city governments tended to bring on greater conflict than their less radical counterparts and were thus less likely to win reelection.[15] Given especially the small number of PT-led statehouses (of a possible twenty-seven, only two PT governors were elected in 1994 and three in both 1998 and 2002), it was important that the party build a strong governing record in the municipal arena. For the better part of fifteen years this was the main context in which the PT gained executive experience. Because the party cut its teeth on several large cities – São Paulo, Porto Alegre, and even Fortaleza – the national media covered these experiences, for good or ill.

Appointing Party Militants to Municipal Offices

As the PT won subnational executive office it gained access to government resources, which complemented selective and collective incentives obtained through movement or union politics. Brazil's biggest cities tend to have large bureaucracies, allowing PT officials to hire some of their associates. Each department head appointment provided an opportunity for the mayor to bring in his or her own aides (Singer 2001: 85). These same cities also tend to have a large number of civic organizations. When the PT attains power, many activists take official roles within the administration or participate in its policy-making councils. For example, mayor Olívio Dutra of Porto Alegre (1989–1992) is well known to have staffed municipal departments with PT activists independent of their expertise or experience (Baiocchi 2005: 33). The same can be said of Raul Pont, mayor of Porto Alegre from 1997 to 2000. Similarly, Edmilson Rodrigues in Belém employed *petistas* from various currents of the party toward the explicit goal of taming radicalism and stemming factional infighting (Guidry and Petit 2003). In short, the party's ascension to executive office brought many radical activists and social movements closer to the state. Because militants thereby gained a concrete and direct stake in the reelection of the PT government, they were motivated to act in ways that increased that prospect. The professionalization of many civil society activists – some of whom gained significant social mobility and economic security as a result – made them less likely to defy elected PT governments. This demobilization of the PT at the local level had an important impact

---

[15] The first time that *individuals* could be reelected as mayors was in 2000, yet the party always sought to place another *petista* in office.

on supporting the moderating efforts of the PT leadership at the national level. Given the structure of leadership selection, whereby lower-level party officials elect those at higher levels (even for party president before 2001), the effects of co-optation arguably filtered upward. Similarly, a diminution of social mobilization and protest activities at the local level enhanced the credibility of Lula's efforts to moderate his proposals for government over various presidential races.

Problems Encountered

The core issue facing the party early on involved reconciling its larger historical project with a realistic and immediate plan of action for governing Brazil's cities. Put concretely by Gianpaolo Baiocchi (2005: 33), the question was, "[s]hould the PT administration's chief focus be managing the capitalist city or manning the trenches in the fight for socialism?... Who would make decisions – the mayor, the party, or social movements?" How in fact would the PT forge a viable plan of action, politically and financially, in line with its guiding historical principles?

The PT had not adequately thought out answers to these questions beforehand, certainly not in 1982 or 1985 but more importantly not even in 1989 when thirty-six PT mayors assumed office, many in cities with serious financial problems. For one, relevant personnel had not decided who would be in charge: the elected official and his or her administration, the party, or unions and social movements. They were also slow to find an appropriate and workable balance between governing for the collective on the one hand and attending to the party's historical constituencies on the other. Moreover, no longer would it be possible to simply assume a negative posture, as the PT did in its opposition role in the legislature. Instead, the party's elected officials would have to show that they could present a true alternative to municipal government as usual yet one allowed by existing structures. Many PT-led municipal governments settled eventually on reasonable and even imaginative compromises but not without first experiencing conflict and even defeat in subsequent elections.

The PT in São Paulo (1989–1992): A Reflection of First-Generation Problems

The 1989–1992 PT administration in São Paulo – headed by Mayor Luiza Erundina – epitomized many of the early PT-led municipal administrations. The core problems Erundina encountered were shared by other

PT governments, for example, in Fortaleza (1986–1988) and some in the same cohort like Campinas (1989–1992). Tensions were rife between the elected government and various other actors: the party (national and local elements), unions and social movements, private business, the city council, and the media. The experience in São Paulo, which led to defeat in the next mayoral election, was pivotal in prompting the party to rethink many of its previous positions about municipal government.

It was to be expected that Erundina's administration would run into problems with business and the private sector. Conflict with these groups was built into the structure of the "inversion of priorities" that PT mayors sought to promote. To divert greater financial resources into pro-poor social policies, PT-led municipalities would need to raise taxes, in part by instituting a more progressive tax structure. Reforming the local property tax law to accomplish this in São Paulo proved difficult. After the municipal legislature passed the law, business groups took Erundina's government to court, contending that the law's progressivism was unconstitutional. Although they did not win in court, they succeeded in hurting the PT government by stalling the tax reform until after it left power. Property owners also strongly resisted changes in property tax rates instituted by mayor Olívio Dutra (1989–1992) in Porto Alegre (Abers 2000: 94–95). A similar reaction occurred in Belém (Guidry and Petit 2003: 67–68).

Intense conflict also transpired between Erundina and her government on the one hand and the party and affiliated unions on the other. Through the lens of rational choice and historical institutionalism, the struggle was between forces that admitted change and those committed to persistence. Whereas the mayor and leading members of her government responded to incentives that encouraged adaptation, PT militants and the party's union base remained wed to norms and practices inherited from the past. The party – influenced by Leninist organizational principles as well as its own opposition origins – maintained that it had a legitimate right to influence the decisions of the elected government, which it saw as central to the PT's long-term ideological project. Party leaders at both the national and local levels viewed the municipal government's actions through the lens of historic party issues, such as the party program, factional power disputes, and accountability to the activist base. Whereas elements in the party clung to an outlook that was forged when the PT was still struggling to emerge, the elected government quickly moved beyond that perspective when faced with the daunting challenges of governing a megalopolis like São Paulo. Though inexperienced, Erundina and her *petista* allies in the government recognized that their new position entailed a new set of incentives and required a higher degree of autonomy from the party. Their task was not simply or even especially to attend to the party's base but rather to meet the needs of as many city residents as possible within the hard economic and political constraints that existed. Against fierce party resistance, Erundina grew strongly committed to an approach that became known as the "PT of results."[16]

Erundina battled with local party committees for the four years she was in power. Although many members stayed in the trenches, she grew increasingly pragmatic and pluralistic with time. Aggravating tensions was the fact that she had distributed all the major posts in her government to factions that had supported her candidacy, alienating others in the process. Given that the PT did not control the city council (it held less than 30 percent of all seats), an initial failure to form an interparty coalition in the municipal legislature hurt her as well. Such an alliance would have put her government on a firmer political foundation and perhaps even shielded it from the constant dictates of the party (Couto 2003: 81–82). Learning from her experience, many subsequent PT officials in executive positions – mayors, governors, and even Lula himself – adopted a more inclusive approach, drawing in not only broader factions of the party but also forming wider interparty alliances.

Strife also existed between the PT administration and some of the party's historical social movement support bases, especially CUT-affiliated unions. In fact, many of the intraparty disputes about the role of a socialist party running a municipal government turned on whether Erundina's administration would give special priority to formal sector workers (the PT's effective core constituencies) or pay equal attention to other sectors of society, including or perhaps especially those less organized and well off. Notably, although many PT mayors had begun their careers in union politics, they quickly came to understand that they could not behave like trade unionists while in the mayor's office (Macaulay and Burton 2003: 136). As with other PT-led municipalities of the 1989–1992 cohort, including the troubled administration of Jacó Bittar in Campinas, Erundina faced cross-cutting pressures between raising the wages of municipal workers and attending to other city residents, including poorer and less organized constituents who had provided an important margin for her victory. The highly contentious municipal employee unions

---

[16] "Contra resistências, Erundina desenvolve o 'PT de resultados'," *Folha de São Paulo*, February 25, 1990.

affiliated with the CUT strongly resisted the administration's attempts to contain salaries or to make major changes in the bureaucratic structure of the government. The party, both national and local, mostly backed the unions over Erundina's government.[17]

City transportation services proved to be an especially controversial area.[18] The most contentious episode took place in 1992, when bus drivers and conductors demanded wage hikes that the financially strapped administration refused to grant. The standoff between their unions and the mayor led to a total shutdown of the public transportation system for nine days and the firing of large numbers of workers. The stance that Erundina took spoke volumes: The longtime PT militant sided with the public interest over the demands of the strikers and local party. The Municipal Directorate of the PT responded by censuring the mayor over her handling of the strike. The National Directorate did not intervene on her behalf even though it recognized that a strike that so impaired the city's functioning was poor press for a party seeking to control the national executive. Even Lula, who would eventually become a vocal voice in favor of pragmatism, condemned Erundina and several other PT mayors for their policies vis-à-vis city transportation.[19] The media were all over the story. Especially because events in São Paulo constituted local news for major media outlets – such as the *Folha de São Paulo* and the financial daily *Gazeta Mercantil* – word of the PT's disunity and inability to govern with minimal order and efficacy was broadcast across the country. Notwithstanding the mostly negative press toward the 1989–1992 generation of PT mayors, the media did note the lack of any hint of corruption in cities governed by the party.[20]

Negative Electoral Consequences from the 1989–1992 Generation of PT Mayors

The 1989–1992 PT administrations fared poorly on the whole. In stark contrast to the euphoric climate that surrounded their inaugurations, most ended on a somber note. Of the thirty-six mayors elected in 1988,

---

[17] "PT acerta contas com prefeitos," *Estado de São Paulo*, January 30, 1990; "Cabresto inaceitável," *Istoé Senhor* 1125, April 17, 1991.

[18] Many of the insights in this paragraph come from an author interview with Paulo Sandroni, head of the Department of Metropolitan Transportation under former PT mayor Luiza Erundina. The interview took place in São Paulo on July 14, 2003.

[19] "PT acerta contas com prefeitos," *Estado de São Paulo*, January 30, 1990.

[20] See for example, "As famosas vidraças do PT," *Istoé Senhor* 1046, October 4, 1989.

twelve left office before their terms ended, either resigning or being expelled by the party. The expectation that PT mayors represent the party's core values was brought home when the leadership expelled five of the thirty-six mayors of the 1989–1992 cohort, accusing them of betraying party principles after winning office. José Dirceu, secretary general of the party at the time, made this statement: "The party does not accept that mayors change shirts after the elections" (Sader and Silverstein 1991: 123). That the PT would take such action shows that it did not seek power at all cost. Commitment to ideology and program meant more than filling offices with people who wore the party label.

Yet the price of such a stance became very clear in the 1992 elections. The PT was reelected in only twelve of the twenty-four municipalities in which PT mayors completed their terms (Macaulay 1996: 227). In fact, the party was voted out of office in many previous PT strongholds, including Campinas, Santo André, and São Bernardo. Worst of all, the right wing and notoriously corrupt Paulo Maluf was elected as Luiza Erundina's successor in São Paulo. Even the generally well-liked and respected PT politician Eduardo Suplicy – whom the party put up as its mayoral candidate – could not command enough votes to keep the party in power. Although the 1992 municipal elections did increase the number of cities that would come under the PT (from thirty-six to fifty-four), given the configuration of wins and losses, the total number of Brazilians who would be governed by the party fell from almost 10 percent of the population to approximately 5 percent. The loss of São Paulo, which figured heavily in this decrease, carried huge symbolic significance. The PT leadership read the election returns as a wake-up call.

REFLECTION AND CHANGE

In response to the problems described in the preceding paragraphs, the national leadership reflected on the party's municipal performance. It did not shy away from openly examining its failures, debating contentious issues, learning from past experience, and conceding the need for some adjustments. More than any other Brazilian party, the PT showed a willingness to undergo such a deliberate process of evaluation. Even some of the most hard-core figures who wanted to use PT-led municipalities to build hegemonic support for socialism conceded that further disasters of the kind witnessed among the 1989–1992 cohort would jeopardize the party's long-term future. Failed governments in capital cities were thought to diminish the chance that PT mayors could use municipal governance as a springboard for capturing statehouses, much less the presidency.[21]

The *Secretaria Nacional de Assuntos Institucionais* sought to identify weaknesses in the PT's administrative experiences and to formulate strategies for improvement. It sponsored a national meeting in August 1991 to evaluate local PT governments and to develop proposals that struck a balance between short-term political realism and the long-term strategic goals of the party. Although appreciating the diversity of Brazil's municipalities, the secretariat sought to define some uniformity in the policies to be enacted by PT-governed cities and to establish mechanisms for their collaboration and coordination with one another. The 1991 meeting resulted in the widely circulated book O *Modo Petista de Governar* (Bittar 1992). In June 1999, the PT held another major conference to analyze the experiences of more recent PT mayors, vice-mayors, and governors and establish an agenda suited to the political and economic conjuncture of the late 1990s and early 2000s. The conference gave rise to *Governo e Cidadania: Balanço e Reflexões sobre o Modo Petista de Governar* (Magalhães, Barreto, and Trevas 1999), which features chapters by many *petistas* who held executive power at the subnational level, including Tarso Genro (mayor of Porto Alegre, 1993–1996), Raul Pont (mayor of Porto Alegre, 1997–2000), Edmilson Rodrigues (mayor of Belém, 1997–2004), Celso Daniel (elected mayor of Santo André in 1988, 1996, and 2000) and Cristovam Buarque (Governor of Brasília, 1995–1998).

In light of these discussions, what were the changes that the party and individual PT mayors decided to make? The PT continued to view municipal government as a stepping-stone to national power, yet it was generally agreed that the mayoral arena not serve as a caldron of highly pitched ideological battles similar to those being waged in the federal legislature. To the extent possible, PT mayors were to adhere to the general guidelines and spirit of the party program while allowing for adaptation to the specific circumstances of implementation. Rather than mirroring the national party at the local level, PT municipal governments would be allowed to develop their own collective identity somewhat apart from that of the party's representatives in other spheres.[22] The party

---

[21] This was a real concern, given the political centrality of governors in Brazil's federal system together with the difficulties the PT has encountered in winning gubernatorial office. The PT's Jorge Viana went from being mayor of Rio Branco to governor of Acre, Vitor Buaiz from mayor of Vitoria to governor of Espírito Santo, and Olívio Dutra from mayor of Porto Alegre to governor of Rio Grande do Sul.

[22] "Prefeitos no poder fazem PT mudar," *Jornal do Brasil*, March 23, 1992.

The PT in Municipal Government

reserved the right to sanction those who assumed postures deemed to flagrantly contradict its national level project, but PT mayors would not be expected to account to the party hierarchy on a strict and ongoing basis.[23] In short, PT mayors were given greater autonomy to make and carry out daily decisions.

It also became evident that the party leadership – especially the dominant *Articulação* tendency – shied increasingly away from nominating figures anticipated to be magnets of conflict. Over time, PT mayors came more from the center of the party and were less closely associated with industrial unions and social movements than their earlier counterparts. This was partly a function of whom the party nominated as well as whom the voters selected at the ballot box.[24]

To reduce friction between elected municipal governments and the local party hierarchy, many PT mayors adopted the policy of including diverse factions in their governments. For example, Belém Mayor Edmilson Rodrigues (1997–2004), himself from the far left *Força Socialista* tendency in the party, deliberately distributed posts across the various tendencies (Guidry and Petit 2003: 72–73). Learning from Erundina's difficult experience, Marta Suplicy (PT mayor of São Paulo, 2001–2004) undertook a similar strategy. Whereas Erundina's appointments did not reflect the relative weight of various groups in the party, Suplicy was careful to include diverse factions as well as people outside the party in her government. Her subsequent ability to avoid intraparty conflicts of the kind experienced by her predecessor is thought to be one reason for her greater success (Couto 2003: 87–88). Likewise, notwithstanding considerable programmatic divergences in the Porto Alegre PT, a long-standing norm and practice of including minority groups worked to the party's governing advantage (Abers 2000: 58).[25]

While PT mayors developed ways to gain autonomy from the party bureaucracy and diminish factional struggles, they also figured out strategies to tame disputes with the party's organized constituencies. Participatory budgeting was one channel used to help shield their governments from the demands and claims of unions and neighborhood organizations. Amid tight financial constraints and widespread public dissatisfaction, the PT municipal government of Porto Alegre led the way in discovering

---

[23] This was discussed before the 1989–1992 cohort assumed office but in fact was not always observed (Keck 1992: 230).
[24] See Guidry and Petit (2003: 72), and "Com vocês, o PT cor-de-rosa," *Veja Online*, October 11, 2000.
[25] See also "O PT gaucho, um PT que não briga," *O Globo*, November 7, 1999.

participatory budgeting's potential in this regard. Among the government's most vocal critics in mid-1990 were CUT-affiliated bus drivers' and conductors' unions as well as activists from the Union of Neighborhood Associations of Porto Alegre. Angry because the municipal government raised bus fares without increasing their wages, the unionized workers went on strike. Leading community organizations were also dissatisfied even though the higher fares were a by-product of trying to broaden coverage to poorer neighborhoods (Baiocchi 2005: 35–36). Like many of its counterparts in other cities, the elected PT government of Porto Alegre reached the disappointing conclusion that it could not count on the support of some of the party's most organized and long-standing constituencies. Instead, such groups raised the most demands and in the most contentious manner.

How would the broadening of participation help diminish conflict? By making the municipal budget transparent and inviting contending groups to air their demands publicly, participatory budgeting put into stark relief the hard financial constraints that existed. By empowering less organized actors and giving them a context for negotiating directly with more established groups, the Porto Alegre government diffused conflict and diminished the latter's dominance. The nature of the process itself lent legitimacy to the decisions that ultimately resulted. Similarly, when the PT regained power in São Paulo in 2000, mayor Marta Suplicy knew it would be crucial to strike a balance between pleasing the party's traditional base (unions and social movements) and meeting the needs of those with less obvious means of voicing their demands. Notably, she turned to participatory budgeting as a way to tame the former and empower the latter (Wampler 2007: 199). As historical institutionalist principles would expect, municipal governments encountered greater difficulties in implementing broadly inclusive participatory budgeting in areas where previous activist networks – PT affiliated or otherwise – were strongly developed. In a related vein, older PT activists have tended to be more critical than their younger counterparts of participatory budgeting's focus on local immediate issues at the expense of engagement in broader, more ideologically charged matters of long-term significance (Baiocchi 2005: 55 and 153). Nonetheless, as the concept of layering suggests, these potential "veto players" were not likely to try to prevent the addition of such new elements as long as their old institutions were protected.

Besides taking measures aimed at reducing the considerable strife and negative media attention associated with the 1989–1992 group of mayors, many individuals in the party felt that more should be done to

The PT in Municipal Government

publicize the party's accomplishments (Macaulay 1996: 227). How could the party make its achievements in local office better known? Competing for "good governance" and "best practices" awards was one strategy that local PT governments pursued. PT personnel in city halls across Brazil made a point of applying for awards issued through national organizations such as the *Fundação Getúlio Vargas* and international agencies like the Ford Foundation and United Nations. Most of the programs that won awards are progressive, but not radical, in nature. Seeking to further equity and social inclusion within limited budgets, they typically entail using relatively small amounts of public money to elevate the life chances and dignity of less privileged citizens.[26] The Brazilian media's coverage of these prizes helped to publicize PT programs and the municipalities in which they developed. Notably, the PT's record in winning prizes was greatly disproportionate to the number of municipalities it governed.[27]

Regardless of why this might be so, the awards helped give the PT recognition and visibility through the positive media attention they generated.[28] For example, the awards granted to *Bolsa Escola* programs in various municipalities induced many major news outlets – including

---

[26] The *Bolsa Escola* and *Orçamento Participativo* (Participatory Budgeting) programs received early recognition by various organizations, both national and international. Examples of programs recognized by the *Fundação Getúlio Vargas* include a job-training program for at-risk youth (ages 13–17) in Betim (an industrial city outside of Belo Horizonte, Minas Gerais), a recycling program for indigent workers in Porto Alegre, and a program for disabled children in Diadema. For examples of others, see Farah and Barnoza (2000).

[27] For example, at a time when the party administered less than 1 percent of all municipalities, PT-administered cities had developed eight of the eighteen Brazilian projects selected by the federal government as examples of innovative local government to be featured at the United Nations' 1996 Habitat II Conference in Istanbul. Similarly, when in the mid-1990s UNICEF sponsored a report devoted to publicizing exemplary education programs in Brazil, five of the fifteen selections came from PT-administered cities (Nylen 2003: 45). Likewise, with respect to the *Fundação Getúlio Vargas* program, PT-led municipalities were granted a total of nineteen awards between 1997 and 2004. Stated differently, the average number of prizes they won during these years was 0.16 compared with 0.01 for municipalities governed by mayors from all other parties (author's calculations).

[28] One must exercise care when drawing causal inferences about the substantially higher rate of prize winning found among PT-governed municipalities. Does the PT have a real edge when it comes to imaginative and effective local administration? Do the party's municipal cadres promote particularly well what they do? Or, are the judges of such awards positively biased toward the PT and its entries? There is probably some validity to all of these factors. Regardless of what the most accurate answer is, however, the significance of PT prize winning for the party's electoral trajectory rests in public perceptions.

Correio Braziliense, Jornal do Brasil, Estado de São Paulo, and *Istoé* – to cover the program and its many benefits (Sugiyama 2007: 100). Some of the less-well-known PT programs in more remote areas of the country also received media attention.[29] Notably, whereas nongovernmental organizations and the progressive public may have applauded recognition of the kinds of programs that won awards, party radicals were markedly less enthusiastic, regarding them as palliatives to social problems that called for more fundamental structural reforms. They were also quick to point out that the much applauded participatory budgeting and *Bolsa Escola* programs were precisely the kinds of measures championed by the World Bank and other international financial institutions to ease the hardships caused by market reform.[30] Nonetheless, because these new elements were added alongside old party institutions, there was a limit to how much radical *petistas* would try to block their implementation.

Especially after enacting such changes, the party found the 1996 municipal election results disappointing. The number of municipalities that the PT won did rise – from 54 to 115. Some of the victories even took place in states where the party had yet to govern.[31] Nevertheless, the returns were less than hoped for. The PT had one of the worst reelection rates among the largest parties. In only 19 percent of all cases did it manage to win reelection and in only 21 percent of large cities did it remain in power, well inferior to the PSDB's rate of 33 percent and the PPB's 36.5 percent in cities of equivalent size. Especially painful were defeats in Diadema and Santos, cities governed by the PT since 1983 and 1989, respectively. Moreover, the number of capital cities the PT held dropped from four to two (Porto Alegre and Belém). Given the specific 115 municipalities it won, only 5.2 percent of the Brazilian population would live under a PT government in the 1997–2000 period. For a party trying to exalt the merits of the *modo petista de governar*, this was

---

[29] See, for example, "Prefeituras petistas ganham prêmio de administração pública," *Folha de São Paulo*, September 20, 1996.

[30] Author interviews with Markus Sokol and João Batista Oliveira de Araújo (Babá). The interview with Sokol, a long-term PT militant and cadre, took place in São Paulo on August 8, 2006. The interview with former PT deputy Babá took place in Brasília on August 6, 2003. See also "Corrente ataca Lula e Genro," *Folha de São Paulo*, August 24, 1997.

[31] Singer (2001: 62) notes that the 1996 elections furthered the spread of the party across the national territory. Only four states (three of them in the Northeast) did not elect a single PT mayor.

not great publicity. An exhaustive discussion and debate of the returns ensued.³²

What did the analysis yield? The party took a close look at cities that it could reasonably have won but did not. PT candidates were defeated in a number of close second-round races in a handful of cities with more than 200,000 voters, such as Ribeirão Preto (São Paulo), Maceió (Alagoas), Pelotas (Rio Grande do Sul), Santos (São Paulo), Natal (Rio Grande do Norte), Aracajú (Sergipe), and Florianópolis (Santa Catarina). In fact, the PT won only two of the eleven races that involved a second round. While having enough core support to make it into a runoff, the problem came in trying to expand its first-round strength into an electoral majority. A broadening of alliances would greatly enhance the probability of achieving victory in the second round, a measure deemed worthwhile by moderate quarters even though doing so would dilute the PT's distinctive image and sometimes entail supporting candidates from other parties instead of running its own. A look at the alliances forged by the PT in the municipal elections of 2000 reflects a move to include coalitional partners not on the left while retaining former allies.³³ For example, in Rio Branco, the capital city of Acre, the PT's alliance for the mayoral race of 2000 included the PL and PSDB. In 1996, the coalition – composed of the PT, PPS, PSB, PSTU, and PV³⁴ – had been clearly confined to the left. Similarly, the PT cast its lot with the PSB, PSDB, PRP, PST, and PRONA³⁵ for the mayoral race of Macapá, the capital city of Amapá. More purely leftist, the 1996 coalition had consisted of the PDT, PCdoB, and PT. Resistance to undergoing this adaptation was greatest in some of the PT's early strongholds, which continued to operate under principles consistent with that of an externally mobilized left party.³⁶

The party also sought to understand what accounted for comparatively strong performances in some states and weak ones in others. Particularly troublesome was the party's less than stellar showing in the state of São

---

³² See "PT assume derrota e decide mudar estratégia política," *Correio Braziliense*, November 18, 1996; "Derrotas podem acelerar mudanças no PT," *Estado de São Paulo*, November 19, 1996; "Partido relativiza tropeço e evita se declarar derrotado," *Folha de São Paulo*, November 19, 1996.
³³ "Votação obtida é ineficaz," *Folha de São Paulo*, November 19, 1996.
³⁴ PSTU stands for the Unified Socialist Workers' Party; the PV is the Green Party.
³⁵ PRP is the Progressive Republican Party; the PST is the Social Labor Party; PRONA is the National Order Reconstruction Party.
³⁶ "PT de resultados," *Istoé*, October 14, 1992.

Paulo, the original home and heart of *petismo*. Although early projections had led strategists to believe that the party had a good shot at securing twenty-five municipalities, in fact only thirteen mayors were elected in the entire state. Besides not capturing the capital city, the party lost in locales generally considered to be PT strongholds, such as Diadema and São José dos Campos. In stark contrast to the state of São Paulo, however, the PT did very well in Rio Grande do Sul, where it went from governing eight to twenty-six cities. It won in two of the three biggest cities in the state (Porto Alegre and Caxias) and came close in the third, Pelotas. The dominant interpretation of these contrasting outcomes was that the São Paulo PT's strong association with unionism and the militant reputation of the CUT hurt its broader electoral appeal. Whereas the principal leadership of the São Paulo PT hailed from the industrial union movement, leading *petistas* from Rio Grande do Sul tended to be more middle class in origin, thereby diminishing an important source of rejection. They also enjoyed support from a wider range of tendencies within the party, avoiding sectarian schisms. This was even true of someone like Olívio Dutra, who was close to the left faction, *Democracia Social*. Finally, the fact that they had less antagonistic relations with business sectors was thought to give its representatives an edge in attracting middle-of-the-road and nonideological voters.[37] In sum, party moderates read the returns as a call for even greater pragmatism, pluralism, and administrative competence.

The municipal elections of 2000 represented an unprecedented victory for the party. The PT elevated the number of cities it won to 187, up from 115 in 1996. Moreover, the total number of votes its mayoral candidates obtained represented a 51.2 percent increase over that achieved in 1996 (Fleischer 2002).[38] The party captured 27 of Brazil's 100 largest cities, up from 9 in 1996, and 12 in both 1992 and 1988. Six of these were capital cities. The party regained São Paulo after losing it in 1992, retained Porto Alegre and Belém, and won in Recife, Aracajú, and Goiânia for the first time. With these victories, the PT would come to govern 17.8 percent of Brazil's population, the equivalent of 29.1 million people, and in 17 cities alone would administer approximately one-fourth of the national GNP.[39]

---

[37] "PT espera crescer, mas não o esperado," *Folha de São Paulo*, October 2, 1996; "PT tenta estabelecer 'hegemonia' gaúcha," *Folha de São Paulo*, November 10, 1996; "PT gaúcho cresce e ocupa lugar do paulista," *Folha de São Paulo*, December 22, 1996; "Lula acusa 'orquestração' em ataques," *Folha de São Paulo*, October 29, 2000.

[38] See also "Números da Reeleição," *Cidades do Brasil*, October 2000.

[39] "Prefeitos petistas vão administrar 23% do PIB nacional em 17 cidades," *O Globo*, October 31, 2000.

Notably, the party was reelected in half of the municipalities where it had held power in the previous term, which the leadership understood as a reflection of the public's growing satisfaction with PT-led local governments. This was a strong showing relative not only to many other parties but especially to its own previous record (28 percent in 1992 and 19 percent in 1996). As with many other parties, the PT's ability to sustain itself in power rose with the size of the municipality. Reelection rates tended to be higher in cities with more than 200,000 people (Bremaeker 2000:4).

Examining which kinds of candidates were victorious in 2000 formed a key basis of the inferences the leadership arrived at and its strategic thinking about the future. Although the party's municipal candidates no doubt benefited from the rising negative sentiment toward the Cardoso government, the most successful were nevertheless those whose campaigns focused on resolving daily problems in Brazil's cities. Administrative experience and good local government were the dominant themes they promoted. Many of the most prominent PT victories that year were from an emerging "PT light" set, moderate mainstream individuals like João Paulo Lima (mayor of Recife), Marta Suplicy in São Paulo, and Tarso Genro in Porto Alegre. Those who maintained a more ideological discourse tended to lose (Fleischer 2002: 90). They included historic union movement figures like Jair Meneguelli and Vicento Paulo da Silva (Vicentinho) in the ABC region of São Paulo, the party's birthplace.[40] Having fairly broad alliances was confirmed as an important determinant of success.[41]

Seeking to do better, the PT leadership identified several areas for improvement. A future goal would be to make inroads into smaller cities across the country. Although the party won 187 municipalities in 2000, this was still only 20 percent of the number governed by a major catchall party like the PFL. The PT's victories still tended to be confined to larger cities: 82 percent of the population it governed was concentrated in cities of more than 200,000 residents. The party had managed to increase its presence in small towns in São Paulo but not in other states where it had worked to do so, such as Minas Gerais and Rio de Janeiro.[42] Made aware anew of its fragile hold in such places, the party sought ways to penetrate

---

[40] "Surra igual, só a de 1974," *Folha de São Paulo*, November 1, 2000; "Segundo turno," *Folha de São Paulo*, October 24, 2000; "O jogo começa agora," *Veja Online*, edition 1,674, November 8, 2000; "Vitória dos moderados," *Correio Braziliense*, October 4, 2000.
[41] "Falta de alianças leva a derrotas no Rio," *Folha de São Paulo*, November 5, 2000.
[42] "PT amplia presença no interior de São Paulo," *Folha de São Paulo*, October 3, 2000.

the *grotões* (hinterlands) of Brazil.⁴³ In particular, the Northeast was still a weak link in the PT's network, although the party won more mayorships in 2000 (twenty-two) than in 1996 (eleven) or in 1992 (eight). A deficit in small towns was also one of the chronic challenges facing Lula in his presidential races, a situation that would change only after the PT had acquired national executive power.

Looking to Lula's prospective presidential candidacy in 2002, the leadership sought to maximize the impression it made in the cities it governed, hoping it would translate into goodwill toward the PT in that crucial national race. The PT national leadership encouraged its cohort of mayors for the year 2000 – especially those governing large and complex cities – to staff their departments with people of high professional quality (even if they were not *petistas*) to reap the most effective results possible.⁴⁴ Toward a similar end, the National Conference of PT Mayors and Vice-Mayors met to discuss ways to better enact and market the social programs central to the party's banner and its governance at the local level.

In sum, over time the party's leadership and its elected officials responded to the difficulties, shortcomings, and failures experienced by many early PT-led municipal administrations by undertaking a series of measures to facilitate the operation of PT-led cities and publicize the party's municipal successes. Although recovery did not occur immediately, local PT governments eventually hit stride and the party's record at the municipal level improved. This in turn generated a dynamic of its own: Party moderates, more likely to be associated with such positive experiences, tended to do better at the polls than their more radical counterparts.

THE UNDERSIDE OF GOOD GOVERNANCE:
CAIXA DOIS ACTIVITIES

While the PT fought to gain traction at the national level, its militants could take heart in the party's victories in local government and sustain their enthusiasm for the larger struggle. Clean government became a hallmark of the PT in large part through its municipal officeholding. Indeed,

---

[43] "O Brasil que sai das urnas," *Folha de São Paulo*, November 5, 2000; "PT traça estratégia para crescer em cidades pequenas," *Folha de São Paulo*, November 12, 2000; "Raio-X-Partido dos Trabalhadores," *Folha de São Paulo*, March 17, 2002. See also "O Brasil que sai das urnas," *Folha de São Paulo*, November 5, 2000.

[44] "PT quer 'Sayads' em novas prefeituras," *Folha de São Paulo*, November 10, 2000.

The PT in Municipal Government

there was much positive to be said about the party's programs and its electoral record at the local level. Unfortunately, not all was as it seemed. Developing beneath the public activities comprising the *modo petista de governar* was an elaborate and centrally organized party financing scheme organized with the help of mayors and their associates in many PT-led city halls, who extracted money from firms that bid on municipal contracts and later channeled these kickbacks into a secret campaign slush fund, the *caixa dois*. From approximately 1994 onward, the treasurer of the national PT sought municipal government complicity in raising funds for important PT campaigns at the national level, most importantly Lula's presidential races.[45] As described earlier, the PT's paltry resource base relative to that of its competitors turned more problematic after the party leadership enhanced the priority it placed on winning elections.

If vote seeking formed the primary motivation for additional resource acquisition, executive officeholding at the subnational level provided the institutional opportunity. Aside from the rare statehouse occupied by the party, municipalities were the main point of access the PT enjoyed to public resources. The more executive offices the party gained, the wider its "off the books" network became. A well-kept secret for many years, this illicit underside was revealed publicly only in 2005, when media and congressional investigations about malfeasance under the Lula government led to an inquiry about past activities as well.[46] The news was shocking and disillusioning to many Brazilians, let alone PT enthusiasts, given especially that many of the cities involved in the *caixa dois* network were PT showcases, such as Santo André,[47] Campinas, São José dos Campos, and Ribeirão Preto. Given the PT's association with policies that reflected principles such as transparency and accountability, even a public long accustomed to malfeasance among its elected officials felt duped.

In short, if the PT's status of difference – especially its historic anti-free-market stance and the modest personal assets of most *petista*

---

[45] The immediate situation prompting this development was Lula's drop in the polls in July and August of that year and the PT's inability to respond in the way that a well-financed organization might have. See "Falta de recursos atrapalha o PT," *Jornal do Brasil*, August 11, 1994.

[46] The party managed to cover up indications that something was awry, such as the protests of one PT figure who discovered financial irregularities in the city halls of Campinas and São José dos Campos. In addition, a handful of historic figures, such as Cesar Benjamin, left the party in 1994 and 1995 over what were then unknown reasons but now appear related to their knowledge of the scheme.

[47] "5 mistérios e uma certeza," *Veja Online*, October 19, 2005.

politicians – was largely responsible for its resource shortfall, the PT took a crucial step into the realm of "politics as usual" in seeking to overcome it. Crossing that line "normalized" the party, arguably lowering the barrier to undertaking other questionable activities such as the *mensalão* many years later. The *caixa dois* scheme run out of many PT-led municipalities thus contributed to the growing pragmatism induced by power holding at the subnational level. Along with all of the other incentives and constraints that operated in the municipal sphere to lead the party toward greater pragmatism, the illicit fund-raising possibilities opened up by executive officeholding at the local level contributed ultimately to undermining a crucial dimension of the party's distinctiveness.

CONCLUSION

Elections and governing experiences at the municipal level thus shaped the balance of forces within the PT as well as the party's public image and support base. Insights from rational choice institutionalism shed crucial light on why the party adapted to the incentives unleashed in the municipal sphere. The rules of winning elections – especially from 1992 onward, which required that victorious candidates in large municipalities receive an absolute majority of valid votes – induced many candidates to shift to the center and form alliances with parties outside the left. Furthering the trend toward adaptation were the challenges encountered in governing and the desire to perform well to benefit the party's reputation.

Initially, the party was unsure of how to approach municipal government. Torn between trying to focus on the larger struggle and solving daily problems, the first PT municipal governments were often too ideological. Insights from historical institutionalism help explain the lag in adaptation. A series of clashes took place early on between local party elements that clung to past visions and principles and elected politicians who felt pressured to respond to more immediate practical problems and collective considerations. By creating an important context for political learning, a significant effect of municipal officeholding was to strengthen internal arguments for pragmatism and adaptation. Control of local government ultimately had a moderating effect, and crucially, the national party learned from the initial experiences and encouraged the pragmatic and highly innovative approach pursued by municipal governments in the 1990s.

By ultimately revealing its ability to compromise and administer within the broader context of a capitalist economy – especially in showcase cities such as Porto Alegre and Diadema – the PT showed a side of itself not easily discernable from its conduct in the Chamber, where its ideological face remained prominent for a longer period of time. Rounding out its public profile no doubt helped the party win favor among less ideological and more middle-of-the-road voters. Thus, PT governance at the local level created an important set of changes within the party. They did not altogether replace former patterns and practices or institutions associated with the legislative sphere; rather, they developed alongside them. Party radicals were not likely to launch a frontal veto of most of these changes, such as participatory budgeting institutions, because they did not strike at the core of older institutions. Over time the changes generated "increasing returns" (Pierson 2000), which enhanced the probability that the PT would take further steps along the same path. Lula's evolution over the course of his four presidential bids as well as the experience of presidential officeholding itself mirrored and reinforced many of these developments.

5

Striving for the Presidency

From Opposition to Government

This chapter examines and analyzes Lula's first four presidential contests and their effects on the party's trajectory. The PT's determination to place Lula in the presidency, coupled with Lula's fierce personal ambition to become president, played a decisive role in pushing the PT in a more catchall direction over time. The party made a number of important programmatic and organizational changes designed to broaden Lula's electoral appeal and empower the moderate factions that backed him. A key institutional constraint – namely the need to win a majority of votes to capture the presidency – made it all the more imperative to extend Lula's electoral reach across broad segments of the electorate, many of which did not respond positively to the party's early radicalism. A decline in Brazil's economic and political volatility after the enactment of the *Plano Real* – that is, better governance and growing state and party institutionalization – rendered a far-left strategy much less likely to be successful than it previously was. Changes the party enacted in response to Lula's first three failed bids (1989, 1994, and 1998) were crucial in securing his ultimate triumph in 2002. The factors responsible for the party's adaptation in the context of Lula's attempts to win presidential office fit well into a strategic framework. Indeed, rational choice institutionalism sheds crucial light on how politics in the presidential arena pushed the party in a more pragmatic direction over time.

Notwithstanding widespread internal consensus on the importance of securing presidential office and on putting forth Lula as the party's candidate, there were tensions at every turn. Fierce divisions existed over how much the PT should conform to behaviors typically employed by parties and candidates that win presidential office in Brazil. The degree of programmatic moderation the party should undergo, the PT's alliances with nonleft parties, and how much Lula's image should be tailored around opinion poll findings were among the most contentious issues facing the party. Internal factions or "tendencies" also battled over organizational changes that, if enacted and observed, would effectively empower the voices of moderation. Principles of historical institutionalism shed light on the forces of resistance to change. In the end, however, the most notable aspects of the PT's trajectory between 1989 and 2002 concern its adaptation, and these are best understood through rational choice institutionalism.

The vote-maximizing pragmatists prevailed first on matters deemed most central to bolstering the PT's chances of securing presidential victory, such as moderating Lula's presidential program and softening his image. Issues that bore a direct relationship to increasing the PT's ability to appeal to the electorate and to key interest groups were tackled before trying to institute internal organizational changes. In several instances party moderates won out, but not infrequently they achieved only partial victories or lost altogether. Electoral defeats, especially those incurred in the 1994 and 1998 presidential races, brought reflection and adaptation. Nevertheless, as a result of intense internal struggles and low leadership autonomy (a product of the PT's history), change occurred in a bounded fashion. It took place less by an all-out frontal assault on established party norms and institutions and more by prolonged efforts at persuasion by moderate factions, informal measures taken by Lula to circumvent the party bureaucracy, and institutional changes placed on top of (but not altogether replacing) existing party institutions. Over time, the separation between Lula and the party organization grew.

The chapter develops a systematic comparison of the following issues by successive elections.

The Strategy Adopted (Policy Seeking vs. Vote Maximization) and the Accompanying Tactics Employed. Expanding on Chapter 2's general discussion of the factors influencing the PT to turn from policy seeking to vote maximization, in this chapter I focus more specifically on how considerations of Lula's presidential prospects influenced the party's approach at given times. Lula's loss to Fernando Henrique Cardoso in 1994 was an inflexion point in this regard. The defeat in 1998 reinforced the resolve of party pragmatists to shift to a vote-maximizing outlook. Accordingly, they led efforts to moderate the PT's proposals for government, soften Lula's image, pursue alliances across the ideological spectrum, conform to trends in public opinion, and find new (if legally questionable) sources of campaign financing. At the same time, they did not employ all of the changes they might have. Some were attempted and failed. Others were not even tried. In my analysis I seek to explain not only why the party instituted the changes it did but why it did not assume a fuller range of catchall characteristics.

How Internal Tensions Were Overcome or Mitigated. Although normalizing measures enhanced Lula's popularity with the broader electorate, they were not always positively received within the party. As Lula and his fellow moderates pursued adaptation they encountered opposition by members of the party's radical wing, which was fortified by various formal structures that had been forged in line with the PT's externally mobilized past. However, various sources of strategic flexibility counteracted such resistance. A key contributor to loosening the grip of these structures was the overwhelming internal consensus that no other PT politician could rival Lula's potential as a presidential contender. This was rooted in the perception (eventually backed by survey research) that no other PT politician held as much simultaneous appeal to organized sectors in the most developed areas of the country and to the rural poor.[1]

This gave Lula much more effective leverage over the party than formal organizational features would suggest. When he could not prevail by persuasion, Lula sought other routes. His efforts to gain autonomy from radical elements in the party bureaucracy included going around established decision-making mechanisms as well as pushing for the development of new institutional mechanisms that would effectively empower party moderates. The leadership role of Lula fits into a strategic analysis of the PT's adaptation insofar as he as an individual, together with a small circle of advisors, proved willing and able to overcome considerable internal resistance and respond to external incentives for change. Lula's ability to use his popularity as leverage to push organizational change was crucial in the PT's adaptation.

The Profile of Lula's Support Base. Lula's electoral base evolved markedly between 1989 and 2002. Given the institutional requirement of winning an electoral majority, presidential campaign strategists – especially in Lula's later campaigns – worked hard to figure out how to attract voters across a wide array of demographic categories. Whereas Lula's

---

[1] Datafolha poll no. 01601 of February 2002 replaced the name *Lula* with that of other PT politicians in investigating first-round vote intentions for the 2002 presidential election. For example, when the name *Eduardo Suplicy* was used, the vote share for the PT declined significantly. Although popular in São Paulo and other areas of the Southeast and South, Suplicy held markedly less appeal than Lula in less developed regions of the country.

early strength rested disproportionately with voters from higher education and income brackets from predominantly urban areas of the South and Southeast, over time he managed to broaden his support among poorer and less educated voters from small towns and less developed regions of the country. Such people were more attracted to Lula's moderated discourse and image than they had been to the previous emphasis on radical change and collective mobilization. Notably, however, whereas Lula succeeded in reaching across lines of education, income, city size, and region, the party – as reflected by its congressional delegation – did not evolve as quickly in this direction. PT deputies continued to come disproportionately from more developed states. The constituency supporting Lula versus the party thus came to diverge more and more over time.

THE PRESIDENTIAL ELECTION OF 1989: POLARIZATION AND PROMISE

Background Context

The 1989 presidential election was the first direct election of a Brazilian president in nearly thirty years. It took place in a context of economic turmoil, ideological polarization, and the delegitimation of the country's political class. Inflation was spiraling out of control. A wave of strikes had wracked Brazil earlier that year. The public mood was one of disgust at the chronic malfeasance of the political class in general and the government of José Sarney (1985–1990) in particular. Many of the social movements that had gained momentum in the era of democratization were still going strong. Against this background the PT was riding high, having clinched important victories in the municipal elections of 1988 (e.g., São Paulo, Porto Alegre, Vitória, Santos, and Campinas). The marked fluidity in the system gave the PT a sense of unlimited possibility. The climate seemed right for the PT to pursue a strategy of polarization and to assume a leading position on the left pole.[2]

The election's first round yielded front-runners on opposite sides of the social and political spectrum. Lula was a factory worker turned labor leader whose early life story of migration from the Northeastern state

---

[2] Many of the insights contained in this section come from author interviews with Luis Gushiken, José Genoino, and Paulo Vannuchi. Excellent sources on the period include Amaral (2003), Mendes (2004), and Campello (2007).

of Pernambuco to the city of São Paulo was shared by millions of poor Brazilians. Victimized by the military regime for the strikes he led in the ABC region of São Paulo in the late 1970s, Lula came from an organized left political party that proposed redistributive change and social transformation. His opponent, Fernando Collor de Mello, descended from an established conservative family with political roots in the Northeastern state of Alagoas. A son of the military regime, he was nominated by the government party ARENA (National Renovating Alliance) in 1978 to be mayor of the capital city of Maceió and in 1982 was elected federal deputy on the ticket of ARENA's successor, the PDS (Democratic Social Party). Collor voted for the notorious rightist candidate Paulo Maluf in the Electoral College that selected the new president in 1985 after the direct elections campaign failed.

Reflecting the extreme fluidity and fragmentation of the political system was the comparatively low combined vote share – 47.7 percent – of the two front-runners in the first round. The parties from which they came were disproportionately small. Collor garnered the biggest share of the first-round vote (30.5 percent) while coming from a splinter party. Little more than a personalist vehicle for his presidential bid, the PRN (Party of National Reconstruction) all but disappeared after Collor's resignation in 1992. Finishing in second place with a vote share of 17.2 percent, Lula came from a party that was the sixth largest in the lower house.[3] Patterns of competition in presidential contests would stabilize after 1994 (as discussed in subsequent paragraphs), but in 1989 the field was wide open. Given the fluid and uncertain political and economic environment at the time, the PT's pursuit of a left strategy was not irrational.

Strategy and Tactics

The 1989 campaign represented an open and unapologetic effort by the PT to place Lula and his party firmly on the left and to identify them with the intention to bring about socialism, however ambiguously defined. The world view depicted was one of winners versus losers, rich versus poor, exploiters versus exploited. Change was envisioned in the form of fundamental breaks and ruptures with the past rather than modest modifications. Party documents and speeches issued fierce criticisms of the status quo, railing against everything from the external debt and

---

[3] The largest party in the lower house (the PMDB) occupied 21 percent of all seats but its presidential candidate (Ulysses Guimarães) garnered a mere 4.7 percent of the vote.

international financial organizations to the existing banking structure, land tenure system, and income distribution in the country (e.g., Partido dos Trabalhadores 1989). Firm opposition was mounted against privatization, which was depicted as delivering the national patrimony over to greedy domestic and foreign interests. Land reform, nationalizing the country's banks, and defaulting on the debt were put forth as central priorities. Proposals of how to change established patterns were lacking in detail, although the agent of development and redistributive change would surely be the state.

Beyond the content of its programs and the tone of its discourse was the image the PT projected. A reflection of the PT's authenticity in 1989 was to have Lula appear before the public as who he really was: a former factory worker with few years of formal education who spoke grammatically imperfect Portuguese and was rough around the edges. This was someone who rose from grinding poverty to become a national union organizer and command an impressive strike of over 100,000 workers in 1979. The image of the bearded labor leader in rolled-up sleeves said it all: The PT in 1989 was not about to engage in a "make-over" operation. Only in subsequent years would the party hire publicists to work on recasting Lula: coaching his speech and inducing him to don a suit and tie, crop his beard, lose weight, whiten his teeth, and stop chain-smoking.

In line with the PT's policy-seeking approach at the time, parties comprising Lula's electoral coalition were unequivocally of the left. The PT's formal allies that made up the *Frente Brasil Popular* were the PSB and the PCdoB. Center-left parties – namely the PSDB and PDT – informally supported Lula in the second round after their own candidates had failed to pan out. After Mário Covas of the PSDB managed to garner only 11.5 percent of the first-round vote share, he and other highly placed *tucanos* went on stage to show solidarity with Lula. It would be the last of such appearances for a long time to come. With 16.5 percent, Leonel Brizola came in less than a percentage point behind Lula. The small edge that Lula gained over Brizola took on enormous symbolic significance and led him to assume the mantle as leader of the Brazilian left. Brizola's support would prove crucial in boosting Lula's second-round prospects in the important states of Rio de Janeiro and Rio Grande do Sul, where he went from bringing in a modest 12.2 and 6.7 percent of the first-round vote to securing a massive 72.9 and 68.7 percent of the second. Notably, the PT did little to cultivate support from the PMDB, even though its candidate Ulysses Guimarães did formally endorse Lula after garnering a mere

4.7 percent of the vote. The PMDB had failed to live up to its progressive roots in opposing the military regime. More immediately relevant, Lula feared the consequences of being identified with the Sarney presidency.

In sum, the strategy and tactics that the PT adopted in the campaign suggested it wanted to win, but not at all cost. It was deemed more important to be right than to secure power through moderation. Those running the campaign stood on principle with respect to several matters even when told that doing so could jeopardize the prospect of electoral victory.[4] One example concerns the party's position on land reform. Advisers informed those who coordinated the 1989 Program of Government that Lula would probably have to sweep the interior of the states of São Paulo and Paraná to secure the presidency. Both states have highly mechanized productive agricultural sectors, which doubtless would have been hurt by radical land distribution. In the end, the campaign chose not to tone down references to agrarian reform or even to propose and clarify that land reform would take place elsewhere in the country. Lula did not even distance himself from the MST and its land invasion strategy. Not surprisingly, he did quite poorly in these regions. Lula's decision not to actively court the PMDB also came at a price. Had he received the nearly 5 percentage points that PMDB candidate Ulysses Guimarães had garnered in the first round, it might have covered his shortfall or at least brought the PT much closer to victory.[5] Nevertheless, these outcomes were part and parcel of the PT's self-conscious choice to *marcar posição* (take a stance) even at the cost of losing.

Trajectory

The Lula campaign, PT activists and supporters of the left in general were ecstatic to learn that Lula had fared well enough in the November 15 election to make it to the second round, scheduled for December 17. It was hard to believe that the same party that had to struggle to gain recognition a few years earlier would have a genuine shot at the presidency. The runoff gave Lula a chance to rethink and reconfigure. Notably, however, PT strategists did not undertake a move to the center in search of votes. Staying on the far left, Lula focused on better explaining

---

[4] Author interview with a confidential source.
[5] More than a decade later, Lula revealed to a journalist that he considered his not seeking a stronger alliance with the PMDB to be an error of historic proportions. "Lula admite error de estratégia," *Folha de São Paulo*, February 10, 2000. See also "Sem o PT a política seria só a do sim senhor," *O Globo*, February 6, 2000.

his positions to the unconverted and continuing to rally the enthusiasm of his base. Perpetually short on funds, the PT depended heavily on the commitment and energy of its militants.

In the end, Lula was able to lift his first-round vote share of 17.2 percent to an impressive 47 percent of total votes. Ready sources of support included people who identified with the left and the organizations and social movements associated with it, individuals who were not necessarily leftists but could not bear to back a candidate with Fernando Collor's profile in the first direct presidential election of the postauthoritarian era, and people who would cast a protest vote out of disgust with the Sarney government. Lula's challenge was to go beyond these groups and appeal to other segments of the electorate – not especially progressive or enlightened – that could put him over the mark.

Collor had many advantages over Lula in this regard. Heavily funded by the business community and the political right, which closed ranks under the specter of a Lula victory, he was able to pull off an impressive campaign. He crisscrossed the country in a private jet and produced slick television spots projecting his good looks and commanding presence. Connections with conservative elites allowed him to draw on established social and political networks. Collor also had the establishment media on his side, most notably the formidable *Globo* network. The mainstream press presented him in the most positive light possible, featuring countless stories that highlighted his travel in sophisticated international circles and ability to speak foreign languages. A knight in shining armor, Collor was portrayed as a man who would ride in and save the country from the evils of corrupt traditional politicians and radical leftists alike.

After a period in which Lula and Collor ran neck and neck, vote intentions for the PT candidate fell in the final days of the campaign and never recovered. A negative television attack the Collor campaign mounted via the publicly funded electoral advertisements (*Horário Gratuito de Propaganda Eleitoral*), watched nightly by at least half the electorate, contributed to Lula's eventual fall (Mendes 2004: 32). Appealing to social conservatives, Collor revealed that Lula had fathered a daughter out of wedlock some years earlier and publicized her mother's denunciation that Lula had urged her to have an abortion. Collor also accused the PT candidate of intending to take away individual savings accounts and divide up houses with more than three or so rooms. It did not help matters that top business leaders threatened to take their money out of the country in the event of a Lula victory. The president of the country's main business federation, FIESP (Federation of Industries of the State of São Paulo), went as far as announcing that 800,000 business people would leave the country if Lula were elected. Given the polarized conception of "labor versus capital" that Lula himself had presented, it was not surprising that business feared his election.

Profile of Support

Where did Lula's 47.0 percentage points come from? In which demographic categories did he fall short? In terms of regions, Lula's strongest support lay in the South and Southeast. He surpassed Collor in the South (51.7 to 48.3) and came close to beating him in the Southeast (49.5 to 50.5). However, he performed poorly in the North and Center-West (29.5 to 70.5 and 36.8 to 63.2, respectively) and was also deficient in the Northeast, where he garnered 44.3 percent to Collor's 55.7 percent. There was nearly a 22 percentage point difference between the regions of Lula's highest and lowest popularity (the South and North).[6] Such a regional distribution hurt Lula's chances. Although the majority of the electorate resides in the Southeast and South, approximately 42 percent of it does not. The Northeast alone contains approximately 27 percent of all voters. Winning an electoral majority thus depends on making inroads across regions outside of the comparatively developed South and Southeast. Clearly, Lula would need to broaden his regional bases of support in the future.

In terms of the education level of his supporters, Lula outperformed his competitor among people with higher levels of schooling but did less well among those with lower levels. According to vote-intention polls, 62 percent of respondents with secondary education and 59 percent of those with higher education said they would vote for Lula, compared with 44 percent of respondents with basic education.[7] Not being able to win among the least educated Brazilians impeded Lula's ability to prevail.

---

[6] Lula carried only four states: Rio Grande do Sul, Rio de Janeiro, Pernambuco, and the Federal District. The first two were strongholds of Brizola, whose support was crucial in helping Lula land these victories. Lula won by a wide margin in the Federal District (62.7 to 37.3), an area dense with public functionaries and educated and affluent individuals. Victory was razor thin in Pernambuco, Lula's state of birth and home to veteran leftist and then state governor Miguel Arraes, who championed Lula's candidacy.

[7] The category of basic education encompasses everyone with up to eight years of schooling. See Tables A.5 and A.6 for presidential vote intentions by education and income level. Table A.7 shows vote intentions by city size for the presidential elections between 1994 and 2006. See also Centro de Estudos de Opinião Pública (2002b) for a comparison of Lula's support base in his four presidential bids between 1989 and 2002.

Given that 70 percent of the electorate has only a basic education (eight years or fewer),[8] it would be hard to imagine capturing a majority of votes in a nationwide contest without gaining massive support among this group.

A similar pattern held true with respect to income levels. For example, Lula had the expressed support of 59 percent of those who earned between five and ten *salários mínimos* (minimum wage levels), yet he won the support of only 43 percent of those who earned two minimum wage levels (then equivalent to approximately 150 dollars per month) or less. Given that far more Brazilians fall in the two-minimum-wage-level category than in the five- to ten-minimum-wage-level group,[9] the absolute numbers favored Collor. In short, Lula's defeat stemmed ultimately from not being able to carry the poorest and least educated sectors of society. This outcome bore out the Brazilian saying, "*Pobre não vota em pobre*" (The poor don't vote for the poor). Although Lula had tried to appeal to this group by emphasizing the demographic characteristics he shared with them, apparently poor and uneducated Brazilians were not yet ready in 1989 to have someone like themselves hold the highest political office in the land.

As for other demographic categories, Lula did far better in larger cities than in smaller towns. Although a majority of the electorate resides in municipalities with more than 50,000 people, not being able to carry a significant share of smaller municipalities can make a decisive difference in a close race (such as 1989): Roughly one-fourth of the electorate lives in municipalities with fewer than 20,000 people. In addition, Lula was comparatively more popular among men than women, a gap that would narrow by 2002. The gender gap that existed in 1989 was estimated to be roughly 10 percentage points (Centro de Estudos de Opinião Pública 2002b: 393). In terms of religious groups, evangelicals voted massively against Lula and for Collor (Freston 1994, 2001).[10] Leaders of the popular *Igreja Universal do Reino de Deus* went on the offensive and accused Lula of being the candidate of the devil and wanting to persecute evangelicals if elected. To the PT's great disappointment, Lula lost even in areas

---

[8] See the *Tribunal Superior Eleitoral* (2002) for a profile of educational distribution among Brazilians.
[9] Nearly 30 percent of the population earned two minimum wages or less, compared with roughly 20 percent in the five to ten range. See the Instituto Brasileiro de Geografia e Estatística (2000) for a breakdown of income levels across the population.
[10] At least 15 percent of all Brazilian voters identify as evangelicals. Evangelical Protestantism is expanding rapidly among the working class.

of the interior where progressive Catholic clergy had done its best to rally support for the PT candidate.[11]

Postelection Analysis

After recovering from the immediate loss, most figures within the party emerged with a sense of optimism about the future. The situation was encapsulated well by Oswaldo Amaral, who said that the PT underwent a "defeat with the flavor of victory" (2003: 101). Especially considering all the material advantages Collor enjoyed and the political networks upon which he drew, PT leaders were heartened and emboldened by Lula's performance. They regarded it as evidence that it was possible to capture executive power by promising Brazilians far-reaching change. That the PT claimed to be the party of the downtrodden but had failed to clinch the backing of the poorest and least educated Brazilians in the most destitute areas of the country was not lost on party strategists. Nevertheless, they did not respond by thinking that a dramatic redirection was necessary. Notably, even pragmatic figures like José Dirceu, who would later lead the party toward the center, maintained that the PT did not lose the election as a result of its radicalism. He and others attributed defeat to factors like media unfairness, an abuse of economic power, the poorly informed nature of the electorate, and widespread prejudice against having a former manual laborer as president. Furthermore, they advocated that the PT stay the course.[12] What the party leadership did not adequately appreciate was how much Lula had benefited from the polarized nature of the campaign and the general climate of economic and political volatility that surrounded the 1989 election. Indeed, many voters settled on Lula in the second round for lack of a more palatable alternative. An economy in the process of stabilization and a less polarized contest against a credible centrist opponent from an institutionalized party would yield a decisive first-round defeat in 1994. In sum, the presidential election of 1989 left a significant mark on Lula, the PT, and the Brazilian electorate. It brought both Lula and the party into the public eye like never before, making them household names. It bestowed upon Lula the leadership of the left. Perhaps most important was that it convinced the PT that winning the presidency was within the range of possibility.

---

[11] "Padres pró-PT derrotam velhos líderes do Nordeste," *Folha de São Paulo*, November 27, 1989; "Militância de padres ajuda PT,"*Jornal do Brasil*, November 26, 1989.
[12] "Dirceu diz que PT deve continuar 'radical'," *Folha de São Paulo*, December 24, 1989.

Striving for the Presidency

The psychological change entailed by this should not be underestimated. For the more strategically minded within the party, coming so close to victory constituted an argument for backing off from the PT's initial radicalism. There was little doubt that Lula would return in 1994.

1994: A PAINFUL DEFEAT WITH LESSONS FOR THE FUTURE

Context

Lula had many things going for him as the 1994 election approached. If the PT had wished for the Collor administration to be less than successful, his abbreviated tenure and abrupt resignation in 1992 amidst a storm of corruption charges exceeded all expectations. The PT continued in opposition mode, assuming a strict stance against the subsequent two-year interim government of Itamar Franco.[13] Lula entered the 1994 campaign as the candidate with the highest name recognition (Almeida 1996: 85). Moreover, many who had voted for Collor in 1989 expressed regret over their vote choice.[14] Although this did not necessarily imply that they would vote for Lula, the PT regarded it as a plus. More generally, it was thought that Lula would benefit from the widespread sense of disillusionment and disgust toward the political class left by the Collor government, especially the corruption scandal that led to its unraveling. Beyond such diffuse support, the PT candidate could count on the core following that the PT had developed: Catholics linked to Christian base communities, union affiliates, members of the MST, and miscellaneous social movement groups.

Coupled with Lula's strong performance on a radical platform in 1989, the fact that the economy and political system were still in disarray in late 1993 and early 1994 encouraged the PT to continue presenting itself as a distinctive alternative to the present order. After all, established politicians and the measures they instituted had not worked to solve

---

[13] Its insistence on not cooperating was exemplified in a swift turn against former PT mayor Luiza Erundina for accepting President Franco's invitation to become a government minister. Notably, it was not just the far-left wing that wanted to see her punished, if not banished, from the party. Lula himself – although stopping short of advocating outright expulsion – supported Erundina's suspension. A public opinion survey showed that 75 percent of those surveyed thought the party judged her with excessive harshness. See "Constelação Ameaçada," *Visão*, February 17, 1993.

[14] Of respondents who voted for Collor, 56 percent said they regretted their vote choice (compared with only 3 percent who voted for Lula). The expressed regret rose to 68 percent among those with higher education (Almeida 1996: 111).

many pressing problems in Brazil's new democracy. State performance was poor by a variety of indicators. Brazilians named rising inflation as the single most serious problem confronting them. An overwhelming percentage (91 percent) of survey respondents rated Brazil's economic situation as either fairly poor or very poor in late 1993, and a majority (55.7 percent) reported being pessimistic about seeing much improvement in 1994 (Weyland 2002: 224–225). Four major economic plans in the nine years since democratization had not succeeded in bringing inflation under control. Throughout 1992 and up until April 1993 (when Cardoso became Minister of Finance in the government of Itamar Franco), monthly inflation rates had hovered around 30 percent. On the political front, volatility remained high. Voters' preferences and patterns had not stabilized and coalesced around a small number of established parties. For these reasons, coupled with opinion polls that showed Lula as the clear front-runner as late as June 1994, the PT was optimistic about winning on a left platform (Azevedo 1995: 213). The campaign it ran reflected this confidence.

Strategy and Tactics

The PT's language of 1994 still evoked radical change brought about by state action. Promises of "transformation" and even "revolution" against the "dominant classes" filled the party's governing platform (Partido dos Trabalhadores 1994). Clearly marking itself as a left option, the PT affirmed that producers of wealth should enjoy the right to appropriate it and that state initiatives would be designed first and foremost to redistribute the very ample wealth found in the country. In terms of specific issues, the PT's government program focused on many of the same concerns raised in 1989: the external debt, land and income concentration, and privatizations.

Nevertheless, in contrast to 1989, the 1994 document did not advocate immediate debt suspension but rather hard-line negotiations; a moratorium should be considered only upon failure to reach a reasonable agreement on repayment. No mention was made of nationalizing the banks. The contradiction between the high productivity of Brazil's agribusiness sector and the malnourished status of 32 million citizens was underscored, but the most profitable land would not be targeted for expropriation. The document also promoted the idea of creating and bolstering mass internal markets, designed to provide momentum for a positive and virtuous circle between salaries, productivity, consumption, and investment. The overarching difference between the 1989 and 1994 programs was that the latter backed away from professing socialism as the ultimate goal. The policies intended to redress problems of development and redistribution would support "socialist objectives" if not socialism itself.

As for the general image that the PT candidate projected, Lula came off as still committed to substantial change but less militant than in 1989. This was evident in his appearances on the publicly funded *Horário Gratuito de Propaganda Eleitoral* and a variety of other media events (Mendes 2004: 36). The zero-sum language of 1989 (e.g., the poor can only gain at the expense of the rich) gave way to the concept of "citizenship" (*cidadania*). The discourse of class conflict remained but the idea of guaranteeing basic rights to the population as a whole was introduced. Thus, the electoral coalition *Frente Brasil Popular* of 1989 became the *Frente Brasil Popular pela Cidadania*.

Lula's image in 1994 remained that of a blue-collar worker, one who had helped reorganize the labor movement at a time when workers had "neither voice nor vote." In this connection, he highlighted his commitment to resolving problems of formal sector workers, such as demanding salary increases and more formal sector jobs. At the same time, Lula began to talk more about his life prior to becoming a labor leader. Emphasizing his difficult childhood and the plight of his long-suffering mother humanized the candidate and showed his capacity to empathize with the millions of Brazilians who endured lives of grinding poverty. It also lent credibility to his commitment to programs – such as agrarian reform and hunger eradication – that would improve their welfare. Thus, if in 1989 Lula was the candidate of organized labor versus that of the "bourgeoisie" (Collor), in 1994 he represented the *povo* (people or popular sectors) versus the "elites." The alliance struck between Cardoso's PSDB and the PFL gave this polarity added bite (Mendes 2004: 38–40).

In line with its program and image, the alliances the PT forged in 1994 were still very much confined to the left. Consisting of parties whose main constituencies were urban and predominantly middle class – the PSB, PCdoB, PPS, PV, and PSTU – the coalition did not give Lula a ticket to penetrate the interior of Brazil. By contrast, the PSDB's alliance with the PFL helped Cardoso draw votes from rural areas of the country, most prominently in the Northeast. Lula recognized the restrictive alliance policy of the party as an electoral impediment. In fact, early in the year he made several trips to the Northeast to try to soften the sectarianism of some state directorates and pave the way for alliances to be widened at the state (if not national) level.[15] He and his close associates also started

---

[15] "Petistas investem em coligações nos Estados," *Folha de São Paulo*, April 5, 1994.

the *Caravanas da Cidadania* (Caravans of Citizenship), a road tour of PT militants through the interior of the country (especially in the electorally important Northeast) as a way to publicize the party and gain support for its candidate beyond the PT's original strongholds.[16]

The financial profile of the campaign fell in line with the picture portrayed here. Private contributions remained meager because big business harbored antagonistic views toward Lula and far-left elements within the party rejected the few overtures made. In May and June of 1994, the Datafolha Research Institute conducted a poll of owners and managers associated with nearly 10,000 firms: 78 percent of the business people polled had a negative view of Lula and only 8 percent expressed a positive view. A full 63 percent listed Lula as the candidate most likely to hurt the business class, far behind the 9 percent who named Brizola. Confidence in Lula was also low among bankers (Almeida 1996: 55 and 138).

For this and related reasons, Lula could not hold a candle to Cardoso when it came to fundraising. The latter conducted a campaign with unprecedented resources: over US $3 million was spent on focus groups and tracking polls alone (Lima and Bustani 1995: 217). Interestingly, one of the first instances of any *caixa dois* activity by the PT began around the time of the 1994 campaign. Paulo Okamoto, a close associate of Lula and effective treasurer of the party, approached a number of PT mayors to inquire about companies that supplied their respective municipalities with services. The objective was to solicit their help in forming a *caixa dois* network to fund Lula's 1994 campaign.[17]

As radical as the program, tone, and tactics of the 1994 campaign were, without the moderating influence of Lula and his associates they would have been markedly more so. Some analysts report that the socialist ethos of many within the PT was as strong in 1994 as it was in 1989 (Federacão das Indústrias do Estado de São Paulo 1994b: 13). In fact, the party leadership shifted further to the left in 1992 and 1993. Large numbers of militants from the party's left wing had won internal elections to head the municipal directorates of various capital cities.[18] This influenced the

---

[16] The idea did catch on eventually and helped overcome the party's prior weakness in rural regions. On the program's initial difficulties, however, see "Caravana de Lula é fracasso de público," *Estado de São Paulo*, May 4, 1993.

[17] "Denúncia abala comissão do PT," *Correio Braziliense*, July 12, 1997.

[18] These were most prominently São Paulo, Rio de Janeiro, Porto Alegre, Vitória, Salvador, Fortaleza, and Belém. See "Esquerda do PT ganha diretórios de capitais," *Folha de São Paulo*, May 16, 1993.

selection of presidents of the respective state directorates, which in turn affected choices for the National Directorate and National Executive Committee. Lula's group, the *Articulação*, had split into two factions the year before: *Hora da Verdade* and *Unidade de Luta*. The former joined ranks with tendencies on the far left to isolate figures from the latter (e.g., Lula and José Dirceu) and their moderate allies within the party (e.g., José Genoino, Eduardo Jorge).[19] The lack of control and risks inherent in the PT's institutional arrangements for selecting top party leaders were made starkly evident in the subsequent period: 56 percent of the delegates at the national party meeting in June 1993 (the eighth *Encontro*) came from left tendencies (moderates totaled only 44 percent), allowing for the approval of a document that put forth a number of extremely radical theses, including an embrace of the *luta revolucionária* (revolutionary struggle) and call for the PT to return to its social movement base.[20] The document rejected any notion of a "third way": It demanded that either the party get on track for fundamental change or see a continuation of misery and marginalization (Partido dos Trabalhadores 1998b: 547–564).

Lula and his closest associates had planned to stay solidly anchored on the left, yet as the party veered to the extreme left they began to fear for the PT's chances in the upcoming presidential election.[21] The radicals' emergence with full force at the national party meeting in June 1993 prompted him to take action. Most immediately, Lula demanded that they give him a margin of autonomy to run his campaign.[22] He also threatened to call off his candidacy if the trend toward radicalization continued.[23] Similar ultimatums would be issued in advance of the 1998 and 2002 elections as well. Lula used the autonomy he arrogated to himself to meet quietly with business leaders and sound out leading figures from more centrist parties – namely the PSDB, PDT and PMDB – about possible alliances. He also took it upon himself to form ideas for moderating the party's

---

[19] For details on internal party shifts and the proposals supported by various tendencies, see "Os que Defendem as Tendências Petistas," *Folha de São Paulo*, June 11, 1993; "Correntes de 'esquerda' repetem aliança e derrotam grupo de Lula," *Estado de São Paulo*, June 12, 1993; "Racha no grupo moderado fortaleceu ala 'esquerda'," *Estado de São Paulo*, June 12, 1993; "Quem é Quem no 'Novo' PT," *Folha de São Paulo*, August 29, 1993.
[20] See "PT assume teses esquerdistas e tenta ocultar esquizofrenia," *Folha de São Paulo*, August 29, 1993.
[21] "Radicalização prejudicará PT em 94," *Jornal do Brasil*, May 30, 1993.
[22] "Lula implora aos xiitas que o deixam fazer campanha," *O Globo*, May 26, 1993.
[23] "Lula ameaça não ser candidato," *Folha de São Paulo*, May 25, 1993.

government platform, some of which he secured in the end.[24] For example, while stressing the need for land reform, the PT's platform for government made clear that the most productive agricultural areas would not be subject to expropriation (Partido dos Trabalhadores 1994).[25] Backing away from saying that privatizations would be blocked outright, it stated that they would be closely audited and regulated.[26] Another item Lula secured over party radicals was the vice-presidential choice of Aloizio Mercadante. His links to the business world and to the military (as a son of an army general) positioned PT Deputy Mercadante to calm fears about the possible ascension of a PT-led government. In style and substance, 1994 marked the first glimmer of the transition that Lula would make from firebrand to conciliator.[27]

A major institutional issue to be resolved, however, concerned who would become the party's next president, a decision that would bear greatly on the direction of things to come. Lula had tried to build support for the candidacy of José Dirceu but left-wing factions (e.g., *Hora da Verdade*, *Vertente Socialista*, and *Democracia Socialista*) resisted.[28] Lula stemmed internecine feuds and radicalization by agreeing to serve as PT president before leaving the next year to run for election.[29] His candidacy as party president met with overwhelming internal consensus despite fierce conflicts over other issues. At the end of the day, it was Lula's popularity among *petistas* and the widespread belief that he was the best candidate the PT could put forth that brought the party back into his fold.[30] Despite an organizational format of low leadership autonomy, Lula found ways to exert authority over the party and to assume

---

[24] "Lula vence radicais e programa é moderado," *Correio Braziliense*, May 2, 1994; "Lula conquista maioria e muda programa," *Correio Braziliense*, May 2, 1994.

[25] Under pressure from the landless movement and its advocates within the PT, however, Lula committed himself to settling 800,000 families. According to calculations by the MST, achieving this would involve an area 5.5 times the state of Alagoas and the cost would be US $6.4 billion. See "Radicais do PT vão pressionar candidato," *Folha de São Paulo*, May 16, 1994.

[26] "Programa do PT preocupa investidores," *Estado de São Paulo*, May 3, 1994.

[27] "Lula passa de incendiário a conciliador," *Folha de São Paulo*, May 1, 1994. See also "Campanha vai deixar de ter comando 'sindical'," *Folha de São Paulo*, August 11, 1994.

[28] "'Esquerda' do PT apóia reeleição de Lula," *Estado de São Paulo*, May 27, 1993.

[29] Lula had been party president from 1990 to 1993 (he was also in from 1981 to 1987) and was reelected in 1993 to serve another term. He left in 1994 to run for president and returned briefly in 1995 until the election of José Dirceu.

[30] As Francisco Weffort openly stated at a meeting of business leaders at the Federacão das Indústrias do Estado de São Paulo, "The radicals won't control Lula partly because they don't want to. They benefit more than they lose from Lula" (author's translation; see Federacão das Indústrias do Estado de São Paulo 1994a).

independent or parallel actions when he could not do so. Nonetheless, it was evident to party moderates that they could not always depend on such informal measures. After the 1994 presidential defeat they would take steps toward developing more institutionalized means to secure their leadership position within the organization.

Campaign Trajectory

With the worst of the internal crisis under control, the situation looked good for the PT candidate until July of 1994. As late as mid-June polls showed Lula running at 42 percent of vote intentions, with Cardoso trailing badly at 19 percent. A continuation of runaway inflation would have been likely to yield a Lula victory, a threat that induced politicians of the center and right to close ranks and support the government's economic program. Many voters would shift their allegiance by late July when the inflation-reducing effects of the *Plano Real* took hold and were felt in their pocketbooks. The lead of more than 20 percentage points that Lula had enjoyed in June disappeared by late July, when the two candidates began to run roughly on par. By mid-August, Cardoso pulled ahead as the clear leader, with 41 (to 24) percent of vote intentions (Weyland 2002: 225). He consolidated this lead by October to land a first-round victory with 54.3 percent of the vote (to 27.0). Indeed, the slogan "*moeda forte, salário forte*" (strong currency, high wages) had gained credibility. Survey data illustrate the strong correlation of rising support for Cardoso and the popularity of the *Plano Real*.

In short, Cardoso's achievement of economic stability ended up undermining Lula's chances. The implication of the election outcome was clear: A national government that performed well on an issue of central importance to most people precluded presidential victory for a party that presented itself as an alternative to the status quo. With the first Cardoso government (1995–1998) the Brazilian state would perform ever better in a variety of areas and become increasingly institutionalized. This would be the source of a powerful moderating pull that would become evident in Brazilian politics in the next few years.

Profile of Support

Cardoso ended up beating Lula in every region of the country. Over the course of the campaign his support grew significantly among the poorest, least educated, and oldest citizens, many of whom resided in the least developed areas of Brazil (Jacob 1997).³¹ In polls asking voters why they were drawn to Cardoso instead of Lula, the *Plano Real* weighed especially strongly among those of lower education levels (Mendes and Venturi 1994: 43, 47). In only two states did Lula command a higher vote share than Cardoso: Rio Grande do Sul and the Federal District, which together contained only 7.3 percent of the population. His third highest vote share (37.0 percent to Cardoso's 53.8 percent) was in Pernambuco, where his strength lay in municipalities with comparatively high levels of urbanization and literacy. All in all, there was little way around the conclusion that the partnership of the modern São Paulo-based party (the PSDB) and the traditional Northern elite (the PFL) was a powerful electoral combination.

At the same time, the PT did benefit from having developed a core following. As mentioned previously, a survey of vote intentions carried out right before the election showed overwhelming support for Lula among respondents who expressed a partisan preference for the PT.³² Their loyalty to the party trumped any immediate considerations about the inflation reduction secured by Cardoso when he was finance minister. Lula was also able to pull in others who were not necessarily PT partisans but who assigned top priority to hunger, unemployment, and other pressing social issues (Almeida 1996: 192–193, Carreirão 2002: 130). Nonetheless, people in these categories constituted a small percentage of the electorate overall. Lula's first-round vote share of 27 percent did not even allow him to compete in a runoff.

The Party's Reaction to Defeat

Lula's loss to Cardoso divided the party. Groups on the left blamed media partisanship, the system of campaign financing that gave candidates like Cardoso an advantage, and the edge that federal government resources conferred on him. Nonetheless, the preponderant view was somewhat more self-critical. Moderate factions (e.g., *Unidade de Luta*³³ and *Democracia Radical*) ultimately concluded that the PT had not been sufficiently in sync with large numbers of voters and what they considered important. It was true that votes migrated from Lula to Cardoso

---

³¹ For demographic data on vote intentions, see Tables A.5, A.6, and A.7 of the Appendix for details.
³² Datafolha poll, no. 00372, September 1994.
³³ *Unidade de Luta* constituted the core of the former *Articulação*.

in droves while left factions (e.g., *Hora da Verdade*) publicly demeaned price stability as a "bourgeois" concern, moderate factions charged that stabilization had been accomplished by squeezing salaries, and members of the Lula camp openly predicted the ultimate failure of the plan. In retrospect, party moderates felt that rather than downplaying the problem of inflation, criticizing how Cardoso had accomplished it, and even seeming to root for the *Plano Real*'s demise, the PT should have communicated that it too was committed to providing a stable currency and had concrete plans for doing so.[34] Another critical observation was that Lula stuck too close to the perspective of the formal working class, defending policies like salary indexation, a luxury not even within the reach of many poor Brazilians who worked in the informal sector.

In the wake of defeat, leading PT figures published editorials in various venues. The PT's main forum for intellectual exchange, *Teoria & Debate*, featured two interesting pieces that underscored the overwhelming backing that the poorest Brazilians gave to Cardoso and the *Plano Real*. Referencing the PT's insensitivity to the burden of inflation suffered by the informal sector poor (i.e., those without the benefit of indexed wages), they called for the party to be more in touch with and responsive to public opinion (Feuerwerker 1994; Weffort 1994). In fact, the PT had not been very responsive to public opinion: Although surveys suggested that issues like price levels and employment far outweighed concerns like debt suspension and land reform, the party paid disproportionate attention to the latter.

Also underscored as problematic were the shortage of funds the Lula campaign had to work with, the rigidity of the party's alliance policy, and the excessive influence that the PT's decision-making structures gave to radical voices in the party bureaucracy (Feuerwerker 1994). One of the most incisive editorials was written by Luiza Erundina, former PT mayor of São Paulo, and published in the *Folha de São Paulo*. Focusing on the defeats the PT had just suffered in three majoritarian races in São Paulo – that of president, governor, and senator – she blamed the party for talking a lot about the "excluded" but failing to present programs that resonated with them, for not cultivating partnerships with the democratic center and center left, and for keeping only one eye on society while focusing the other on sectarian internal struggles.[35] Notably, many of those expressing

---

[34] Author interview with Paul Singer, long-term economic adviser to the PT. The interview took place in Brasília on August 16, 2006.
[35] "PT: crescimento, derrota e perspectiva," *Folha de São Paulo*, October 14, 1994.

such sentiments also urged the party to use the executive positions it held at the local level (that is, PT mayorships) to demonstrate responsiveness to citizens and their expressed concerns with concrete results.

In internal party meetings, party moderates referred to the difference between Brazil and Chile, where a mere plurality of just over 36 percent of the popular vote was sufficient to elect Salvador Allende on a socialist platform in 1970. Lula would need to capture a majority of all voters. The problem with pursuing a left strategy was that most Brazilian voters did not identify with the left. Furthermore, because more Brazilians appeared sympathetic to the figure of Lula than to the party as such, strategists concluded that more should be done to cultivate Lula's personal image.[36]

In this light, moderate leaders engaged in strenuous efforts to convince their radical counterparts to be more realistic about the given parameters of competition. After Lula's 1994 defeat they emphasized that it was erroneous to think that his strong 1989 showing (on a radical platform) could be repeated. In retrospect, they saw that it was the special circumstances of that campaign – a highly polarized contest between a populist right-wing candidate associated with the military regime and a candidate who represented a break with that style and era – that yielded such a positive result. A less polarized contest involving a credible centrist opponent from an institutionalized party not linked to the military had brought a decisive first-round loss in 1994.

Indeed, as rational choice institutionalism would suggest, the majoritarian requirements of winning presidential office played a central role in debates that shaped the PT's future. The evidence pointed to an unavoidable conclusion. Efforts to secure the backing of more middle-of-the-road voters, especially poor people, the elderly, and women, seemed to require a centrist ideological shift as well as measures that would modify the party in organizational terms, deemphasizing programs and highlighting personality (i.e., the figure of Lula) and even the provision of concrete immediate material benefits.[37]

---

[36] This assessment was made by comparing Lula's first-round vote share to that of the party in simultaneous races. Public opinion research confirms the average Brazilian to be more drawn to Lula than to the PT (Samuels 2006a).

[37] José Genoino and Paulo Vannuchi stressed in author interviews the difficulty of gaining internal acceptance of the view that the PT should reorient its strategy around the premise that most poor people cared less about the PT's ideological vision and more about the personal appeal of Lula and any immediate benefits they could receive from him as president. Their instincts received strong confirmation in the groundswell of support that Lula received in his bid for reelection (2006) from recipients of the conditional cash transfer program, the *Bolsa Família*.

Post-1994 Adaptations

Looking to 1998, Lula and his closest allies took important strides to modify the workings of the party. These changes fit well into a rational choice framework of analysis. The most immediate goal was to get more moderates elected to the National Directorate in 1995 and to build support for the election of José Dirceu as party president that same year. Securing the party leadership in the hands of moderates would facilitate the process of adaptation. They were pleased when José Dirceu won the presidency in August 1995, carrying the votes of 54.02 percent of the National Directorate to the 45.98 percent that voted for left candidate Hamilton Pereira. When Dirceu assumed office he enjoyed solid but not overwhelming control over the National Executive Committee, which would be crucial in influencing the tone and substance of Lula's next presidential campaign.[38] Of the twenty-one members comprising that body, thirteen belonged to moderate factions whereas eight came from the party's left wing.[39] Importantly, Lula and his group took the lead in promoting more lasting institutional changes to enhance the probability of keeping the party leadership in the hands of moderates. Set in motion shortly after the 1994 defeat, these would come to fruition only with time.

A series of post-1994 changes involved Lula's efforts to gain autonomy from the party. Lula blamed his 1994 defeat partly on having to abide by a decision-making body on which his allies did not hold a majority and hence wanted greater room to maneuver in 1998. The slim margin by which José Dirceu was reelected party president in August 1997 reflected the continued prevalence of radical opinion within the party.[40] Lula's most public informal response to the prospect of enduring constraints was to demand virtual autonomy to run his 1998 campaign or not accept his party's nomination. This threat held sway even among radical figures like the head of the MST, who argued that Lula was the only figure in

---

[38] One of the problems in 1994 was that radicals like Markus Sokol were members of the National Executive Committee, which positioned them to be on the committee that coordinated Lula's bid for presidential office.

[39] "PT decide se renovar para alcançar o poder," *Jornal do Brasil*, November 27, 1994; "Ala moderada quer dar novo perfil ao PT," *Gazeta Mercantil*, October 24, 1994; José Dirceu vence em eleição tumultuada," *Folha de São Paulo*, August 21, 1995; "Dirceu aposta na Executiva para impor moderação ao PT," *Jornal de Brasília*, August 22, 1995.

[40] A mere 28-vote advantage in a voting body of 541 separated him from left candidate Milton Temer. "Vitória de Dirceu acirra a divisão do PT," *Folha de São Paulo*, September 1, 1997.

the PT who could conceivably unite the opposition and lead the party to victory.[41]

Another path that Lula and his allies pursued was to found the *Instituto Cidadania*, a nongovernmental organization funded through individual donations, corporate sponsors of specific research projects, and the PT itself. One of the *Instituto Cidadania*'s primary original purposes was to provide a context in which Lula could meet with members of the business community free of the party's interference.[42] It became a context for the analysis and development of sector-specific programs to prepare for Lula's presidential campaigns. Lula called upon progressively minded professionals with expertise in various sectors and topics (e.g., social security, labor relations, energy, hunger eradication, violence, and internal security) to discuss ideas and develop proposals away from the sectarianism that often plagued debates within the party. The *Instituto Cidadania* was viewed with suspicion by *petistas* committed to vetting all decisions through established party institutions. Although they were not pleased with Lula's efforts to go around the party bureaucracy, their opposition was lessened by the fact that the *Instituto Cidadania* developed alongside the party rather than replacing its functions altogether. The work carried out at the *Instituto Cidadania* would prove crucial in the elaboration of Lula's 2002 government program. Moreover, some of the same individuals who participated actively in the *Instituto Cidadania* (such as economist Guido Manteiga) were brought into the government after Lula was elected president.[43]

Moving the party's national headquarters from São Paulo to Brasília was another "layered" change that Lula got underway. Shortly after the 1994 defeat he began to assess the desirability of moving the party from its original home in São Paulo (with all that the city implied symbolically and concretely) to the seat of national government. The motivation was in part to gain distance from the PT's social movement base in São Paulo and the ideological groups associated with the party's founding.[44] Notably, it would take twelve years before such a transition would be fully enacted. The decision would need to be approved by a party congress – the third in

[41] "MST afirma que só Lula une a oposição," *Folha de São Paulo*, August 31, 1997.
[42] Author interview with Paulo Vannuchi.
[43] Articles on the *Instituto Cidadania* include "'Bunker' de Lula toma lugar do PT na elaboração de programas," *Folha de São Paulo*, March 17, 2002; "A Corte de Lula," *Folha de São Paulo*, March 17, 2002; "Entidade recebe verba de partido e fundações," *Folha de São Paulo*, March 17, 2002.
[44] "Baixo teores de radicalismo," *Istoé*, November 2, 1994.

twenty-six years – scheduled for 2007. Until then, the party set up a dual set of offices and structures, symbolizing the gradual nature of change marking the PT's evolution.

Another important post-1994 shift was to start tracking public opinion in a more systematic fashion. This represented an important shift away from the earlier vanguard approach of the party, with its emphasis on leading rather than following societal preferences. In this connection, in one of Dirceu's first interviews as party president he announced, "The PT is undergoing changes to be more in tune with public opinion" (author's translation).[45] The party hired a top pollster, who was also a *petista*, to build internal support for public opinion polling. His response to those who voiced the historic PT rejection of opinion polling – that the party should raise people's consciousness rather than conform to preexisting views – was that changing citizens' views rested on knowing better what they were. Although the adoption of opinion polling meant that the PT would try to figure out what the public actually wanted by listening from the "bottom up," activists could still try to convince voters from the "top down" to adopt the party's values. This was another example of change taking place but not entirely at the expense of previously established practices. Focus groups would also become part of the PT's strategic arsenal, allowing the party to get a better handle on why some groups were reluctant to support Lula and what could be done to win them over. The party's major think tank (*Fundação Perseu Abramo*) began to commission focus group and survey research on issues thought to be important to the PT but inadequately studied by the major commercial polling firms.[46]

Another major line of adaptation pursued was in the realm of alliances. Lula, José Dirceu, and José Genoino went on an all-out campaign to convince party militants of the odds against winning the presidency without loosening the party's restrictive alliance policy. Lula announced that he was not going to be the PT's 1998 presidential candidate unless he saw a relaxation on this issue, at least in state races.[47] While he admonished the PT against always insisting on launching its own people instead of joining with reasonable candidates more likely to win (a viewpoint increasingly shared by party moderates), factions further to the left

---

[45] "Esquerda do PT perde disputa por secretaria," *Folha de São Paulo*, October 30, 1995.
[46] One of these issues concerned why Lula suffered from a deficit of women voters (author interview with Gustavo Venturi).
[47] "Convenção nacional deve ter equilíbrio," *Folha de São Paulo*, July 29, 1997.

(e.g., *O Trabalho*, *Democracia Socialista*, and *Força Socialista*) continued to argue that alliances for 1998 be limited to the traditional leftist camp.[48] With the exception of bringing the PDT into the coalition, little concrete would change for the 1998 presidential campaign. A crucial breakthrough, however, would come in 2002.

1998: THE PT ON THE DEFENSIVE

Context

The 1998 campaign was in many ways the most difficult of Lula's presidential bids for which to develop a strategy. The political polarization of the late 1980s and early 1990s was gone. So was the atmosphere of economic turbulence that obtained in the years preceding the two previous campaigns. President Cardoso was generally viewed as serious, honest, and competent, leaving Lula and the PT with little to credibly oppose with regard to character. Moreover, he had a solid record he could point to. In 1998 Cardoso still benefited from the dramatic inflation reduction achieved with the *Plano Real*: That year, Brazil registered its lowest rate of inflation in thirty years. A majority of Brazilians reported having a positive assessment of recent changes in their well-being. Market reform had certainly not solved or even improved all of Brazil's economic ills – especially not unemployment – but Cardoso made a case for needing another four years to attack other fronts as effectively as he did the problem of inflation. Solid support based on his accomplishments together with the significant weight that voters assigned to his experience and leadership qualities in safeguarding Brazil from future economic catastrophe put Lula in an exceedingly difficult position indeed. Moreover, the PT's problems of campaign financing continued. The efforts of the CUT to raise funds for Lula outside the doors of factories, hospitals, and universities were a poor match for the ample resources enjoyed by Cardoso (Samuels 2006b: 144).

It made little sense to launch a far-reaching critique of a president the public regarded so positively. Given also the considerable public support that existed for key aspects of the government's market reform program – such as trade opening and even privatizations (especially in some sectors, such as the telephone system) – Lula had less room to maneuver than in previous campaigns. The PT's challenge was to find credible points of

---

[48] "Tese de grupos expõem divisão do PT," *Folha de São Paulo*, August 24, 1997.

opposition within a fairly confined center-left political space. The Lula campaign was acutely aware that it faced an uphill battle (Mendes 2004: 54). Absent was the exciting sense of possibility that marked the 1989 runoff or the optimism that animated the party during the first half of 1994. Although Lula would have to work within a similarly restricted ideological range in 2002, by then there would be considerably more latitude to oppose a competitor who stood for continuity. In the years between 1998 and 2002 much would change. Brazilians' appreciation of the *Plano Real* would plummet with the 1999 devaluation crisis. The limitations and shortcomings of the market model would become clearer. Regarding victory as unlikely, Lula ran the 1998 campaign with one eye focused on the present contest and the other directed at the future.

Strategy and Tactics

Unemployment and social injustice formed the core focus of the 1998 program (Partido dos Trabalhadores 1998a). It was conceivable that the PT could make headway on these issues while simultaneously toning down its previous radicalism. However, the PT found itself hemmed in and unable to offer clear alternatives to the Cardoso government. Unemployment was a central problem in the Brazilian economy and in the minds of voters. The control of hyperinflation had entailed costs. Partly as a result of high interest rates, economic growth slowed to roughly 3 percent in 1996 and 1997. Poor growth, combined with the loss of jobs brought about by various privatizations and business efforts to adapt to foreign competition, led to increased unemployment. The PT campaign criticized the policies of the Cardoso government for having exacerbated Brazil's long-standing employment problems but it did not go as far as proposing a clear alternative economic model that would ensure full employment for all, as it did in 1994 when it stated that it would be "fundamental to articulate a new model of economic and social development in order to guarantee the right to work" (author's translation).[49]

Lula's 1998 campaign addressed problems with privatization but did not question outright the need for it or launch a frontal attack on the process itself. It emphasized the deterioration in the quality of some public services brought on by the sale of some state enterprises and stated that the PT would conduct a sector-by-sector review and regulation of privatized

---

[49] "PT vai dar ênfase a desemprego," *Jornal do Brasil*, March 17, 1998; "Emprego é o carro-chefe da oposição," *Jornal do Brasil*, March 31, 1998.

firms.⁵⁰ In an interview with *Veja*, Brazil's leading news magazine, Lula stated clearly that the PT would not undo the privatizations that had already been carried out, if only because laws passed by the Congress should be respected. This shift was partly the result of the decision to take public opinion polls more seriously. With survey outcomes in mind, one suggestion was to refer to privatization as "denationalization" because the latter term seemed to conjure up more negative sentiments (Kucinski 2000: 37). Opening up a new chapter, Lula discussed the difficulties of market reform not only as far as workers were concerned but national industrialists as well. Unlike in previous years, there was not even a hint of debt repudiation; nor was the International Monetary Fund discussed in incendiary language, because research suggested that most Brazilians did not necessarily view the organization unfavorably (Kucinski 2000: 211–213).

The 1998 program called for agrarian reform but broadened the previous focus on land distribution to issues like credit and irrigation, especially in drought-stricken areas of the Northeast. Rather than focusing on agrarian reform as a matter of social justice, reform efforts were framed more in terms of transforming Brazil into a developed country. Previous rhetoric to the effect of redistributing land to smash the "landowning classes" was greatly toned down. Instead, the focus was on production. When the press asked about his view on land invasions and occupations of the kind the MST typically carried out, Lula responded by saying that he did not think occupations were a necessary tactic given the amount of available land to be settled.⁵¹ The land reform issue was made all the harder to address because Cardoso had distributed a considerable amount of land in his first government (Ondetti 2008).

As for matters of image, the 1998 campaign marked a turning point in Lula's recasting. Many changes first appeared then that were accentuated and developed further in 2002. Considerable internal consensus existed of the need for change, but less obvious was what the precise content of Lula's new image should be (Mendes 2004: 60). Although identified as the leader of the opposition, Lula sought to appear less obstructionist and more constructive than he previously appeared. In 1998, compared with 1989 and even with 1994, his use of expressions like "class struggle" and "conquest over the dominant classes" was minimized. Even more than in 1994, the campaign deemphasized Lula's days as a labor leader and

---

⁵⁰ "Subsídio não é palavrão," *Jornal do Brasil*, July 14, 1998.
⁵¹ "Falta auto-estima," *Veja*, August 12, 1998.

emphasized his early life story: being born into a large family of tenant farmers and having a mother who traveled from the rural misery of the Northeast to the *favelas* (shantytowns) of São Paulo in search of a better life. This was a saga shared by millions of poor Brazilians. Public television spots portrayed Lula as simple, dignified, and serious, as someone who could identify with the downtrodden because he himself was from the heart of the *povo brasileiro*. They featured Northeasterners of humble origins who swore that Lula never lost touch with his past. Departing from the PT's prior emphasis on the need for collective mobilization and political organization, Lula emphasized the importance of having a dream and believing in oneself (Mendes 2004: 60, 62).

The effort to depoliticize and soften Lula's image extended to downplaying the PT and the candidate's possible subordination to it. This was very different from the situation in 1989, when Lula's candidacy was more intimately linked with the party. Opinion polls and consultations with business elites suggested that Lula was seen as more reasonable than the PT but subject to domination by party militants should he become president (Almeida 1996: 215). Another quality that the campaign worked hard to promote was that of the professional competence and preparation of Lula's prospective governing team. Television spots showed Lula surrounded by technocratic experts drawing up proposals aimed at developing the country, a collaboration that was actually happening within the walls of the *Instituto Cidadania*.[52] Without over-referencing his union leader past, the campaign portrayed Lula's own sphere of professional competence as that of a negotiator. The transition in Lula's image from obstructionist radical to conciliatory pragmatist was indeed underway.

The coalition forged to lead Lula's 1998 presidential bid consisted of the PT, PDT, PCdoB, and PCB.[53] The left wing of the PT had advocated forging "left only" alliances against Lula's stated desire to sound out support from center-left politicians like Ciro Gomes and Itamar Franco.[54] The PDT joined as a formal member for the first time. Although this brought in the following of Brizola, who ran as Lula's Vice President, it did little to extend the PT candidate's reach into less developed areas of the country or to enhance his appeal among centrist urban sectors.

---

[52] "PT tenta atacar imagem de despreparo de Lula," *Folha de São Paulo*, September 10, 1998.
[53] As I explained in Chapter 3, PCdoB is the *Partido Comunista do Brasil* or Communist Party of Brazil; PCB stands for the Brazilian Communist Party.
[54] "Disputa define os rumos do PT," *Jornal do Brasil*, August 10, 1997.

As in 1994, Cardoso's coalition was rooted in the marriage between centrist urban-based reformists with a technocratic bent and traditional politicians based in the less developed Northeast. Lacking such a broad base – especially a parallel to the PFL – would limit Lula's advance.[55]

Evidently, the main concerns raised by the opposition – unemployment and social justice – were viewed as less urgent and fundamental than the issue of economic stability. A majority of Brazilians still had a positive or neutral assessment of recent changes in their well-being and ultimately hedged their bets on the candidate that represented the best chance of continuity. The vote trajectory suggested that most Brazilians were not willing to risk the country's (and their own) economic future to Lula when Cardoso had a proven track record. The specter of serious new problems – brought on by the midyear outbreak of the Russian crisis – only seemed to boost the importance attached to economic stability (Weyland 2002: 240). The 1998 outcome showed that Brazilians were not willing to go out on a limb in the face of reasonable incumbent performance. President Cardoso won reelection in October with 53.1 percent of the vote to Lula's 31.7 percent. Even with problems of unemployment, drought in the Northeast, stock market fluctuations, and charges of vote buying to approve his reelection amendment, the incumbent president was able to carry a majority in the first round.

A closer look at the numbers, however, suggested that the political left made some headway. Lula's first-round vote total of 31.7 percent was slightly higher than the 27.0 he garnered four years earlier. Moreover, adding together the first-round vote share won by PPS candidate Ciro Gomes (11 percent) with that of Lula (31.7 percent), the left experienced a 12.46 percentage point increase from 1994. At least some segments of the public appeared less than satisfied and open to change. Perhaps Lula's prospects would improve in 2002 if the achievements of the Cardoso years were to wear thinner and existing problems were to become exacerbated. However, it would also rest on Lula to enhance his public appeal and on his party to put forth a credible set of proposals that simultaneously

---

[55] Even getting Brizola on the Vice Presidential ticket was trickier than one might have imagined. In exchange for having Brizola support the presidential candidacy of Lula, the PDT in Rio de Janeiro wanted the PT not to run its own gubernatorial candidate but rather to support the PDT's candidate, Anthony Garotinho. The Lula campaign fought bitterly with the radical wing of the party in Rio de Janeiro to prevent it from launching a PT candidate. PT radical Milton Temer led the Rio directorate of the party in vetoing this decision and trying to put forth PT radical Vladimir Palmeira. In the end, however, the national party won out. This reflected once again the fact the PT was different: It was hierarchical and the national leadership would prevail. See "PT terá candidato próprio no Rio," *Jornal do Brasil*, April 27, 1998.

embraced the market while proposing ways to modify its workings in more palatable and socially progressive directions. Several developments led to a downward turn in Cardoso's approval ratings over the course of his second presidential term, principally the devaluation of the *real* in January 1999, public utility and fuel price hikes, electricity blackouts in major cities, and persistent unemployment. This inspired hope that Lula's time would finally come in 2002.

In the meantime, an institutional reform designed to bolster the leadership possibilities of party moderates was finally enacted. Lula's group had worked hard to build internal support for the PED (*Processo de Eleições Diretas* or Process of Direct Elections). In 2000, years after the external features of the party began to shift in a catchall and electoral-professional direction, the PT reformed its statute such that party members would directly elect the president of the party, the members of the National Directorate, and the presidents of state and municipal directorates. Previously, party delegates to the annual national convention chose the party president and the National Directorate. The latter, in turn, elected the National Executive Committee. By increasing the weight of average party members over delegates, who by virtue of linkages with the party bureaucracy were more likely to be radical, the change was designed to favor the moderate leadership. Similarly, the new statute's provision of internal plebiscites with participation of the rank and file diminished the influence of organized factions. The public argument for instituting these changes was that they would make the party more democratic, reflected in the slogan "*um militante, um voto*" (one party activist, one vote). Toward the goal of reducing the occurrence of factional conflict, the reform also extended the party president's term of office and that of other leaders from two to three years. The party's left wing opposed the reform to the party statute, suspecting it was a way for Lula and his allies to ensure domination over the party. Its members argued that the reform would reduce deliberation and that people only minimally engaged in the life of the party would be allowed excessive influence.[56] In the end, though, the forces of change won out. José Dirceu won reelection to the party's presidency in 2001 with a slightly higher vote margin than before.[57]

---

[56] Author interview with PT Deputy João Batista Oliveira de Araújo (Babá), Brasília, August 6, 2003.

[57] Informative articles on the PED include "PT quer se reorganizer internamente," *Jornal do Brasil*, February 7, 1999; "Disputa interna volta a agitar o PT," *Jornal do Brasil*, September 12, 1999; and "Todo poder `as bases," *Istoé*, December 8, 1999. See also http://ped.pt.org.br/ (last accessed on January 20, 2010).

2002: SUCCESSFULLY BALANCING OPPOSITION AND CONCILIATION

Context

Opposition to Cardoso grew markedly over the course of his second administration. Alongside the relief brought about with inflation reduction, key elements of the Cardoso-era market reforms produced negative side effects felt by the population. In particular, the government limited spending, introduced new taxes, and maintained unusually high interest rates to preserve much needed capital inflows and secure the stability of the currency. Low inflation and higher government revenues resulted, but they were at the cost of dampening domestic business investment and formal sector employment. To stem the massive outflow of resources emanating from a mounting exchange rate crisis, the *real* was devalued in January 1999, decisively shattering the magic of the *Plano Real* and causing permanent damage to Cardoso's popularity. The major problem cited in public opinion polls was unemployment. If in 1989 Brazilians named inflation as their primary concern, by 2002 they were most worried about unemployment (Centro de Estudos de Opinião Pública 2002b: 372–373). Further undermining the government's credibility was a series of blackouts in major cities, which were particularly troubling in light of widespread concerns about personal security.[58] Indeed, many Brazilians were ready for a change.[59]

Yet Lula would have to tread with caution. The market model may have left some things to be desired, but Brazilians were not calling for an all-out overhaul of the economic order.[60] Lula would need to criticize government policies but not launch a fundamental indictment of

---

[58] Many Brazilians blamed these blackouts on privatization in a blanket sense, and they failed to distinguish between the aspects of generation, transmission, and distribution. Inadequate investment in generation was where the Cardoso government ran into problems.

[59] Two informative sources on the economic problems of the late 1990s are Weyland (2002: 239–243) and Amaral, Kingstone, and Krieckhaus (2008: 137–160).

[60] *Latinobarómetro* polls after 2003 asked two questions that yielded responses reflecting this point. The first is, "Do you strongly agree, agree, disagree or strongly disagree with the following statement: 'Only with a market economy can Brazil become a developed country?'" Between 2003 and 2005, 65 percent of all respondents said they strongly agreed or agreed. However, when asked, "In general, would you say that you are very satisfied, fairly satisfied, not very satisfied or not at all satisfied with the way the market economy works in Brazil?," only 34 percent of respondents (in those same years) said they were "very satisfied" or "fairly satisfied."

neoliberalism, much less of capitalism itself. If a frontal assault on the status quo and an associated strategy of polarization made sense in 1989, the situation in 2002 called for walking a finer line between opposition and commitment to the basic contours of the market model.

The problems just described, coupled with Cardoso's plummeting popularity, led all candidates in the 2002 presidential contest to position themselves around the theme of *mudança* (change). In addition to Lula, this held for Ciro Gomes (PPS), Anthony Garotinho (PSB), and even for José Serra himself, running on the PSDB ticket. A former member of the PSDB and government minister under Itamar Franco in 1994, Gomes' attempt to distance himself from the Cardoso group was not entirely credible. Widespread accusations of Garotinho's misuse of public funds as governor of Rio de Janeiro (1999–2002) made him look like the rest of the country's political class. Needless to say, José Serra's efforts to separate himself from some of the Cardoso government's policies proved difficult given his close and long-standing personal relationship with the president, the two cabinet positions he held under him (Minister of Planning and Minister of Health), and the fact he was Cardoso's hand-picked successor. No matter how much moderation Lula underwent in 2002, he was the candidate who could most credibly claim to represent an alternative given the PT's history and the role he had played in the three preceding presidential contests (Almeida 2008: 52).

Nonetheless, to walk the necessary line between opposition and adaptation, Lula had to manage his race carefully. With even greater insistence than previously, he demanded autonomy to run his own campaign. Among other matters of concern, the party's national meeting held the year before (2001) in Olinda (the twelfth *Encontro*) yielded a party program far more radical than the government platform Lula envisioned putting forth (Partido dos Trabalhadores 2002a). Also worrisome was the fact that, in mid-2002, markets began to react in an apprehensive fashion to a likely PT victory (Jensen and Schmith 2005). The independence Lula asserted vis-à-vis the party was exemplified in the *Carta ao Povo Brasileiro* (Letter to the Brazilian People) published in June 2002 (Silva 2002). Directed to the domestic and foreign investment community more than to ordinary citizens, Lula pledged to maintain many of the Cardoso-era economic policies, pay the public debt, keep a balanced budget, and honor agreements that Brazil had signed with the International Monetary Fund. The *Carta ao Povo Brasileiro* annoyed PT radicals, but because Lula presented it as a letter from himself and not the party per se, there was little they could do to veto it. In this way, the *Carta* never displaced anything but was added alongside party documents. The *Carta*'s opening line said it all: "*O Brasil quer mudar. Mudar para crescer, incluir, pacificar*" ("Brazil wants to change in order to grow, include, and pacify").

Strategy and Tactics

Another demand Lula made was to hire Duda Mendonça, a highly paid publicist who had overseen many winning political campaigns, most notably on the political right. Mendonça would devise a broad strategy as well as specific tactics for the campaign. His point of departure was the estimate that Lula could count on roughly one-third of the electorate to support him, that another one-third would probably not back him under any circumstance, and that the remaining one-third was up for grabs and needed to be won over.[61] Voters in the last group included those at the very lowest levels of education and income, as well as women,[62] older citizens,[63] and members of Brazil's very heterogeneous middle class. Necessary to court them effectively would be the promise of reform – aimed at preserving the market model's best features and revising its shortcomings – delivered in a highly accessible and nonthreatening "light" fashion.

The moderate nature of the program Lula endorsed ran parallel with the series of images he projected. Notably, the words *socialist* or *socialism* did not appear anywhere in the 2002 government proposal (Partido dos Trabalhadores 2002b). The program was short on specifics but the discourse was one of "reforms within capitalism" and the "democratization of the market." The overarching stated goal was to establish a "social contract" between the government, business, and workers with the aim of resuming economic growth, creating more jobs, and achieving a better distribution of income. The 2002 platform raised the issue of land distribution but in a novel twist underscored its centrality to reducing conflict in the countryside. Furthermore, for the first time, Lula professed an explicit commitment to upholding the interests of agribusiness. To lend credibility to that promise, one of his television spots featured a rancher from Mato Grosso do Sul as he hailed the economic benefits as

---

[61] "A tese dos três terços," *Folha de São Paulo*, December 17, 2001.
[62] See Centro de Estudos de Opinião Pública (2002b: 350) for a profile of Lula's social base by gender from 1989 to 2002.
[63] See Centro de Estudos de Opinião Pública (2002b: 349) for a profile of Lula's social base by age from 1989 to 2002.

well as social peace the PT governor had brought to the state (Mendes 2004: 89).

The campaign worked hard to get Lula's image right in 2002. Because the issues were breaking his way anyway, the atmospherics were at least as important as the substance of the platform he endorsed. Duda Mendonça went quickly to work casting Lula in a more "presidential" style and formulating catchy yet unobjectionable slogans like "*Lula, Paz e Amor*" ("Lula: Peace and Love") and "*O PT: para um Brasil Decente*" ("The PT: for a Decent Brazil"). Two key images of Lula were projected: that of national unifier and of competent administrator and modernizer. Gone was the prior rhetoric of polarization, which focused on the irreconcilability of interests between popular sectors and elite groups. Instead, Lula would oversee a government for all Brazilians. Much less heavy and negative than in previous campaigns, the tone sounded in 2002 was positive and optimistic.

At the same time, Lula was portrayed as competent, professional, and experienced. If this was suggested with subtleness in 1998, it was emphasized in 2002. Lula's television campaign ads showed the candidate surrounded by well-groomed and highly educated experts in various sectoral areas. The suggestion was that Lula would have well-qualified advisors even if he lacked an impressive academic background himself. To give further credence to the idea that a PT-led government would administer the country well, the campaign emphasized the PT's record of governance in Brazil's cities. The idea was to piggyback on the party's executive record at the municipal level and suggest the promise the PT held for national government.

Attention was also paid to winning over targeted constituencies through more specific appeals. Mendonça's reaction to previous campaigns was that the discourse was too academic for people with exceedingly low levels of education. He urged Lula to communicate in simpler, more concrete, and immediate terms to reach this group while at the same time trying not to lose the middle and upper classes.[64] As for seeking to redress the "gender gap," the target audience was the female electorate with fewer than eight years of schooling. Several of Lula's campaign ads featured leading women of the PT – Benedita da Silva, Marta Suplicy, Marina Silva, and Heloísa Helena – testifying to Lula's ability to identify with the challenges facing women. Lula invoked his mother anew,

---

[64] "Marqueteiro de Lula vê em Serra seu maior adversário," *Folha de São Paulo*, December 15, 2001.

speaking in the sincerest of terms about the many hardships she had experienced.[65]

With respect to the issue of alliances, Lula and his group had raised the matter again soon after the 1998 defeat. They sought to maintain partnerships with left parties but to start attracting more centrist elements, such as part of the PMDB and even the PTB. Left-wing members wanted to bar even the PDT and PSB from inclusion.[66] Party president José Dirceu contended as early as 2000 that it would be essential to secure the support of Itamar Franco, governor of Minas Gerais (1999–2002). He and Lula viewed the PMDB governor's backing as essential to a victorious center-left alliance. In the national party meeting of 2001, the PT approved an "ample alliance" for the 2002 race. Perhaps to first gain approval for the general idea, there was no specific mention of the *Partido Liberal* (Liberal Party or PL) as a member.[67] Roughly one-third of the PL's federal delegation consisted of deputies linked to evangelical churches. Ultimately, Lula did gain the National Directorate's approval of an alliance with the PL and of placing José Alencar on the ticket as Vice President. A businessman, Alencar was chosen partly to defuse business fears. He was also from Minas Gerais, the state with the second largest number of electoral votes in the country and where Lula had done quite poorly previously, especially outside of areas with concentrations of organized workers and mobilized social movements.[68] The approval granted these measures, which were stark deviations from the party's radical past, validated Lula's previous efforts to shape the governing body in a more moderate direction. The formal coalition for the 2002 race consisted of the PT, PCB, PL, PCdoB, and PMN.[69]

Lula's Support Base

After securing 46.4 percent of the first-round vote, Lula then managed to win 61.3 percent of all valid votes in the runoff election against José Serra.[70] The 2002 election results suggest that the PT had evolved to the

---

[65] "Na TV, partido busca agradar as mulheres," *Folha de São Paulo*, May 8, 2002.
[66] "Moderados do PT consolidam power," *Folha de São Paulo*, November 21, 1999.
[67] "PT quer aliança com centro, mas suprime menção ao PL," *Folha de São Paulo*, December 15, 2001.
[68] In 1994, Lula managed to garner only 21.9 percent of the vote share compared with Cardoso's 64.8 percent. In 1998 he came in with 28.1 percent of valid votes compared with 55.7 percent by Cardoso.
[69] PMN stands for Party of National Mobilization.
[70] Serra had received 23.2 percent of all votes in the election's first round.

point of striking that crucial but difficult balance between retaining an alternative identity and assimilating to the political environment, a challenge for former ideological parties seeking to broaden their support base. As encapsulated well by Otto Kirchheimer, "[t]here is need for enough brand differentiation to make the article plainly recognizable, but the degree of differentiation must never be so great as to make the potential customer fear he will be out on a limb" (1966: 192). In short, although the adaptations the PT made helped expand its vote share, it continued to benefit from the broad contours of the political and economic profile it had established in earlier years.

The PT's more assimilated profile widened the range of voters to whom the party appealed, readily discernable by comparing polls of the same demographic categories across all presidential elections since 1989. Notably, the regional base of support for Lula evened out strikingly over time. Whereas in 1989 the PT followers were concentrated in the wealthier and more industrialized South and Southeast regions, by 2002 the party was even able to carry a majority of voters from the less developed North and Northeast, along with the Center-West. In 1989 Lula lost to Fernando Collor in every region except the South, but in 2002 he beat contender José Serra in all regions of the country. Whereas in 1989 a 22.2 percentage point difference existed between the regions of Lula's highest and lowest popularity (the South vs. the North), the gap narrowed to only 5.7 percentage points in 2002 (see Table 5.1).

In addition, whereas Lula's early following was short on people from the lowest education and income brackets (a large group numerically), in 2002 he managed to carry far more people in these categories. In the 1989 runoff, vote-intention polls suggested that Lula would win the votes

TABLE 5.1. *Regional Breakdown of Second-Round Presidential Election Results: 1989 versus 2002*

Region	1989		2002	
	Lula	Collor	Lula	Serra
North	29.5	70.5	58.2	41.8
Northeast	44.3	55.7	61.5	38.5
Southeast	49.5	50.5	63.0	37.0
South	51.7	48.3	58.8	41.2
Center-West	36.8	63.2	57.3	42.7
Brazil: Total	47.0	53.0	61.3	38.7

Sources: Nicolau, Jairo. *Banco de Dados Eleitorais do Brasil (1982–2006)*; Tribunal Superior Eleitoral.

of approximately 44 percent of Brazilians with only a basic education, as compared with the 56 percent won by his competitor.[71] Although he was more popular among Brazilians with higher levels of education,[72] the much larger number of people with little education disadvantaged Lula in absolute terms. By 2002, Lula's support across educational groups had evened out. Vote-intention surveys suggested that his second-round vote share would be well distributed across those with basic education (64 percent), secondary education (69), and higher education (67 percent). A similar pattern and trajectory exists for income. In the first and second rounds of 1989, Lula's weakest showing was among the poorest Brazilians: those from families earning less than two minimum wages. Beginning in 1994, the gap in support among poorer and more affluent voters began to narrow. By 2002 there was roughly comparable backing for Lula across income categories.[73]

Notably, the PT candidate also extended his support over a larger portion of the ideological spectrum, with the exception of people who classified themselves on the far right (Centro de Estudos de Opinião Pública 2002a). Although he suffered initially from a deficit of support among older Brazilians, by 1998 and 2002 he had made significant headway in that regard (Centro de Estudos de Opinião Pública 2002b: 349). The gender gap narrowed, but Lula would come even closer to closing the gap in 2006. In short, if the aim of PT strategists was for Lula to pick up more middle-of-the-road voters, he succeeded in doing so. In 2002, efforts to enhance his support among groups that had backed him weakly before did not lead Lula to lose standing from previous core backers. This would change in 2006, when Lula gained overwhelming support from the least educated and poorest citizens, especially from the Northeast, but suffered losses among more educated and affluent Brazilians concentrated in his previous regional strongholds.

There can be no doubt that Lula gained from adaptations the PT had made. At the same time, he benefited from the party's long-standing opposition role and its previous focus on policy seeking and organization building. Clearly, many votes cast for Lula in 2002 were rooted in the PT's historic profile. A binomial logit analysis based on Brazil's National Election Survey of 2002 (Centro de Estudos de Opinião Pública 2002a)

---

[71] See Table A.5 in the Appendix for the entire series.
[72] Vote-intention polls suggested that Lula would garner 62 and 59 percent of the valid votes cast by Brazilians with secondary and higher education, respectively (as compared with 38 and 41 percent for Collor).
[73] See Table A.6 in the Appendix for further detail.

suggests that respondents' reservations about economic liberalism and their attachment to modern political principles had a positive and significant impact on voting for the PT in the first- and second-round presidential contests (Hunter 2006: 20–21). Pro-state attitudes and anticlientelist political orientations were important predictors of siding with Lula even though anti-incumbent sentiments had also figured prominently. Indeed, had the PT moderated and become "catchall" in approach sooner than it did, Lula would have had less credibility in casting himself as an alternative. Had the party followed a more pragmatic path earlier, it might well have gone the way of FREPASO in neighboring Argentina, a mere flash in the pan of contemporary Argentine politics (Levitsky 2003). Although responsible for some dysfunctional lags in adaptation, the institutional history that continued to influence the PT and its most significant electoral leader had a positive side as well.

The network that the PT had organized over the course of two decades in the opposition served Lula well in other ways. PT affiliates supported Lula through "thick and thin." The importance of having such a network can be appreciated by looking comparatively at the candidacy of Ciro Gomes, who at one point in the campaign had managed to rise into second place. However, when a series of gaffes caused the "atmospherics" on him to turn negative, there was no organization in place to catch his fall (Baker, Ames, and Rennó 2006). By contrast, Lula's support rested on a far more solid grassroots base and institutionalized party organization, both of which contributed decisively to his eventual path to power.

CONCLUSION

Lula's successive races for the presidency were a key factor in motivating many of the adaptations made by the PT over time. The institutional requirement of winning a majority among an electorate that did not lean to the left to begin with and that became ever more open to the market economy over time induced Lula and his advisors to implement a series of changes strategically designed to broaden the party's support base. A rational choice perspective would predict these changes. Understanding the primacy of Lula and the likelihood that he as an individual (together with his advisors) would respond to external incentives more rationally and readily than would a mass institutionalized party sheds additional light on the PT's adaptation. Environmental and organizational factors interacted. Given that the PT was an institutionalized left party, Lula could not bend it to his every whim. Historical institutionalism helps explain why the process of adaptation was gradual, bounded, and therefore ultimately preserved many of the PT's founding ideals and core backers, which itself had various positive implications in the long run.

Examining the platforms and tactics of presidential campaigns from 1989 to 2002 reveals the transformation of the PT from a radical policy-seeking organization to something closer to an office-seeking catchall party.[74] The first changes made were highly visible to the electorate, such as the moderation of the PT's policy proposals, the softening of Lula's image, and the forging of broader alliances. Slower to come about and more difficult to achieve were organizational changes designed to reduce the influence of the internal bureaucracy (and the radical factions associated with it) and orient the PT more toward ordinary party members as well as the electorate. Notably, Lula also carved out a sphere independent of the party (e.g., forming and working through the *Instituto Cidadania*) and took specific actions around it (e.g., the Letter to the Brazilian People) when he deemed that doing so would bolster his electoral prospects. With the exception of instituting the PED (Process of Direct Elections), Lula tended to promote change in an additive or layered fashion, thereby avoiding frontal confrontations with party cadres who were more deeply attached to the PT's historical commitments, practices, and institutions.

Lula's support base expanded in line with many of the adaptations made. The winning formula for his electoral majority in 2002 involved retaining his initial backers while gaining followers among more conservative or nonideological members of the electorate who had shied away from supporting him earlier, such as Brazilians in the lowest rungs of education and income, especially those who lived outside the South and Southeast regions of the country. Indeed, the evolving profile of Lula's support base suggested the benefits of moderation in the broader context of a history of difference. The PT's origins as a disciplined and ideological mass party no doubt slowed the party's adaptation, kept it in the national opposition for a considerable period of time, and gave it an enduring following and solid base to rely on over time. In other words, the internal resistance waged against undergoing a more rapid and thorough adaptation, which historical institutionalism helps to explain, had some clear advantages. Discussed at greater length in the book's conclusion, this stands in marked contrast to other left parties, exemplified by

---

[74] Many of the changes implemented also fit into the distinctions that Panebianco makes between the features of mass bureaucratic parties and electoral-professional parties (1988: 264).

the FREPASO in Argentina, which was forged in 1994 by dissidents from other parties, by 1997 allied with the *Unión Cívica Radical* (UCR) to form *La Alianza*, and in 1999 entered national government under Fernando de la Rúa, all to collapse in 2001 at its first crisis.

Brazil's political landscape underwent significant convergence and consolidation between 1989 and 2002. If the 1989 election was marked by polarization, 2002 saw a convergence between the two final competitors. Lula made a striking move toward the center while José Serra sought to retain some claim to center-left credentials. Such convergence reflected the weight of external pressures and incentives, both economic and political. The strength of support for the broad contours of the market model amidst improved governance under Cardoso induced the PT to move toward the center while the widespread desire for improving specific aspects of the economy's functioning rewarded its presidential candidate for his long-standing criticisms of the Cardoso government.

The political rise of Lula between 1989 and 2002 both reflected and contributed to a more stable pattern of electoral competition over time. Whereas in 1989 the combined first-round vote share of the two front-runners was less than 50 percent (47.7), by 1994 and 1998 it had risen to over 80 percent and in 2002 remained high at 70 percent. (In 2006 it rose to just over 90 percent). Moreover, after the 1989 race, the top two finalists came from established parties – the PSDB and the PT – that had developed more consistent and significant representation in the lower house.

After the 2002 election the question that loomed in the minds of many was whether Lula as president would continue to successfully balance a commitment to the PT on the one hand – to many of its founding ideals and organizational practices – and to honoring the essentials of the reform process and economic stability begun under Cardoso on the other. Many of the adaptations the PT made and the challenges it encountered between 1989 and 2002 previewed things to come. Lula himself became even more pragmatic in orientation but could not always circumvent the party. Four years of a PT-led government followed by the campaign resulting in Lula's reelection in 2006 heightened tensions between the president and his party. In the end, though, both the PT and especially Lula would move further along the path of normalization.

6

New Challenges and Opportunities

The PT in Government, 2003–2009

On January 1, 2003 Lula assumed office. Leftist circles in Brazil and abroad rejoiced over this long-awaited event. Nevertheless, remaining tensions – the radicalism of some PT factions on the one hand and Lula's efforts at moderation on the other – raised the question of which direction his government would take. Would the PT stand by its core programmatic ideals and historic principles or adapt to the constraints of the global economy and the institutionally derived incentives of Brazilian politics? Would it carry out the party's vision of redistributive state-led economic development, progressive social policy, and ethical government or would it conform in wholesale fashion to contemporary economic trends and the structure of Brazilian politics? With respect to these questions, many wondered whether Lula would be able to control the radicals inside the PT. Just as external economic and political constraints had eroded some of the PT's distinctiveness in the opposition, would the process of adaptation be furthered with the PT in government? How would the PT, as well as its relationship to Lula and his government, change as a result of government decisions? This chapter contends that the experience of government made it even more difficult to retain the norms, commitments, and policy orientations of the past and therefore contributed crucially to the PT's normalization.

Lula's victory meant that, for the first time in Brazil's history, a highly organized party with a sense of ideological purpose and deep roots in society would head the government. Although organization and ideological commitment had helped the PT to grow and eventually reach the presidency, it was less clear how these features would fit with the compromises generally required of presidents within the institutional context of Brazilian politics, where majorities are required but difficult to muster in light of high party fragmentation. A significant constraint on the party was that it held nowhere close to a legislative majority; in fact the PT held less than 20 percent of seats in the Chamber of Deputies and the Senate. Lula's ability to come up with a sufficient support base in Congress was made more difficult by the strict organizational standards that effectively precluded migration into the PT from other parties. The PT's insistence on dominating the cabinet and other state positions – another vestige of its "externally mobilized" past – impeded its adaptation to governing within the constraints of Brazil's political system. The situation created by these organizational rigidities exacerbated the age-old dilemma of multi-party presidentialism: how to forge a workable majority within a highly fragmented legislature. Lula would need to find some way to increase his legislative support within the constraints allowed by the PT. Would his choices reflect the party and its history or a rational attempt to conform to the existing logic of the system? In other words, would the content of government decisions and the process by which they were made reflect the expectations of historical institutionalism or those of rational choice? Historical institutionalism would expect Lula to be tightly hemmed in by the demands of PT militants and to make decisions accordingly. Rational choice would anticipate that Lula would respond primarily to the incentives and constraints of Brazil's political system.

The main points of the chapter are these: The PT-led government adapted more readily to external pressures on the economic policy front than it did to the political constraints of multiparty presidentialism. The macroeconomic policies of both Lula governments (2003–2006, and 2007–2010) were quite conventional. The arena in which the PT's remaining distinctiveness made the most significant impact on the government concerned executive–legislative relations, especially in Lula's first term. Although many in the party took issue with the mainstream tenor of the economic and social policies the government enacted, they were more effective in blocking the conventional approach that Lula tried to use in managing executive–legislative relations: that of bringing allied parties into the cabinet at rates roughly proportional to their size in the legislative coalition. The dynamic that unfolded reflected Lula's efforts to placate the party while simultaneously trying to rise to the demands of the system. Caught between the restrictions his party imposed and the need to come up with a legislative majority (and in some cases a supermajority required for constitutional amendments), the Lula government resorted to bribing individual allied legislators to vote with it. The resulting corruption scandal – known as the *escândalo do mensalão* – caused the PT to *appear* more like a conventional Brazilian party. In fact, however, the method Lula adopted to secure allied support stemmed from the incompleteness of the party's transformation into a fully catchall, electoral-professional party. It was the PT's distinctiveness that limited Lula's flexibility and reduced him to resort to the *mensalão* in the first place. Ironically, the resulting scandal tarnished the PT's image as the standard bearer of ethics in politics and caused it to lose support among citizens previously drawn to it for this reason.

If governing presented heightened constraints, it also brought new opportunities, perhaps most importantly privileged access to federal resources. Especially after corruption charges had eroded support for the party and government among citizens from higher education and income brackets, Lula intensified efforts to reach the poorest and least educated sectors of society through executive power and central state resources. An income transfer program, the *Bolsa Família*, was the cornerstone of this effort. Greatly expanding coverage of this concrete benefit allowed Lula to consolidate a social base among the poor, who had responded only weakly to the party's previous promise of redistributive change through collective mobilization. The PT, however, benefited far less than the president himself from government investment in social policy. In 2006, Lula won reelection by a solid margin while the PT's congressional delegation shrank for the first time ever (although with eighty-three seats the party was still the second-largest delegation in the Chamber). Moreover, the striking inroads that Lula made into the poorest and least developed regions of the country caused his geographic support base to diverge ever more from that of the party.

MAJOR TRENDS IN ECONOMIC, SOCIAL, AND FOREIGN POLICY

Macroeconomics

The macroeconomic policies of the PT-led governments reflected a notable degree of adaptation to contemporary economic trends and pressures for a deepening of market reform. This degree of moderation is quite remarkable given the origins and background of the party. Before Lula took office, foreign investors, multilateral institutions, and members of the domestic business community were understandably apprehensive about a party that had called for socialism less than a decade earlier. They feared that under the PT's influence the new government might default on part of Brazil's large debt and fail to maintain the business-friendly investment policies of the Cardoso government. Knowing this, members of Lula's economic team turned sharply against the party's left wing and went to great lengths to signal their commitment to the market.

As I discussed earlier, Lula began his dramatic shift toward economic orthodoxy in the months leading up to his 2002 election. Those he appointed to top positions immediately after his victory indicated a continued commitment to such an orientation. Henrique Meirelles, a prominent market-oriented economist and former president of the Bank of Boston, was selected to head Brazil's Central Bank. Well-established figures from the world of business and agribusiness, such as Luiz Fernando Furlan and Roberto Rodrigues, were appointed to head up the Ministry of Development, Industry, and Foreign Trade and the Ministry of Agriculture, respectively. Although he was from the PT, Finance Minister Antônio Palocci held highly pragmatic views on the economy. Regarding investor satisfaction as a crucial economic and political necessity, he managed to convince many of his PT allies that enhancing the welfare of poor Brazilians would depend first on maintaining economic stability and achieving growth.

The PT-led administration set financial interests at ease by maintaining the tight monetary policies of the Cardoso government and running a large fiscal surplus, even exceeding the fiscal target stipulated by the International Monetary Fund. Whereas the Cardoso administration's goal was to maintain a primary budget surplus of 3.75 percent of the gross domestic product, this was increased to 4.25 percent under the first Lula administration (Roett 2010: 49). The hike was intended not only to reassure skeptics in the short run but also to safeguard Brazil's financial reserves should new international crises emerge. The economic team's calculations turned out to be correct. By January 2008, Brazil had become a net foreign creditor, and by mid-2008 rating agencies had elevated Brazil's status to "investment" grade (Maxwell 2010: 44). The maintenance of high interest rates and fiscal tightness in general left no doubt about the government's commitment to continuing the policies of the Cardoso era.

Another notable achievement of Lula's presidency was to reduce inflation. With an average inflation rate of 6.9 from 2003 to 2008, Lula could claim an even better outcome than his predecessor. Inflation reduction was accomplished for several reasons: The government made a major effort to balance Brazil's fiscal accounts, it pursued restrictive monetary policies, and it supported greater openness toward international capital (Kingstone and Ponce 2010). The trade-offs it incurred – for example, preferring to maintain macroeconomic stability with low inflation rates to increasing government expenditures and stimulating growth and employment – are not ones typically made by leftist governments. In sum, the continuity that obtained in macroeconomics was so pronounced that critics often referred to Lula's first term as "the third term of President Cardoso."[1]

Although the Lula administration favored the maintenance of macroeconomic stability with low inflation to stimulating economic growth and employment, Brazil's economy did expand. It grew at an average annual rate of 4.1 percent between 2003 and 2008, compared with 2.3 percent under the Cardoso administration (Kingstone and Ponce 2010). In 2007 and 2008, economic growth was calculated to be over 5 percent (Roett 2010: 51), with strong export growth and increased foreign direct investment taking a turn upward. Employment and the purchasing power of Brazilians also improved under Lula. Per capital income increased at an average annual rate of 2.7 percent between 2003 and 2008, compared with 0.7 percent under Cardoso (Kingstone and Ponce 2010).

Needless to say, this positive economic performance was due only partially to the decisions of the Lula administration. The policies set in place under Cardoso's presidency (many of which Lula continued) and the favorable conditions for trade in the world economy – helping to fuel Brazil's export growth – made crucial contributions. Nonetheless, most Brazilians are content with contemporary economic trends and give Lula credit for presiding over them. Throughout 2007 and 2008 the government enjoyed high popularity, with upward of 80 percent of Brazilians surveyed rating it as either "positive" or "okay." Lula's personal approval ratings typically climbed even higher than those of his government (Confederação Nacional do Transporte–Sensus, September 15–19, 2008). His high popularity across various income groups continued well into 2009 (Confederação Nacional da Indústria–Instituto Brasileiro de Opinião Pública e Estatística, June 2009). In January 2010, Lula's approval rating was estimated at 83 percent (Santander 2010: 1).

Pension Reform. Continuity in macroeconomic policy was matched by efforts to advance "second- generation" reforms in social policy.[2] The most noteworthy achievement of this kind was the passage of a social

---

[1] Numerous analyses underscore the similarities in macroeconomic management between the two presidents and their administrations (e.g., Amann and Baer 2006; Amaral et al. 2008; Kingstone and Ponce 2010).

[2] Whereas "first-generation" reforms refer to macroeconomic stabilization, privatization, tariff reduction, and the like, "second-generation" reforms include measures that affect issues such as the distribution, quality, and delivery of social services.

security bill at the end of Lula's first year in office. Designed to ameliorate the spiraling deficit in Brazil's special pension system for government employees, the new legislation (Constitutional Amendment 41) increased the effective minimum-retirement age, lowered benefit ceilings, reduced survivor benefits, and instituted taxes on pensions for better-off individuals.³ Because the reform proposal cut into the privileges of civil servants, a core support base of the PT, its approval required Lula to use his persuasive powers as well as the enforcement of party discipline to secure the votes of PT members of Congress. Notably, as I discussed earlier, the PT delegation had consistently and vociferously blocked a similar reform effort undertaken by President Cardoso. The subsequent reversal of this historical position was a clear indication of normalization.

In the end, the government prevailed over the vociferous objections of important historical constituencies within the PT. Lula made good on his threat to punish dissidence: The party expelled four PT politicians – three deputies and one senator – for voting against the proposal.⁴ These dissidents went on to form a new party, the PSOL (Party for Socialism and Liberty). Securing reluctant party votes for this important second-generation reform exemplifies the reference "using Leninism in the service of liberalism" (Hunter and Power 2005: 131). The dynamic of the bill's passage reflects the idea of programmatic change taking place alongside organizational continuity, namely the norm of party discipline.

Although PT pragmatists supported the reform and the programmatic content it represented – as a result of a combination of external pressures and recognition of fiscal constraints that made it necessary – it was a long-standing organizational feature of the party that saw the effort through. In other words, even though the substance of policy shifted, continuity prevailed on the organizational front, pressuring the reluctant to go along. Indeed, the PT was unique in its expectation of party discipline. Not all PSDB deputies had voted with the Cardoso government in 1998, but those who did not go along were not subject to punishment.

Lula's adherence to macroeconomic orthodoxy and market reform succeeded in winning the trust of investors and the praise of international financial markets and institutions. It no doubt helped lay the basis for the economic growth experienced in Lula's second term (2007–2010). There

---

³ For an explanation of the changes and a comparison with the previous provisions, see Deud (2007). See also Meneguello (2005) for an analysis of public opinion around this reform effort.
⁴ The deputies were Luciana Genro, João Fontes, and João Batista Oliveira de Araújo (Babá). The senator was Heloísa Helena.

were drawbacks to such a thoroughgoing commitment, however, as the following sections illustrate. First, fiscal tightness limited the resources available for other policy areas, most prominently social policy. Second, the subsequent alienation of the party's left wing caused its members to intensify their preexisting demands for positions in the state. This shrunk the space available for the PT's allies and in turn heightened their dissatisfaction with the government.

Social Policy

The PT-led governments assumed a conventional and unimaginative approach in social policy as well. Limitations imposed by orthodox economic policies in the context of modest economic growth and a broader commitment to moderation account for the lack of far-reaching reform experiences in this area. Expenditures for health, education, and social policy in general remained restricted. This was not surprising because one-third of the expenditures cut to reach the initial fiscal surplus target affected the social area. Social policy funding as a percentage of total federal government expenditures increased slightly – from 23.45 to 26.5 – over the four years of Lula's first government. However, most of this increase was taken up by social security, whose leap (from 16.60 to 18.09) was inherent in the system rather than subject to government discretion. The other major hike came from social assistance, which went from consuming 0.96 to 1.83 percent of the federal government budget. As I subsequently discuss, the income transfer program that benefited from this increase was not particularly left leaning in its orientation. Spending on education and health held roughly steady (the former declined from 1.62 to 1.48 and the latter increased only slightly from 3.10 to 3.38).[5] No significant changes occurred in the second term.

It is noteworthy that so little occurred in the mainline ministries of education and health, where reorienting spending patterns and developing key programs have the potential to make a major difference in poor people's life chances over the long run. Although it extended preexisting programs and instituted modest new ones, the government made no significant effort to redistribute existing funds to produce more progressive social effects in these areas. It sustained the trend toward increased school enrollments, improved literacy, and better basic health among the

---

[5] This picture remains the same when education and health expenditures are measured as a share of the gross national product.

very lowest income groups, and it prevented some of the most striking regional disparities from widening further. The combination of fiscal constraints and the manifest desire to avoid challenging privileged interests apparently inhibited the government from instituting major redistributive reforms in the key ministries of education and health.[6]

Land Reform

The record of Lula's presidency on land reform, a historic PT banner, was also exceedingly modest. Notably, under Lula the government redistributed less land and provided fewer inputs and services for settlers than did the Cardoso government, especially in its first four years (1995–1998). Furthermore, most of the plots distributed came from public land rather than from private holdings expropriated as a result of underutilization. This timid approach did little to alter the highly unequal agrarian structure in Brazil because it did not add new holdings to the total stock of land available to the landless. It is also notable that Lula did not repeal a legal measure that Cardoso pushed through in May 2000 in an effort to discourage the MST from undertaking land invasions. The provision stipulated that occupied land would not be considered for distribution.[7]

Compatible with the tight fiscal policies of the Lula government, the credit extended to settlers was restricted, especially compared with the situation that existed under the Cardoso presidency. The land reform agency, INCRA (National Institute of Colonization and Land Reform), spent less per year under Lula than it did under Cardoso. Such restrictions were but one source of friction between the MST and the PT government (Ondetti 2006, 2008).

Given the PT's long-standing ties to the landless movement and its commitment to reforming Brazil's deeply unequal landholding structure, the short shrift the government gave to agrarian reform warrants attention. Why did so little progress occur, especially in light of the fact that the preceding center-right coalition with strong ties to landowners achieved so much more? Given the intensity of Lula's interest in demonstrating market-friendly credentials to the domestic and international business community, together with the minimal economic justification to be made for small-scale agriculture, it is safe to conclude that he chose

---

[6] See Hunter and Sugiyama (2009) for a discussion and evidence of these points. For data on social indicators, see also http://www.ipeadata.gov.br.
[7] See Ondetti (2008: 184–188) for a discussion of this decree.

deliberately not to pursue an ambitious project of land redistribution.[8] The distance Lula put between himself and the MST, which increased markedly between the late 1990s and the 2002 presidential campaign, widened further over the course of his government.[9] Needless to say, activist groups became ever more disillusioned with the president.

Social Assistance: The Conditional Cash Transfer Program, *Bolsa Família*

While shying away from redistributive reforms that would have challenged property and privilege, the PT-led government made advances in social assistance, one of the few areas that enjoyed an increased share of the social budget after 2003. The conditional cash transfer program *Bolsa Família* comprised the social policy centerpiece of Lula's presidency. Operating squarely within existing fiscal and political boundaries, it provided minimal social protection to the poor without threatening more expensive well-established social programs enjoyed by the middle and upper classes.

After assuming office in 2003, Lula formed the *Bolsa Família* by unifying four previous poverty-alleviation programs and creating a single registry of poor families.[10] The *Bolsa Família* is highly targeted: Upward of two-thirds of its recipients are extremely poor. Before the income transfer program, most were living on less than a dollar a day. By potentially doubling their household income, the *Bolsa Família* grant establishes a minimum safety net for families living in extreme poverty. The program is conditional, at least in principle: Children enrolled in the program are required to attend school regularly and to receive basic preventative health care.[11] The Ministry of Social Development administers the *Bolsa Família*

---

[8] In addition, the Cardoso government expropriated the easiest properties, leaving difficult areas untouched. Moreover, land values were higher between 2003 and 2006 than they were in the 1990s because of the international commodity boom in crops like soy and other grains. High land values make land reform more expensive because the owners of expropriated estates must be compensated (in bonds) at the market value of their property (Ondetti 2006:3).

[9] "Presidente Lula não é convidado para congresso do MST," *Folha de São Paulo*, June 12, 2007.

[10] These separate programs, administered by different ministries, consisted of educational stipends to boost school attendance, maternal nutrition, food supplements, and a household gas subsidy.

[11] For details on the program, its eligibility requirements, and method of operation, see Ministério do Desenvolvimento Social (2006) and Lindert (2006).

in conjunction with Brazil's municipal governments. In geographic terms, the program is heavily skewed toward the states of the Northeast and the poorest sections of Minas Gerais.

Prominent supporters of the *Bolsa Família* – including domestic technocrats and international financial institutions – have focused on its cost effectiveness. For a relatively small amount of money the program can keep the poor from falling below subsistence levels (Hall 2006: 692–694). However, not everybody has been enthusiastic about the program. Far-left members of the PT deride it as *"assistencialismo,"* an approach based on handouts. In their view, the means-testing and conditional aspects of the program are paternalistic and demeaning. Moreover, they reject the fact that the *Bolsa Família* conforms so closely to the targeted social programs championed by international lending institutions for their efficient capacity to placate the poor and thereby facilitate the "politics of adjustment." As one PT deputy exclaimed, "We didn't struggle for two decades in the opposition for this!"[12] Such objections constitute an extension of the kind of criticism voiced by the far-left faction of the party in the 1990s toward the *Bolsa Escola* in PT-led municipalities.[13]

Skepticism toward the income transfer program formed part of a much broader internal criticism of the timid character of most government policies under Lula. Discontent reared its head early on. In May 2003, thirty PT deputies (nearly one-third of the delegation) issued a manifesto entitled, *"Tomar o rumo do crescimento já!"* (Growth Now!") They argued that a fundamental contradiction existed between the government's orthodox economic orientation and its ability to institute progressive social policies: The administration's submission to the "logic of financial interests" and a "recessionary trap" imposed excessive restrictions on the social expenditures needed for the kinds of programs that could truly boost people's life chances. The signatories urged the government to lower interest rates, invest in production, attack infrastructural bottlenecks, make credit available for small businesses and micro enterprises, generate jobs, redistribute income, and mobilize the Brazilian Development Bank (BNDES, or *Banco Nacional de Desenvolvimento Econômico e Social*) and other state agencies for a new phase of development. They reminded the president that income distribution and social inclusion had been core commitments of the PT's historic struggle as well as central

---

[12] Author interview with Deputado João Batista Oliveira de Araújo (Babá), Brasília, August 6, 2003.
[13] See "Corrente ataca Lula e Genro," *Folha de São Paulo*, August 24, 1997.

promises of the 2002 campaign.¹⁴ Developments in the sphere of foreign policy would make up partially for some of this dissatisfaction, yet not everyone was to be appeased through policy-based compensations.

Foreign Policy

Although the government's economic and social policies conformed in large measure to the Washington Consensus, Lula maintained closer adherence to the PT's historic views in the sphere of international relations (P. R. Almeida, 2004, 2006). The PT in opposition emphasized the need for autonomy and solidarity among developing countries in the face of domination by more affluent powers. In the 1980s, it strongly supported Nicaragua and Cuba, where several key PT figures had spent time in exile. In the 1990s, it developed strong ties with the *Alianza* in Argentina and the *Frente Amplio* in Uruguay, and after 1998 with Venezuelan president Hugo Chávez (Cason and Power 2009). Resembling this past were the substance and rhetoric of the PT-led government's foreign policies. Some of the people Lula appointed in the area and the process by which they made decisions also bore a *petista* stamp. Although Lula was not prepared to frontally attack the United States government or break with leading international institutions, initiatives he could reasonably undertake would allow him to live up to the PT's historic ideals and compensate for diminishing progressive credentials at home (Hurrell 2008).¹⁵ Foreign policy afforded a degree of decision-making autonomy not present in other spheres, where fiscal pressures and the institutional constraints of legislative politics weigh more heavily. If PT militants rejected the government's economic and social policies, they found greater satisfaction with developments on the international front. It was here that Lula salvaged some claim to promoting a leftist project.

The PT-led government came in announcing that it would pursue new directions in Brazil's international relations.¹⁶ International trade policy constituted the most significant substantive departure it took. The new administration quickly went to work in multilateral trade negotiations. Brazil played a leading role in forming the Group of 20, better known

---

¹⁴ "Tomar o rumo do crescimento já!" Manifesto signed by thirty PT deputies, May 29, 2003 (see pt.org.br).
¹⁵ See also "Desvio ideológico," *O Globo*, February 6, 2007.
¹⁶ "A volta dos círculos concêntricos," *O Estado de São Paulo*, December 27, 2002.

as the G20, which made its debut at the World Trade Organization meeting in Cancún, Mexico in September 2003.[17] A coalition of developing countries within the World Trade Organization, the G20 set out to dismantle the extensive web of tariffs, quotas, and subsidies used to support U.S. and European Union farmers. The South–South orientation of the PT-led government's commercial diplomacy also became evident in Brazil's strong resistance to the Free Trade Area of the Americas, which was a U.S.-inspired proposal for a hemispheric-wide trade agreement. Brazil's actions were decisive in blocking the proposal, which was viewed by many as a threat to the country's industrial base as well as policy-making autonomy in the hemisphere.[18] While opposing the Free Trade Area of the Americas, the government pursued a countervailing emphasis on strengthening the *Mercado Comum do Sul* or Common Market of the South as a collective tool for negotiating on more even terms with advanced industrial countries (Ondetti and Rhodes 2007).

The emphasis on cultivating relations with other developing regions had undergone a period of lag in Brazil's foreign policy. President Cardoso had paid central attention to fostering relations with the United States, international financial institutions, and other South American countries but placed less emphasis on Brazil's relations with other developing countries. The Lula government reemphasized the developing world, seeking to use strengthened relations with countries in Asia, Africa, and the Middle East to increase Brazil's bargaining power with advanced industrial powers. Although his government's international trade orientation resonated with the PT's historic advocacy of enhancing Third World sovereignty, the costs of maintaining this stance were not very high. Unlike many of the domestic programs championed by PT activists, promoting a South–South orientation in trade diplomacy as part of a broader progressive approach to foreign policy put no obvious pressure on the federal budget. Support of trade missions to Asia, Africa, and the Middle East at the time of a tremendous export boom allowed historically *petista* ideals to find common ground with commercial interests. Brazil's agribusiness elite welcomed a way to liberalize the farm policies of wealthy countries through the G20. Furthermore, many Brazilian industrialists feared that an agreement like the Free Trade Area of the Americas would cause the country's

---

[17] India and South Africa were also central to the effort.
[18] "Brasil só tem a perder com a Alca, diz embaixador," *Folha Online*, April 14, 2001.

manufacturing sector to falter under increased competition. There is little evidence that the United States punished Brazil for its rejection of the agreement and concomitant focus on strengthening trade with developing countries. Brazil's maneuvering room has no doubt been widened to the extent it is perceived as a buffer against more radical governments like that of Hugo Chávez in Venezuela and Evo Morales in Bolivia.

Apart from substantive outcomes, perhaps what most distinguished the PT government from its predecessors were the people appointed to leading positions and the development of a partisan decision-making track that ran parallel to traditional channels of Brazilian diplomacy. Appointments made early in Lula's first term foretold changes to come. Samuel Pinheiro Guimarães, a diplomat well known for his outspoken views against the Free Trade Area of the Americas, was chosen Secretary General of the Ministry of Foreign Relations (*Itamaraty*). President Cardoso had dismissed Guimarães in 2001 for being too outwardly anti-American in his position as director of research within *Itamaraty*. Longtime PT insider Marco Aurélio Garcia – appointed Special Adviser to the President on International Affairs – constituted another key leg of Lula's foreign policy team (Cason and Power 2009). A career diplomat, not a party cadre, normally held that position. The presence of such a partisan figure at the center of foreign policy decision making was novel indeed in the Brazilian context. A veteran *petista* who lived in exile in France as well as Cuba, Garcia had served for ten years as the party's Secretary of International Relations. In this capacity he extended the PT's networks with left-leaning movements and governments throughout the region. Appointed to head the ministry was Celso Amorim, a respected establishment figure. Amorim, Guimarães, and Garcia coexisted in a government with cabinet ministers that included orthodox economists, high-powered industrialists, and agribusiness elites.

At the center of greatest controversy was Marco Aurélio Garcia, who on several key occasions acted independently of and even at odds with *Itamaraty*, whose insulated core of career diplomats had historically dominated Brazil's international relations. He entered the stage in December 2002 (even before Lula's inauguration) by overseeing the delivery of Brazilian oil to Venezuela in the midst of an oil workers' strike that had threatened to destabilize the government of Hugo Chávez. Many observers questioned the appropriateness of sending Garcia – a highly partisan figure with previous ties to Chávez – to assume this role. The Venezuelan opposition perceived Garcia's efforts to prop up the Chávez government as tantamount to meddling in the internal affairs of another country.[19] So did established figures within Brazil's Ministry of Foreign Relations, which traditionally has tried to stay clear of internal politics.[20] Another source of controversy were concerns that Garcia had maintained contact with groups – including the FARC (Revolutionary Armed Forces of Colombia) – with whom the PT had ties but the Brazilian government did not have formal relations. Precisely because he was not a representative of the foreign ministry, Garcia enjoyed comparative flexibility in such matters.[21] These and related episodes led one veteran observer to refer to international relations under Lula as "the most politicized foreign policy ever adopted by a Brazilian president" (Albuquerque 2007: 25).[22]

If a key motivation behind Lula's Third World diplomacy was the PT's desire to satisfy its core supporters, the available evidence suggests that the policy has been successful. A poll taken at the PT's 2006 national meeting revealed that party militants were more supportive of Lula's foreign policy than of any other aspect of his government (Amaral 2006). The margin by which this held was considerable. When evaluating the Lula government in four areas – foreign policy, social policy, the economy, and politics – 75 percent of PT militants rated the government as "very good" in foreign policy, compared with 29.6 percent in social policy, 25.3 in the economy, and 12.2 percent in politics. In sum, foreign policy constituted a partial exception to the trend of moderation observed by the PT-led government. Given the internal discontent that arose from Lula's failure to uphold historic PT commitments in other policy spheres, foreign policy allowed the president to retain some credibility among the party's most ideologically motivated followers. For some, however, this was little consolation.

POLITICS: EXECUTIVE–LEGISLATIVE RELATIONS

The major arena in which the PT's distinctiveness made a difference in governing concerned executive–legislative relations. Normalization came

---

[19] "Enviado de Lula indicou inclinação a favor de Chavez," *Folha de São Paulo*, December 26, 2002. When Chávez asked Lula to forge a Friends of Venezuela alliance, many critics expressed concern that it would be a Friends of Chávez group. See "Chavez pede a Lula clube de amigos," *Folha de São Paulo*, December 21, 2002.
[20] "Assessor de Lula gera crise no Itamaraty," *Folha de São Paulo*, January 16, 2003.
[21] On this note, see "F@rc-os e-mails que comprometem," *Veja*, August 6, 2008.
[22] See also Barbosa (2008). Others, however, feel that Lula democratized foreign policy by diminishing *Itamaraty's* power and giving some play to an official who was at least from the same party as the elected president.

up against strong resistance in this sphere, especially initially, yet ultimately Lula fell into greater alignment with the pressures of Brazil's political system. Unique features of the party played a decisive role in shaping how Lula approached the dilemma faced by all Brazilian presidents of how to build legislative majorities in a highly fragmented and multiparty Congress. Presidential victory in 2002 shifted the incentives facing the PT from the electoral to the governing arena, opening up new requirements and leading the party into an unprecedented web of contradictions. From then on, the party would face the disjuncture between holding the Presidency and controlling less than 20 percent of seats in the Chamber and Senate. The ten parties that made up the initial government coalition held appreciably less than 50 percent of the bicameral Congress.[23] To make matters worse, approval of market-oriented constitutional reforms in areas like social security and taxation would require supermajorities. How Lula would translate his electoral coalition into a workable governing coalition would crucially affect the future of his government and party.

The combination of presidentialism and multipartism has generated considerable conflict for executives in Brazil as well as elsewhere (Mainwaring 1993; Ames 2001). That most Brazilian executives come from weakly organized nonideological parties, however, gives them some room for maneuver (comparatively more than Lula enjoyed) within the requirements and tensions produced by this system. One phenomenon that has tended to expand the government's support in Congress is that of party switching. Brazil has some of the highest rates of party switching in the world. The executive branch's control over public resource distribution provides legislators with an important incentive to join the party of government or at least the governing coalition. Rules that accommodate floor crossing and the weak commitment that Brazilian legislators often have to their parties make for a highly fluid political market. Presidents have typically welcomed new party members in exchange for congressional votes, and seldom have their own parties objected to the joining of newcomers (Mainwaring 1999; Melo 2000; Desposato 2006).

Brazilian presidents have also built legislative majorities by the deliberate and systematic distribution of pork barrel and jobs. Cabinet positions, through which considerable patronage is filtered, comprise the most important of these positions. A core strategy of interparty coalition building is known as *presidencialismo de coalizão* or coalitional

---

[23] Together they occupied 48 percent of the Chamber and roughly one-third of the Senate.

presidentialism (Abranches 1988), which involves allocating cabinet positions by estimating how many legislative votes can be secured on the basis of patronage distributed by prospective ministers to their respective parties and states. Ministries well known for their patronage-yielding potential include Education, Health, Agriculture, Transportation, and Mines and Energy.[24] Strategic cabinet distribution has brought in votes for many presidents and stabilized their governments. President Cardoso elevated coalitional presidentialism to an art form, especially in his second term. Intent on building a broad and stable majority coalition in the Congress, he looked the other way while cabinet ministers greased their clientelistic networks.[25] Although questionable from the standpoint of optimal resource usage, this form of presidential coalition building was at least not illegal.

The organizational weakness and catchall character of Brazil's political parties allowed previous presidents to take advantage of these tactics and thereby operate with greater ease within the institutional constraints they faced. Switching into the party of government rests on its members being open to newcomers, who are generally driven more by opportunism than by deeper commitments. Similarly, a precondition of coalitional presidentialism is that the president's party be willing to share power with other members of the coalition. The PT was different from most parties, however, which effectively restricted Lula's options. Because it demanded such high levels of discipline and loyalty (not to mention a significant financial contribution), few deputies from other parties ever considered joining. Moreover, existing organizational rules specified criteria that tightly limited the ranks of those who could even potentially assume the PT label. That only *two* deputies switched into the PT during the entire 2003–2006 legislature testifies to this important aspect of organizational continuity in the PT.[26] By comparison, *forty-two* deputies shifted over to the PSDB in the first Cardoso government (1995–1998), the equivalent of a 47.6 percent increase in the delegation (Melo and Miranda 2006: 12).

Moreover, the PT did not want to share power with other parties. Why did *petistas* seek to monopolize state positions? Much of the answer goes back to the party's creation by social movements external to the legislature and its subsequent struggle to develop against great odds.

---

[24] See Figueiredo and Limongi (2008) for a list of investment money attached to various ministries under the Cardoso government.
[25] See Ames (2001: 166–167) and Madrid (2003: 159).
[26] Notably, however, thirty-seven deputies switched into the allied PL.

The sacrifices endured by large numbers of activists and their crucial contributions to the PT's advance made it hard to swallow a systematic handing over of influence to individuals who did not share this common history and commitment to the party. Although militants lowered their profile to support Lula's 2002 election prospects, they were loathe to see his government subordinate their ideological project entirely. They objected not only to the substance of many appointments but also to the process by which they were made: The party's National Directorate had not been consulted.[27]

Ideological considerations aside, party militants felt also that their dedication to the PT deserved to be rewarded with jobs in the federal administration. Without *petistas* in control of top cabinet positions, others were less assured of receiving jobs in the second and third echelons of the federal bureaucracy. In addition, beyond the concern that too few *petistas* of any current would occupy top-level positions, left-wing leaders feared that the moderate *Campo Majoritário* faction would dominate among those selected. This was the group close to Lula that included the former *Articulação* and *Democracia Radical*. Representatives of *Democracia Social*, such as Raul Pont, and of *Força Socialista*, such as Ivan Valente, demanded that the party's left wing receive its share of positions as well.[28] Still comprising about one-third of the seats in the National Directorate and between one-fourth and one-third of the party's delegation in the Chamber of Deputies, party radicals were not a force that Lula could ignore altogether.[29] Lula would have to offset the appointment of moderate *petistas* by others who enjoyed more credibility with the left.[30] However, being mindful to distribute public offices among the various factions of the PT further reduced the number of ministries that Lula could allocate to other members of the coalition (Flynn 2005: 1,226).

---

[27] The only individual spared from criticism was Minister of Finance Antônio Palocci because he was at least from the party. "Petistas radicais vêem 'desastre' e 'equívoco'," *Folha de São Paulo*, December 14, 2002.

[28] "Esquerda do PT articula pressão sobre Lula," *Folha de São Paulo*, October 30, 2002; "'Esquerda' petista vai cobrar cargos no governo'," *Folha de São Paulo*, December 4, 2002; "Até agora calada, esquerda do PT reinvindica espaço," *Folha de São Paulo*, October 28, 2002.

[29] For a breakdown of party factions on the eve of the PT's assumption of power, see "O PT Sob o Microscópio," *Folha de São Paulo*, October 28, 2002.

[30] For example, whereas moderates controlled major economic positions, such as the Ministry of Finance, more radical tendencies were granted influence over other ministries, such as *Cidades* (Cities) and *Desenvolvimento Agrário* (Agrarian Development). The former went to Olívio Dutra and the latter to Miguel Rossetto, both from the radical *Democracia Socialista* faction of the PT.

New Challenges and Opportunities

Lula's challenge as president was thus to placate the party while simultaneously satisfying his allies in government. Historical institutionalism would expect Lula to give the party and its cadres first priority. In this connection, students of mass bureaucratic parties observe that dedicated activists are often awarded with public office and spoils for having performed demanding organizational tasks (Strøm and Müller 1999: 15). Rational choice would expect Lula to respond first and foremost to the pressures of the system. Lula tried to balance these competing imperatives. Caught between the PT (and all of its history) and the requirements and structure of legislative politics (and all of its peculiarities), he could not rely on conventional means to gain legislative support. Instead, he and his closest associates turned to tactics that ended in the *mensalão* corruption scandal, namely bribing individual legislators for as much as $12,000 per month to lure them into allied parties or buy their votes on specific pieces of legislation.[31] They *purchased* interparty collaboration rather than placing allied members into a greater number of ministerial posts. That Lula was unable and unwilling to overcome party pressures against a more proportional distribution of cabinet seats is obvious from an examination of ministerial selections.

A quick glance at appointments to the most central and constant cabinet positions in Lula's first term – especially in the first two and a half years – suggests a clear overrepresentation of figures from the PT.[32] In the initial coalition (January 2003 to December 2003), the PT represented 36.4 percent of the legislative coalition (in the Chamber) and 47.8 percent of the cabinet. In the second coalition (January 2004 to July 2005), PT politicians made up 30 percent of the governing coalition in the Chamber and 43.5 percent of the cabinet. By comparison, the PT's allies – most prominently the PMDB and PTB – had a disproportionately low number

---

[31] This section is informed by Pereira and Power (2005), Amorim Neto and Coelho (2007), Hunter (2007b), Samuels (2008), and Sola (2008: 39–41).

[32] See Table A.8 in the Appendix for a comparison of the Lula and Cardoso governments regarding the weight of parties in the legislative coalition in relation to their representation in the cabinet. For the sake of a direct comparison, the analysis covers twenty-three central ministries and not some of the entities created over time that gained ministerial status. The twenty-three include Agriculture, Science and Technology, Communications, Culture, Defense, Agrarian Development, Industry and External Commerce, Education, Sports, Finance, Justice, Environment, Mines and Energy, Planning, Social Security, Foreign Relations, Health, Labor, Transportation, Tourism, and National Integration. Also examined are the Ministry of Cities and the Ministry of Social Assistance, which was eliminated and later substituted by the Ministry of Social Development and Hunger Reduction.

of cabinet seats in relation to their presence in the governing coalition.³³ For example, the PTB – the second largest allied party in the Chamber – made up 16.4 percent of the legislative coalition but occupied only 4.3 percent of the cabinet in the first coalition. The party gained no more cabinet seats in the second coalition (January 2004 to July 2005) to bring it into alignment with its congressional weight. Similarly, the PMDB made up 23.1 percent of the legislative alliance but occupied only 8.7 percent of the cabinet in the second coalition. Although the PMDB was the second largest party in the coalition, it held only two ministries: Communications and Social Security. These two parties – from which many of the *mensaleiros* hailed – felt insufficiently rewarded for the working majority they gave to Lula in the Congress. By 2005, dissatisfaction had been growing within the PMDB for some time. Not only was it and other allied parties discontent with the number of major ministries they commanded but also they complained that the PT was overrepresented in secondary cabinet positions as well as in second-echelon positions within the federal administration.

Within the framework of their reasoning, discontent had an empirical basis, especially when we consider that the aforementioned figures actually understate the PT's full cabinet presence. A number of departments (*Secretarias*) – some of which Lula created – enjoyed ministerial status, such as the Department of Women's Affairs, the Department of Fishing, and the Department of Human Rights. When we consider such entities, the PT's occupation of ministerial positions actually rose to 60 percent in the first coalition, 54.8 percent in the second, and 46.5 percent in the third, as I subsequently explain. The PT was clearly overrepresented in the cabinet in relation to its numbers in the legislative coalition.

Petistas also figured prominently in second-level positions within the bureaucracy, such as in executive jobs in federal banks, regulatory agencies, and public enterprises.³⁴ The Brazilian state has roughly 20,000 jobs that are exempt from merit-based selection criteria and are the prerogative of the federal executive to fill. Lula added close to 2,700 additional posts in January 2004, giving himself more room to maneuver (Pacheco 2004: 9). A survey of personnel in the highest category of the second echelon (known as DAS-6) revealed that nearly 40 percent were from

---

³³ "Bem Me Quer, Mal Me Quer," *Veja*, March 9, 2005.
³⁴ The practice of distributing posts to *petistas* was especially marked in the Brazilian Company of Agribusiness Research, the Brazilian Institute of Environment and Renewable Natural Resources, the Brazilian Development Bank, and the post office (*Correios*).

the PT versus only 7.5 percent from allied parties, with the rest claiming no particular party affiliation (D'Araújo 2007: 38). Many who occupied these positions had a union background (D'Araújo 2007: 44), which is not surprising given that thirteen ministers alone in Lula's first cabinet were former union leaders (Rodrigues 2006: 13). One observer writes that this "politicization of public administration" was "at odds with the unspoken rules of coalitional presidentialism" (Sola 2008: 40).[35] Without a doubt, the PT's allies were disgruntled by what they viewed as being inadequately rewarded at lower levels as well.

Apparently, Lula, who was more strategically minded than many in his party, had originally wanted to encourage a wider and more stable coalition by including more parties in the cabinet. In particular, he tried reaching out to PMDB leaders shortly after the election but encountered resistance from within the PT about incorporating the party in a central way. *Petistas* had long criticized the PMDB as a bastion of corruption and *fisiologismo* (clientelism) in Brazilian politics. Back in December of 2002, Lula's soon-to-be chief of staff José Dirceu pieced together an agreement with PMDB leaders that would have awarded two choice ministries to the party: Mines and Energy, and National Integration. At the last minute, though, Lula canceled the deal, saying that the PT could not tolerate sacrificing its image as Brazil's most ethical party with notorious PMDB *fisiologismo*. The PT's feelings about the PTB were similar. Many in the PMDB stayed out of the coalition when the posts it wanted were not forthcoming.

After the *mensalão* scandal broke in July 2005, Lula was under further pressure to include more allied parties in the cabinet. The corruption charges launched by Deputy Roberto Jefferson (PTB) motivated the formation of a new cabinet.[36] Although this post-*mensalão* cabinet (July 2005 to December 2006) reflects some change in the direction of political pragmatism, there was not as much change as one might expect. Lula needed to negotiate hard with the PT to gain what he did. He had tried to wrangle four ministries for the PMDB but was able to free up only three. While making up 24.1 percent of the legislative coalition, the PT still held 43.5 percent of the cabinet. The PMDB went from two to three ministries. Although losing Social Security, it ended up maintaining

---

[35] Although overrepresenting the PT had important political drawbacks for the government, it is worth remembering that the party's coffers benefit from the dues paid by members who hold such positions. In addition, having *petistas* occupy some state offices allows the party to take more credit for some projects than it could otherwise.

[36] "Reforma ministerial foi motivada por denúncias de Jefferson," *O Globo*, July 21, 2005.

Communications and gaining (at the expense of the PT) the Ministry of Mines and Energy, and the Ministry of Health, both of which hold significant patronage potential.[37] It was not until the second Lula government began in 2007 that a fuller accommodation took place.

It is instructive to compare the situation that existed in Lula's first term with that which obtained under Cardoso, whose government operated comparatively smoothly and without scandal. For most of Cardoso's first term (1995–1998), the PSDB fluctuated between representing 18.4 to 21.7 percent of the legislative coalition (in the Chamber) and holding between 21.1 and 27.8 percent of all cabinet seats. In other words, there was a rough correspondence between the PSDB's weight in the legislative coalition and the cabinet, with the party holding even fewer cabinet positions than warranted based on its numbers in the Chamber. The four cabinets that existed in Cardoso's second term (1999–2002) reflect an effort to limit the PSDB's cabinet holding. Whereas the average legislative weight of the PSDB across these four coalitions was 30.9 percent, it held on average 22.5 percent of all cabinet seats. This allowed the PSDB's allies to be better represented in the cabinet than were the PT's allies in the first Lula government. Beyond the sheer number of cabinet positions they held, the PFL and PMDB held a number of important ministries from the start. For example, the PFL held Mines and Energy for the entire first term and most of the second. It also commanded Social Security for nearly all of Cardoso's time in office. Similarly, the PMDB held Transportation for virtually the duration of Cardoso's two terms, National Integration for the whole second term, and Justice for the whole first term and part of the second. This comparison suggests that whereas the PT tried to "have its cake and eat it too," the PSDB and President Cardoso knew the name of the game, accepted it, and played it straight up.

It was thus in executive–legislative relations that the party's distinctiveness created the most difficulties in governing. Never before did Brazil have a highly organized governing party with strong ideological commitments and a large core of activists that would have to navigate the dilemmas contained within a system that combined presidentialism and multipartism. It was these residues of the PT's past that impeded Lula's

---

[37] Articles that highlight the pressure put on Lula by the party include "Lula pede ao PT que não atrapalhe mais," *Jornal do Brasil*, November 17, 2006; "Lula avisa ao PT que terá de dar espaço ao PMDB," *O Globo*, November 17, 2006; "Lula rejeita pressão do PT por cargos," *Gazeta Mercantil*, November 17–20, 2006; "Esquerda cobra mais espaço no governo do PT," *O Globo*, December 14, 2006.

New Challenges and Opportunities 167

ability to follow his predecessors and employ their methods of building legislative support. A new set of dynamics emerged when the PT governed as a legislative minority in conjunction with parties that did not share its ideological background and organizational features.

The concentration of ministerial power that arose in the first Lula government suggested that the PT had not left behind its past enough to stand on solid ground in its new position. Traces of the PT's history as an externally mobilized party worked at cross-purposes with the institutional constraints the party faced in its new governing role. As with its illicit campaign-financing scheme – a result of wanting to play the electoral game but without doing what it took to receive the financial backing of business through legal channels – the PT wanted to govern but to avoid playing coalitional politics as usual. The result was the *mensalão*: illegally purchasing collaboration with others through individual bribes rather than legally sharing power via the time-honored practice of coalitional presidentialism.

The solution Lula chose – awarding *petistas* a disproportionate number of state positions and buying off allies through individual payments – placed the party in an awkward in-between position: not fully above "politics as usual" but not comfortably situated in the conventional ways of Brazilian politics. Lula wanted to compete in the mainstream political game but was constrained by a party that was not willing to play by its rules. Insights from historical institutionalism as well as elements of strategic reasoning are borne out in the dynamic that unfolded. The party's resistance to undergoing a more complete transformation reflected the weight of history. The *mensalão* represented a strategic attempt on Lula's part to work around this resistance and yet meet the demands of the system.

THE SCANDAL AND ITS EFFECTS ON LULA'S 2006 REELECTION CAMPAIGN

The consequences of the scandal effectively furthered the party's normalization. The most immediate repercussion was the resignation of several historic party figures suspected of playing a central role in the vote-buying scheme. All were from the *Campo Majoritário*, the group close to Lula that included the former *Articulação* and *Democracia Radical*. They included Lula's Presidential Chief of Staff José Dirceu, Minister of Finance Antônio Palocci, Minister of Communications Luis Gushiken, and PT president José Genoino. Their departure meant the loss of people who had played an important role in linking the government to the party as well as to various societal groups. A number of longtime militants also left the party out of disillusionment. Some headed for the PSOL, the new party led by former *petista* senator Heloísa Helena who had been expelled from the PT over Lula's 2003 social security reform.

The vote-buying scandal had other decisive effects on the PT, on the president, and on their relationship to one another. Most importantly, it tarnished the image of the PT as the party of ethical governance. Opinion polls suggest that the PT's image as being different in this regard suffered considerably (Fundação Perseu Abramo 2006). The blow to the PT's reputation was made worse by the fact that the *mensalão* charges had a cascading effect. The extensive *caixa dois* network that operated in PT-led municipalities was eventually revealed after investigators began to question where the money to operate the *mensalão* had come from. Media coverage of the PT's involvement in wrongdoing was intense, dominating the news for months after PTB Deputy Roberto Jefferson spilled the beans in June 2005. Lula's efforts to protect the party rather than submit more systematically to the power-sharing incentives of the system had clearly backfired. All too ironically, if the unsavory character of parties like the PMDB and PTB was one of the main reasons that sectors of the PT had wanted to avoid placing more of their members into the cabinet, the *mensalão* scandal ended up sullying the party's public image far more than power-sharing ever would have.

The scandal also marred the image of Lula, who admitted obliquely to wrongdoing but quickly shifted blame to the dilemmas inherent in the system and the missteps of certain individuals within his own party. One year before the October 2006 presidential election, opinion polls suggested that Lula might lose by a significant margin to either of two potential opponents from the PSDB, José Serra or Geraldo Alckmin. Overall, however, Lula emerged from the scandal less scathed than the party. His popularity remained more intact among voters from lower education and income brackets. For example, between June and September 2005, when the *mensalão* and *caixa dois* made headlines on a daily basis, polls evaluating the public's trust in Lula showed only a 9 percentage point decline (from 62 percent to 53 percent) among respondents with less than a high school education, as compared with a 20 percentage point decline (from 56 to 35 percent) among those with secondary education or higher. Less educated voters either did not know much about the scandal, exempted Lula from personal blame and held the party responsible instead, or cared more about the material benefits they received from the government (Hunter and Power 2007: 10–14).

With an eye toward the 2006 presidential election, Lula reacted to the public's evaluation of the scandal by both distancing himself from the party and casting his lot with less educated and poorer demographic groups. The effort to separate himself from the party was reflected symbolically in the vastly reduced size of the PT's emblematic red star that appeared on Lula's campaign advertisements and his scarce mention of the party during allotted public television time. These and related measures went a significant step further than those he had taken in previous campaigns (especially 2002) to gain autonomy from the party and its comparatively radical platforms.

Because opinion polls showed the corruption charges to be most disconcerting to voters of higher income and education levels (Lula's strongest backers in previous elections but possible defectors in 2006), the president's reelection prospects appeared to depend more than ever on gaining massive backing among the poorest and least educated sectors of Brazilian society. Control over federal government resources would finally give Lula an opportunity to appeal to them in a way that he couldn't from the sidelines of power (Fundação Perseu Abramo 2006; Hunter and Power 2007: 11–14). He thus staked his reelection bid on minimum wage hikes and on expanding the *Bolsa Família* program, which together with inflation control and a favorable export climate expanded significantly the purchasing power of poorer Brazilians. Together with previous increases, the president's authorization of these wage hikes amounted to a 23 percent real rise in the minimum wage over the course of his first term. The government also intensified its efforts to expand the *Bolsa* in the final two years. By the time of the election, the *Bolsa Família* had appreciably reduced poverty levels in the country.[38] That Lula, no stranger to grinding poverty, closely identified himself with the program gave the matter a poignant personal touch.

These measures generated sweeping support for Lula among the poorest and least educated sectors of society. Their backing, which had been elusive in previous presidential contests, proved essential in his October 2006 reelection. After winning 48.6 percent of all first-round votes, Lula then went on to beat Geraldo Alckmin in the runoff by capturing almost 61 percent of the vote share. The decline in extreme poverty that the

---

[38] See Soares et al. (2006) on the contribution of the *Bolsa Família* to poverty reduction and the decline of inequality.

TABLE 6.1. *Regional Breakdown of Second-Round Presidential Election Results: 1989, 2002, and 2006*

Region	1989		2002		2006	
	Lula	Collor	Lula	Serra	Lula	Alckmin
North	29.5	70.5	58.2	41.8	65.6	34.4
Northeast	44.3	55.7	61.5	38.5	77.1	22.9
Southeast	49.5	50.5	63.0	37.0	56.9	43.1
South	51.7	48.3	58.8	41.2	46.5	53.5
Center-West	36.8	63.2	57.3	42.7	52.4	47.6
Brazil: Total	47.0	53.0	61.3	38.7	60.8	39.2

Sources: Nicolau, Jairo. *Banco de Dados Eleitorais do Brasil (1982–2006)*; *Tribunal Superior Eleitoral*.

Bolsa Família helped to produce led to a historic shift in the composition of Lula's electoral base, even since 2002.[39] In 2006, Lula captured between 60 and 86 percent of the vote share in the poverty-stricken North and Northeast states, long established oligarchic strongholds that typically voted for conservative options. For the first time ever, gender parity was achieved in Lula's support base, and his backing in small municipalities (fewer than 20,000 inhabitants) was on par with his national average (Nicolau and Peixoto 2007).[40] Accompanying this heightened support among the poor, however, was a corresponding loss of backing among voters at higher levels of income and education, most concentrated in the South and Southeast. In short, executive power and federal resources enabled Lula to finally consolidate his party's proclaimed social base, which had previously responded only weakly to a more party-based strategy of grassroots mobilization for progressive change (see Table 6.1).

Notably, however, the impressive support that Lula received in areas dense with *Bolsa* beneficiaries was not shared by PT candidates in congressional races. This is not surprising because resources for the *Bolsa* were not distributed through party networks but channeled directly from the executive to municipalities.[41] Many citizens who voted for Lula cast their lot with other parties in the legislative arena. It is thus safe to conclude that their attachment to the president was not a reflection of

---

[39] Changes that occurred in Lula's electoral support base are discussed in Hunter and Power (2007), Nicolau and Peixoto (2007), Soares and Terron (2008), and Zucco (2008).
[40] See also Tables A.5, A.6, and A.7 in the Appendix.
[41] Grindle (1996: 165) notes that the design of the National Solidarity Program in Mexico was such that the president's popularity was boosted more than the party's.

underlying partisan commitment. They were clearly more taken with the concrete benefits that Lula provided and the solidarity he displayed with their plight than with the PT's more ideological profile. Although Lula maintained the 61 percent vote share that he received in 2002, the numbers of votes cast for the PT in Chamber races shrank for the first time ever. Support for the PT in the lower house fell from 18.4 to 15.0 percent of all valid votes, which translated into a reduction from 17.7 percent of seats in 2002 (ninety-one seats) to 16.2 percent (eighty-three seats) in 2006. As for its trajectory by region, the delegation grew slightly in the Northeast (increasing from seventeen to twenty-three seats) and lost ground in its historic strongholds of the Southeast and South (falling from thirty-seven to thirty seats in the former and nineteen to fourteen in the latter). Needless to say, the slight rise in the PT delegation's Northeast component was not commensurate with the remarkable growth of support experienced there by its presidential candidate. Chart 6.1 compares the regional trajectory of Lula versus the PT over time.

The popularity of Lula compared to the party organization was not lost on PT partisans and militants, especially those from outside the *Campo Majoritário*. Although recognizing that Lula's personal popularity had always exceeded that of the party and given the PT a degree of standing it probably could not have attained otherwise, they feared that the president's recent maneuvers overshadowed the party and overstepped the boundaries of the previous "marriage of *lulismo* with *petismo*." In the end, they argued, *petismo* needed to prevail over *lulismo* because the appeal of a single individual could not carry the party into the future.[42] In their view, the Lula government's support for programs that diverged significantly from the party's historic orientation eroded the PT's profile of difference excessively. Although Brazil's positive economic performance and improved social indicators raised high barriers to the capacity of critics to redirect the government's economic and social policy course, they nonetheless called for a "refounding" of the party and defended the party bureaucracy's continued influence over core issues. However, even in the immediate aftermath of the *mensalão* scandal and the resignation of party president José Genoino, their call for a refounding of the PT and attempt to place one of their own into the party's presidency (Raul Pont of *Democracia Socialista*) against a highly compromised figure from

---

[42] "'Petismo' deve prevalecer sobre 'lulismo,' diz dirigente do PT," *Folha Online*, November 13, 2006; "Com bancada enfraquecida, PT usa Lula para puxar votos," *Folha Online*, July 16, 2006.

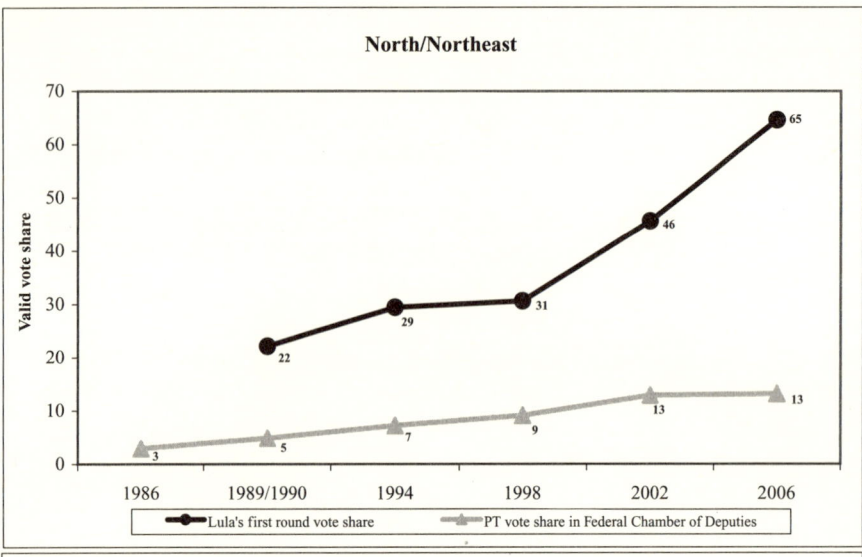

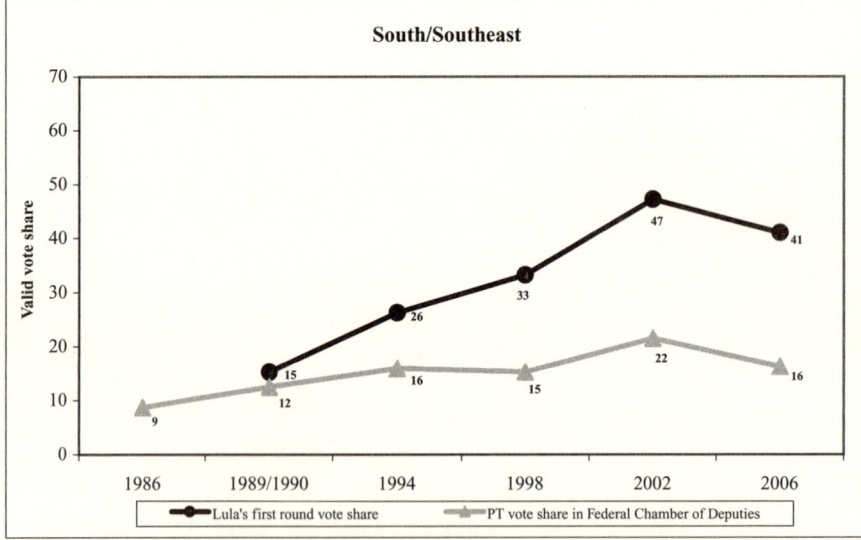

CHART 6.1. Evolution of vote shares by region: Lula vs. the PT. (Source: *Tribunal Superior Eleitoral*.)

the *Campo Majoritário* (Ricardo Berzoini) did not win sufficient support from the membership at large.[43]

---

[43] Berzoini won 51.6 percent of the vote in the election for party president against the 48.4 won by Raul Pont in October 2005. He was Lula's social security minister during the controversial 2003 pension reform.

ABSOLVING SARNEY: ANOTHER STEP TOWARD NORMALIZATION

Following the *mensalão* scandal, there was an important episode in Lula's second term in which the PT acted in a manner at odds with its past advocacy of ethical conduct in government. The immediate issue at hand concerned whether to vote in favor of or against an investigation of allegations that the president of the Senate, José Sarney, was involved in financial wrongdoing and other irregularities. The larger issue at hand concerned maneuvering to boost the prospects of the PT's presidential candidate, Dilma Rousseff, for the 2010 race. Rousseff, who had served as Lula's Chief of Staff in the presidential palace, was Lula's preferred candidate. Notably, she was not a historic *petista* who had come up through the party's ranks but rather had become affiliated with the PT only a decade before becoming Lula's hand-picked favorite.[44] This was a point of considerable tension among PT militants. Just as Lula's races for the presidency had promoted adaptation and normalization, seeking to better position Dilma Rousseff for the 2010 presidential race caused the PT to diverge from its past emphasis on ethical conduct and to engage in "politics as usual." Ultimately, the behavior of three PT senators and the party leadership directing them, together with the fallout from their actions, reflected a further normalization of the Workers' Party. The PT suffered one more round of damage to its reputation. Moreover, the incident resulted in the decision by two PT politicians with untainted records and public images to leave the party.

By way of background, Lula and the group close to him had long recognized and accepted the centrality of PMDB support for the PT's presidential prospects in 2010. Apparently, they were willing to take far-reaching measures to obtain the PMDB's backing, including absolving one of its kingpins against accusations of financial irregularities and abuse of power. José Sarney, president of the Senate, was notorious for playing fast and loose with the rules. This reputation dated back to his days as an ARENA politician under the military regime and was reinforced during his tenure as president of Brazil from 1985 to 1990. It was therefore not surprising when questions about him arose in mid-2009. Senators from various opposition parties brought charges against Sarney, accusing him of nepotism, shady business dealings, and diverting public funds to his foundation.

---

[44] After having engaged in clandestine activities under the military regime, which led to a three-year prison sentence, Dilma Rousseff went on to become active in the PDT in the state of Rio Grande do Sul.

The Senate Council of Ethics and Parliamentary Decorum was responsible for deciding whether to investigate or archive the allegations against Sarney. With three senators, the PT effectively held the balance on the Council.⁴⁵ There were fifteen members in all, five opposition senators and ten from the government bloc. Had the entire opposition voted against Sarney and the three PT members joined it, the result would have been eight against seven and an investigation against Senator Sarney would have gone forth. Instead, when the vote took place on August 19, 2009, all three PT senators sided with the government bloc. Sarney was thereby absolved.⁴⁶ Numerous reports suggest that Lula and the PT's national president Ricardo Berzoini leaned heavily on the party's three senators to achieve the desired outcome.⁴⁷

In short, the PT faction of Lula and Berzoini got the votes it sought to absolve Sarney and ingratiate the party with high-ranking members of the PMDB. Soon after the decision, it became public that the vice-presidential slot on Dilma Rousseff's ticket would go to the PMDB. The PT paid a price for its opportunism, however, one that went beyond further tarnishing its reputation. Absolving Sarney and the politicking surrounding that episode appear to have been the final straw in *petista* Marina Silva's decision to leave the party. Marina Silva grew up poor and illiterate until the age of sixteen, when Catholic nuns in her Amazonian home state of Acre housed and educated her. Working with Catholic activists and the rubber tappers' union were stepping-stones for her to become a state deputy, federal Senator, and eventually Minister of the Environment under Lula (2003–2008). A national and international icon for her defense of the Amazon rainforest, Marina Silva held important symbolic significance for the party. Similarly, Flávio Arns, who joined the PT in 2001 and subsequently won a Senate seat in 2002, also left the party in the wake of Sarney's absolution. He departed with a public statement about his disappointment with the party's willingness to stoop that low in the pursuit of electoral success.⁴⁸ Even Lula's longtime political associate,

---

⁴⁵ They were João Pedro from Amazonas, Ideli Salvatti from Santa Catarina, and Delcídio Amaral from Mato Grosso do Sul.

⁴⁶ The actual vote was nine to six because one senator from the government bloc joined the opposition's call for an investigation.

⁴⁷ See, for example, "Presidente do PT pede que senadores arquivem denúncias" (noticias.terra.com.br/brasil/noticias/0,,OI3930249-EI7896,00.html).

⁴⁸ "Flávio Arns diz querer sair do PT após decisão de Sarney" (http://gl.globo.com/Noticias/Politica/0,,MUL1273230-5601,00); "Flávio Arns volta a se filiar ao PSDB e deve disputar Câmara em 2010" (http://www1.folha.uol.com.br/folha/brasil/ult96u631790.shtml).

PT Senator Aloízio Mercadante, let his individual opposition to the vote become public. Evidently, he came close to resigning his own Senate position over the affair until Lula engaged in arm twisting, persuading him to stay on.[49] Notably, especially given that Dilma Rousseff was not even from the heart of the party, historic *petista* militants felt that her candidacy itself – not to mention what was done to advance it – represented a victory of *lulismo* over *petismo*.[50]

Nonetheless, calls to "refound" the PT and return to its original ideals were unsuccessful again in the party's internal elections of November 2009, in which José Eduardo Dutra became party president in 2010. From *Construindo um Novo Brasil* (a new designation for the *Campo Majoritário*), Dutra represents a continuation of the faction controlling the PT since José Dirceu was elected PT president in 1995. Simultaneous elections to constitute a new national directorate also returned to office some PT figures who were closely associated with the *mensalão* scandal. These developments suggest that efforts to turn back the clock lack sufficient support and are unlikely to succeed.

CONCLUSION

In conclusion, the central policies enacted under Lula's presidency were far more moderate than what the PT had promised in its opposition role, especially in earlier years. Whereas radical reforms to develop Brazil and redistribute its substantial wealth characterized the party's program well into the 1990s, conforming to market dynamics became the order of the day in the macroeconomic policies of the first Lula government. Similarly, social policy saw few innovations, notwithstanding the significant extension of the popular income transfer program *Bolsa Família*. Land reform was kept to a minimum. The government pursued new directions in foreign policy that resonated with the PT's historic discourse but were also largely market conforming in character. The overall logic of government policies, even those that helped the poor, was to stay well within fiscal limitations and not threaten privileged interests.

Such policies were the result of significant external pressures – from business as well as voters – and learning on the part of pragmatic leaders

[49] "Em carta, Lula diz que Mercadante é imprescindível `a liderança" (http://www.estadão.com.br/.../nacional,em-cartalula-diz-que-mercadante-e-imprescindivel-a-lideranca,422569,0.htm).
[50] See "Candidatura de Dilma é uma vitória do lulismo," *O Globo*, February 21, 2010.

within the PT. One drawback to such a high degree of adaptation, however, was that significant elements within the party opposed it and therefore sought compensation, namely positions in the cabinet and federal bureaucracy. The goal of PT partisans was not only to retain marginal policy influence but also to be rewarded for their sacrifice to the party. Factions of the PT clung to the hope of remaining different. Historical institutionalism would expect this. The *mensalão* represented a clash between a PT-led government seeking to respond to multiple pressures and a party resisting full accommodation to the system. The scandal to which the vote-buying scheme gave rise was the most serious crisis of the first Lula government. It laid bare the complications of seeking to maintain a status "in between" that of adaptation and difference.

Ironically, the protection of the PT ultimately led to the expedient of bribery for guaranteeing support in Congress. The resulting *mensalão* scandal ultimately furthered the normalization of the party and increased the divide between it and Lula. By tarnishing the PT's image as a party of ethical government, the scandal eroded a key basis of the party's claim to distinctiveness. Having Lula in the presidency no doubt diminished the party's interest in undertaking a process of internal criticism and reform. Its failure to discipline high-level *petistas* involved in wrongdoing suggests that being in power unleashes various forces that reinforce convergence. Moreover, the scandal motivated Lula – in anticipation of the 2006 presidential election – to deepen his support among the least ideologically inspired voters. The measures he took to win over the most destitute and poorly educated Brazilians, precisely those who seemed to know or care the least about the PT's illegal fund-raising and vote-buying activities, involved focusing on concrete and immediate "bread and butter" issues at the expense of more ideologically infused policies (e.g., land reform) that the party had advocated to win over their support.

Lula's reelection, followed by the tremendously high public approval he would enjoy when economic growth took off in the first half of his second term, made it difficult for radical factions to criticize the government. How could they credibly oppose a president who had presided over a set of policies that yielded growth, kept inflation at bay, diminished poverty, and appeared to make some inroads into Brazil's long-standing socioeconomic inequality? Without being able to bring the party membership over to its side in internal elections, they had even less of a leg to stand on. In the end, the experience of government added a crucial layer of normalization to the party.

7

Analytical Implications and Comparative Perspectives

The PT is a case of the successful and fairly gradual transformation of a radical institutionalized mass party into a more electorally competitive professional party. Given its start as exceptionally ideological and grassroots oriented, it was the kind of party we might least expect to have reoriented in a vote-maximizing way. Ultimately, the PT did adapt but its adaptation was fairly slow – arguably slower than, for example, the Argentine Peronists, the Chilean Socialists, or the Argentine FREPASO. After three failed presidential bids, the PT went on to win two consecutive presidential contests, an unprecedented feat for the left in Brazil. Although Lula had responded rationally to externally induced incentives (and persuaded significant elements in the party to go along with him), there was also internal resistance to change. The PT's origins and structure created lags and distortions in adaptation but also some real advantages, namely endowing the party with credibility as the voice of opposition in 2002, discipline in passing difficult reforms once Lula became president, and a reliable foundation that would help it weather a number of serious crises.

In this chapter I return to the analytical approaches that frame the book. I draw out the broader theoretical implications of the book's analysis after first revisiting the reasons for change within the PT and comparing anew the features of its adaptation that are explained by a strategic framework to those that historical institutionalism helps to understand.

The next section examines comparative experiences of left-party adaptation in Latin America. It applies the arguments developed in the book to help us understand why, how, and to what extent other left parties have adapted in democratic or at least democratizing contexts. Notwithstanding some notable differences, the *Frente Amplio* in Uruguay shares key similarities with the PT and its evolution over time. It was an institutionalized left party that developed grassroots support and competed for the presidency various times before its popular leader, Tabaré Vázquez, won election in 2004. Along the way, the *Frente Amplio* enacted various adaptations. Argentina's FREPASO, which never built up a mass activist base or credibility as a distinctive party, is analyzed as a contrast case of inadequate institutionalization, overly rapid transformation, and quick demise. The *Izquierda Unida* (United Left) in Peru reflects excessive organizational rigidity, ideological sectarianism, and failure to adapt despite the presence of a popular leader who sought strategic transformation.

The book ends by pondering the PT's future and considering how various factors might influence the direction it will take in coming years. Will the old and the new continue to coexist, however uneasily at times? Or will change, which started on the external front, continue and make inroads in the interior of the party, thereby bringing into alignment elements that have been slow to adapt? Will new layers overtake the old over time such that the PT will evolve into an organization that bears little resemblance to its former self?

EXTERNAL PRESSURES AND ORGANIZATIONAL HISTORY

What has created the particular mix of features that characterize the PT? The roots of the PT's adaptation lie in the external environment: the international economy, the structure of electoral competition, and Brazilian institutions. Clearly, economic pressures and trends, coupled with the institutionally based incentives of winning majority elections in Brazil, provided strong impulses for the adaptations enacted by the party while in the national opposition. Growing international momentum for market reform together with public support at home for key aspects of economic restructuring and opening put significant pressure on the party leadership to adapt to changing times. That the program of market reform was well underway by the mid-1990s made it hard to reverse course. Although the PT could reasonably stress the shortcomings of the new market model and point out modifications to improve the welfare of Brazilians, it found itself under increasing pressure to endorse the general contours of a market economy.

Enhanced governance and the strengthening of the state and party system that occurred in the 1990s – reflected in outcomes such as controlled inflation, lower ministerial turnover, and a downward trend in party system volatility – also set considerable limits on the left's ability to keep pursuing a radical strategy and come out ahead. That Brazilians perceived their situation as having improved from the crisis-racked conditions of the late 1980s and early 1990s rendered them unlikely to support a party that called for a drastic reorientation away from the very policies associated with these improvements. However, they might well support one that promised to retain the best features of the new market model while addressing some of its shortcomings, and to promote more ethical standards of political conduct and greater societal participation as well.

When much of the party leadership conceded that realizing the PT's transformative aspirations was out of the question, a clearer shift toward vote seeking and electoral professionalism occurred. With this redefinition or reordering of goals, the PT became more susceptible to the institutionally derived incentives of Brazil's political system. In the broader context of an electorate that was largely nonideological, especially not left leaning, the need to win a majority of votes to capture the presidency induced a shift in a more catchall direction. Lula and fellow pragmatists moved the party toward the center programmatically, enhanced the public appeal of its candidates and the images they projected, and sought alliances with parties that were not from the left. Lula's efforts to gain leverage over the party, and to separate himself from it when he could not, gained momentum in the period leading up to the 2002 presidential election. His issuing of the famous *Carta ao Povo Brasileiro* in the wake of financial market volatility was a prime example of this.

This divide deepened after Lula entered the presidency and was induced to institute and maintain an orthodox economic program, in no small part to signal market friendliness and abide by the international agreements he had pledged to honor. When Lula's popularity soared with the upturn in the economy's performance after 2006, party radicals had even less of a leg to stand on than they did before. Their legitimacy was especially weakened because the PT-led government could credibly claim to have overseen a reduction in extreme poverty and perhaps even some improvement in Brazil's long-standing income inequality.

The dramatic changes that occurred on the external front coexisted with stickiness in the interior of the organization. For the most part, internal organizational features bear less directly on a party's capacity for vote getting and hence are less subject to outside pressures. Moreover, they enjoy greater protection because they tend to be more institutionalized. For example, whereas modifying candidates' images does not necessitate a change in bureaucratic rules and procedures, matters like how candidates are selected and their obligations if elected are codified in party statutes. Their revision thus rests on the approval by cadres who frequently have a long history of entrenchment in the party's bureaucratic apparatus. More so than their electoral counterparts, many such figures harbor a bunker mentality from the party's externally mobilized past, stand to lose power and status with reform, and are well positioned organizationally to block change.

The external changes the PT has undergone can be summarized as follows: Most notably, the programmatic stances it supports have softened. The majority of the PT's electoral candidates have ceased to advocate socialism and major redistributive programs. Their emphasis on societal participation and ethical government has also become less marked. Beyond the substantive content of their platforms, the images projected by PT candidates and elected officials have grown less radical over time. Whereas union and social movement associations marked most of them in earlier years, the majority of their current counterparts do not cut a particularly militant image.[1]

Reiterating the organizational issues on which the party maintains greater traces of the past, the bureaucratic apparatus of the PT remains intact and continues to influence vital decisions. For the most part, decisions made at the national level still take precedence over those of organs at the subnational level. Candidate selection procedures still make previous involvement in the party or a related social movement a precondition for entry. The PT remains highly restrictive toward outsiders seeking to run on its label. It also maintains the right to sanction the campaign publicity of all its candidates. Organizational continuity includes the survival of internal tendencies, a phenomenon unique to the PT. Finally, the historic reputation of PT politicians for discipline, loyalty, and commitment remains well deserved. PT legislators are still expected to vote according to leadership directives, an obligation to which recent expulsions attest. Switching in and out of the party continues to be rare. Furthermore, hefty financial contributions remain integral to the personal commitment a PT politician is expected to make.[2] This requirement holds even though,

---

[1] See "Com vocês, o PT cor-de-rosa," *Veja Online*, October 11, 2000.

[2] The top amount levied, however, was reduced from 30 percent to 20 percent in 2001. See "Partido dos Trabalhadores arrecada R$20 mi ao ano com 'dízimo'," *Folha Online*, March 17, 2002. Dues for members were also reduced in 2001 in an attempt to expand the party membership. See "PT reduz 'dízimo' para atrair filiados," *Folha Online*, March 3, 2001. In an author interview with Raimundo Júnior, in his role as assistant to former

since entering the government, the party enjoys greater donations from business than it used to. Notably, corporate contributions still make up a smaller percentage of the PT's campaign funds than they do for other major parties.[3]

ANALYTICAL IMPLICATIONS

What are the broader theoretical implications of this study of the PT? The story of uneven adaptation that has unfolded suggests that certain dimensions of a party bear the weight of the past more than others. Change is most likely to start on the outside and proceed to the inside only with time or perhaps not at all. Tension or even dysfunctionality may result from this sequence of change and the gaps that result in the process. Rational choice sheds light on the visible external adaptations a party is likely to make initially. Historical institutionalism appreciates and explains better why some elements lag behind. Either analytical framework alone cannot explain the complex nature of change that has occurred in the party. Insights from both are necessary: Together they form a useful and powerful explanation of change that, however slow, halting, and layered, may nonetheless result in an organization's transformation over time. The analysis thus bears out the need to combine rational choice and historical institutionalism in productive ways (Hall and Taylor 1996; Thelen 1999; Katznelson and Weingast 2005). Relying on both traditions offers a richer account of the PT's evolution than either alone can provide. Bearing out Hall and Taylor's assessment of these two strands of institutionalism (1996: 955), "[e]ach seems to be providing a partial account of the forces at work in a given situation or capturing different dimensions of the human action and institutional impact present there."

The most visible aspects of the PT's evolution between 1989 and 2002 suggest the transformation of a radical programmatic party into a catchall party. Much of this story can be told from a rational choice perspective.

party president José Genoino, the PT official emphasized the need to go beyond the activist core and broaden the membership. Reducing membership dues was one aspect of this effort. This interview took place in Brasília on July 29, 2003.

[3] Average corporate contributions from winning PT deputy candidates as a percentage of their total campaign spending went from 26.5 in 1994 to 25.9 in 1998 to 43.3 in 2002 to 47.8 in 2006. For a comparison, the average percentage that corporate contributions comprised for the other major parties (PDT, PPB, PTB, PMDB, PSDB, and PFL) was 62.0 in 1994, 55.3 in 1998, 57.5 in 2002, and 52.8 in 2006. I thank David Samuels for compiling and sharing these figures.

Approaching the PT's evolution with this analytical lens focuses attention on the strategic situation the party faced at different moments and the associated choices it made. Conduct at the broadest level, such as whether the party pursued policy seeking and difference or vote maximization and accommodation, can be understood in these terms. New incentives and pressures that unfolded by the mid-1990s induced a shift away from policy seeking and differentiation and toward vote maximization and moving closer to the center of the vote distribution. The party began to employ many of the tactics of its catchall competitors in order to capture the majority of votes necessary to win presidential elections. The shift was unexpected in light of the PT's previous radicalism and the important role the party had played in anchoring the left.

Testimony to the powerful role that external incentives exert on political parties is the fact that even the PT, with a committed core of militants and a history of radicalism, adjusted eventually to them. If even the PT could not resist employing the logical instruments of a vote-maximizing strategy with the economic and political developments that unfolded, it is unlikely that any other party could have. That the very individuals responsible for implementing these changes had played a prominent role in the party's founding and once supported radical platforms bears out a strategic understanding of political change.

Nevertheless, the PT has not become "just like any other Brazilian party," contrary to a frequent charge leveled in the Brazilian media. Insights from historical institutionalism add a crucial layer of complexity and nuance to the story. The party's history conditioned which modifications it made and the rate at which it made them. After modifying its strategic motivations in the mid-1990s, the PT responded to a dense and complex mix of parameters and preferences that pulled it in conflicting directions at times. A full account of the party's evolution requires explaining positive aspects of continuity (e.g., high internal discipline) as well as distortions in some of its efforts at adaptation (e.g., the *caixa dois* and *mensalão* phenomena). Rather than conforming fully to the expectations of a strategic framework, the party's conduct was influenced by enduring historical commitments and norms. The resistance to quick and wholesale change created by organizational entrenchment explains unevenness in the party's adaptation. That the party did not adapt overnight or change on all fronts had some beneficial effects on its overall success but also created problems for a party operating in Brazil's competitive environment.

The aforementioned analysis thus suggests that political institutions, the focus of rational choice institutionalism, are insufficient to explain the

Analytical Implications and Comparative Perspectives 183

adaptation of left parties. Whether or not radical parties even choose to reorient themselves and respond to given institutional incentives depends on the broader economic context and structure of political competition that prevail. Even when they choose to reorient themselves, their adaptation may well be incomplete. Transformation on any given dimension can be distorted by historical norms and commitments within the party. Likewise, change can occur more on some issues than on others. For example, Downsian logic may induce a party to moderate on a key dimension of competition, such as the market versus state cleavage. However, the same party that succumbs to such logic may successfully retain a left or alternative identity on other issues. Strategic perspectives thus need to recognize the issue-specific nature of change within parties.

In conclusion, the present study has demonstrated the usefulness of drawing both on rational choice and historical institutionalism to explain the transformation of the PT over the course of the past two decades. As this party turned from an ideologically radical and politically isolated fringe party toward a moderate, electorally oriented catchall party that entered pragmatic coalitions, it underwent changes that over time added up to a profound transformation. This transformation, however, did not come in one fell swoop but gradually as the product of a series of small changes. Thus, it did not follow the pattern of long stretches of stability punctuated by dramatic change that is encapsulated in conventional models of path dependency, the prototypical concept of institutional change advanced by historical institutionalism.

Nonetheless, although the PT underwent significant change in response to institutional incentives and external challenges (especially the global downfall of socialism and the Latin American wave of market reform), these changes were not as adaptive, flexible, and thorough as rational choice would expect. Instead, reformers confronted a good deal of institutional stickiness; active and passive resistance prevented the PT from reacting optimally to the new opportunities and constraints that it was facing. Thus, change was more halting and it produced more tensions than the optimization postulates of rational choice would predict.

As a result, neither one of the ideal-typical versions of institutionalism that many political scientists embrace can, on its own, account for the transformation of the Brazilian Workers' Party. Therefore, it makes sense to combine the two approaches in a systematic fashion, as this book has attempted to do. On the one hand, rational choice can best account for the fact that a party as radical, disciplined, and distant from the mainstream of Brazilian politics did come to respond to the electoral incentives of party competition in the new democracy. The PT started out as the "least likely case" for such adaptation because it had arisen by explicitly rejecting accommodation to the system. However, self-enclosure in a political ghetto limits electoral success; after the close result of the 1989 contest whetted the PT's appetite, the party and especially its leader did change ways, moderate their campaign platforms and, later, their program, and move slowly but surely to the center, where most voters clustered. Rational choice explains this change most convincingly. As its adherents claim, the instrumental incentive of winning power and office gradually softened the rigid insistence on ideological purity and dogmatic policy seeking. As rational choice scholars highlight, one needs to win elections to be able to implement one's program, and the leaders of the PT sooner or later came to understand this fundamental point and to push for the necessary changes in their own party.

If rational choice is important for explaining the impetus and direction of change, historical institutionalism is crucial for explaining the obstacles that PT reformers faced on their arduous path. While it was surprising how much the PT adapted to the incentives and constraints of Brazil's political system, this change was not easy. Instead, the moderating party leadership encountered resistance at almost every point. The established institutional apparatus and the entrenched ideology anchored the party so firmly that the transformation had to proceed step by step; a dramatic overhaul or refounding of the party was out of the question. The slow advance of change thus demonstrates the importance of the institutional stickiness that historical institutionalism highlights (Mahoney and Thelen 2010). In addition, the fact that the PT's transformation in this context of stickiness provoked a number of tensions, which contributed to the scandals plaguing the PT during the past decade, proves historical institutionalism's point that institutional adaptation is far from optimal and "efficient" (March and Olsen 1984). The preceding study documented the frictions and disjunctures that are central themes in historical institutionalism's image of institutional change.

Both versions of institutionalism are important for making sense of the complex processes under investigation in this book. Over the past twenty years, adherents of the two institutionalisms have spilled plenty of ink combating and trying to disprove the arguments of "the other side." Although such discussions can initially be useful for clarifying the contributions and limitations of these approaches, including the assumptions underlying them, the time has come to move beyond this academic struggle and focus on understanding various empirical phenomena that are the subject matter of political science. For this pragmatic purpose,

Analytical Implications and Comparative Perspectives

both approaches can make important contributions. In fact, with respective strengths, they can compensate for the other side's weak and thus complement each other. Rational choice is better at expl change, whereas historical institutionalism helps in understanding stasis and resistance. As the present case study shows, political change displays both sides of the coin, the impetus for transformation and the stickiness of established structures. Therefore, it makes most sense to draw on both approaches to shed light on these two sides, which are intimately linked.

THE PT IN COMPARATIVE PERSPECTIVE

Are the main findings of this book specific to Brazil or do they have broader applicability to other leftist parties in the region? South America has seen several externally mobilized left-wing parties arise in recent decades, and their political and electoral fate has varied greatly. Can the arguments derived from rational choice and historical institutionalism that have shed light on the transformation of the PT elucidate the advances and setbacks experienced by these other parties as well? If the arguments made about rational choice have broader application, parties with outstanding personal leaders will respond to electoral incentives and undergo significant steps toward transformation. This is because individuals, more so than complex organizations, can be expected to adjust more readily to external changes. If strong organizations prevail, especially in the absence of singularly popular leaders, the weight of the past will be slower to lift and adaptation to changing conditions will be harder.

The following comparative assessment focuses on several important leftist parties that experienced different degrees of adaptation under South America's democracies since the "third wave of democratization," namely Uruguay's *Frente Amplio*, Argentina's FREPASO, Venezuela's *La Causa R* or LCR, and Peru's *Izquierda Unida* or IU. The *Frente Amplio* has charted a similar course as the PT and has attained steadily increasing electoral success, capturing the country's presidency in 2004 and winning reelection in 2009. By contrast, the other three parties have not ended up being successful in electoral terms and have withered away in organizational terms as well. FREPASO and LCR achieved early electoral success but failed to transform it into a lasting advance; in fact, they faded from the political scene as quickly as they had burst onto it. *Izquierda Unida*, in contrast, did not get off the ground.

The next few sections show that the factors that shaped the PT's trajectory also played a major role in the success or failure of these other parties. Like the PT, Uruguay's *Frente Amplio* struck a balance between institutionalization and personal leadership, and it therefore prospered. By contrast, FREPASO and LCR failed to build strong institutional structures. This allowed leaders to take advantage of initial opportunities and quickly win respectable vote shares, but this proved to be a flash in the pan as organizational weakness prevented these parties from building on their early success and exposed them to severe setbacks when they confronted problems or crises. *Izquierda Unida*, in turn, had great organizational strength, but that left little room for personal leadership. The party therefore remained confined to its core constituencies and failed to take advantage of the political appeal of its erstwhile personal leader, suffering electoral stagnation and decline. Thus, excessive reliance on personal leadership (FREPASO and LCR) or on entrenched organizational attributes (*Izquierda Unida*) kept leftist parties from attaining the political and electoral success that the PT and *Frente Amplio* achieved, as the examination of each party in the following pages demonstrates.

The *Frente Amplio*: Gradual Adaptation and Sustained Progress

The development of the *Frente Amplio* in Uruguay mirrors that of the PT in important ways. The *Frente Amplio* was created in 1971, with the merging of sectors from the Communists, Socialists, Christian Democrats, and other left and center-left parties. Similar to the PT, it evolved from a labor-based mass party that struggled against the military regime (1973–1985) to one that attracts a cross-section of voters, including those in the informal labor market and from the rural population. Vanguardist in its early approach, it has become increasingly electoral-professional and catchall in orientation. Notably, the *Frente Amplio* found ways to moderate the ideological platforms it espoused while at the same time opposing Uruguay's two traditional parties, the *Blancos* and *Colorados*. Like the PT, the *Frente Amplio*'s electoral trajectory is one of gradual and sustained growth over time (Luna 2005: 367). Its vote share has expanded in the municipal, legislative, and presidential arenas. After several consecutive defeats,[4] the party's candidate – Tabaré Vázquez – eventually won the presidency in 2004.

---

[4] Liber Seregni ran and lost in 1971 and 1989. Tabaré Vázquez ran and lost in 1994 and 1999 before winning in 2004. Yaffé (2005) traces these contests and the party's evolution around them.

The *Frente Amplio*'s shift toward the center of the political spectrum was motivated by some of the same considerations that prompted the PT to undertake a similar series of moves. Neoliberal economic change had limited the viability of remaining on the far left of the political spectrum. At the same time, it opened up space for a new party by disrupting the foundations of the former coalition based on a model of import substitution industrialization. Given the *Frente Amplio*'s long-standing role outside the government, it could take advantage of this opportunity by credibly representing the opposition. At the same time the global context of market reform and the high degree of institutionalization in Uruguay's party system moderated the ideological tenor of the *Frente Amplio*'s campaigns. Moreover, as in Brazil, the majority runoff system approved in Uruguay in 1996 induced its presidential candidates to move to the center and attract non-working-class voters, many of whom were enmeshed in the clientelistic machines of the *Blancos* and *Colorados* (Lanzaro 2010). Pragmatism and moderation were necessary to expand the *Frente*'s support base over time.

If these factors unleashed incentives to adapt, what allowed the *Frente Amplio* to actually do so? As with the PT, a balance between party organization and charismatic leadership influenced the *Frente*'s adaptive capacity. The two factors together contributed to the *Frente*'s gradual and sustained electoral success. Although organizational features of the institutionalized mass party probably slowed the pace of change, they also contributed to keeping the support of the party's grassroots base. At the same time, the ability of key leaders – namely Tabaré Vázquez but also José Mujica – to bypass organizational constraints when deemed necessary for the party's electoral advance boosted the *Frente Amplio*'s success. If the party's central electoral challenge has been to retain strong links to its historical constituency while winning over less organized groups and middle-of-the-road voters (Luna 2007: 5), the ability to combine organization and personal leadership seems to have helped crucially in this regard.

A high level of internal democracy and commitment to consultation between base organizations and the party leadership characterizes the *Frente Amplio*. Various rules and mechanisms institutionalize consultation over preferred party platforms, strategies, and policy options. Despite reductions in the degree of deliberation and debate within the *Frente Amplio* since the time of its emergence, such features have continued to define the party organization. Honoring such patterns and practices has contributed to the *Frente*'s ability to maintain a strong grassroots presence and lasting ties with its original leftist support base (Pribble 2008: 87–95). It has no doubt also engendered the "very high level of party activism among left partisans in Uruguay, particularly with respect to party work, which involves more initiative and commitment than attending meetings" (Handlin and Collier forthcoming).

The popular leadership of Tabaré Vázquez has served as a crucial source of flexibility and pragmatism, allowing the *Frente Amplio* to extend its reach far beyond its core left following. Like Lula, his appeal to the broader public has given him internal leverage over otherwise recalcitrant elements within the party. It has sometimes helped him circumvent radical factions and overcome internal organizational blockages, such as in his push to forge electoral alliances with centrist groups outside the party as well as to moderate the *Frente*'s image and policy platforms (Luna 2007). Given that the *Frente Amplio* faced no serious challenger to the left, it could only benefit from doing so. There was clearly a strategic rationale for undertaking such moves, and it helped to have a popular leader to sponsor and see them through. In sum, whereas organization gave solidity to the *Frente Amplio*, popular leadership helped its support to spread. Drawing on Kirchheimer's definition of a catchall party, Jorge Lanzaro (2010), attributes the *Frente*'s success to the ability to "exchange effectiveness in depth for a wider audience and more immediate electoral success" (Kirchheimer 1966: 184) while nevertheless maintaining a "brotherhood" with trade unions and social movements. This combination was responsible for the *Frente*'s rise in an incremental but steady and sustained fashion.

FREPASO: Rapid Rise and Fall

Whereas organization and popular leadership facilitated the gradual and sustained rise of the PT and *Frente Amplio*, the FREPASO (*Frente por un País Solidario* or Front for a Country in Solidarity) lacked the former and brought to bear only the latter. The FREPASO is quite different from the PT in many ways, yet it makes for an interesting comparison. The FREPASO was "a media-based party that did not invest in party organization" (Levitsky 2003: 211) and whose success was based largely on the ability of its leaders – namely Chacho Alvarez and Graciela Fernández Meijide – to communicate directly with voters (Novaro and Palermo 1998: 65). FREPASO's lack of institutionalization is arguably the feature that separates it most consequentially from the PT and the *Frente Amplio*. Although this gave it a fluidity and flexibility that facilitated its strategic adaptation to the economic and political context of the 1990s, a lack of organization hurt FREPASO's staying power. Its disintegration in 2001 took place as rapidly as its initial formation and dramatic electoral ascent.

The FREPASO was a confederation of different groups with a fairly unified political platform and leadership. Center-left dissidents who had misgivings about the Peronist party in the wake of President Carlos Menem's market reforms spearheaded FREPASO's formation in 1994. Leading figures included José Octavio Bordón, Carlos "Chacho" Álvarez, and Graciela Fernández Meijide. They clearly knew how to take advantage of being in the right place at the right time. Only one year after FREPASO's inception, its presidential ticket won just short of 30 percent of all votes cast in the country. In the Federal Capital, it captured nearly 45 percent of the vote share, exceeding in popularity both traditional parties, the Peronists and the *Unión Cívica Radical*. Although insufficient to win presidential office, this performance was stunning nonetheless. In 1997, FREPASO allied with the *Unión Cívica Radical* to form the Alliance for Jobs, Justice and Education (*La Alianza*) and swept the legislative elections held that same year. Chacho Álvarez won in the Federal Capital and Graciela Fernández Meijide in the province of Buenos Aires. In 1999, the *Alianza* was elected to national government with the *Unión Cívica Radical*'s Fernando De la Rua as president and FREPASO's Chacho Álvarez as his vice president (Seligson 2003: 465).

The broader context for FREPASO's emergence was the series of market reforms pursued by the Menem government and the transformation of Argentina's two traditional parties, which had opened up political space on the left (Novaro and Palermo 1998). As in Brazil with the PSDB's move to the center right, the *Unión Cívica Radical* had shifted following the presidency of Raúl Alfonsín. By the early 1990s both of Argentina's traditional parties had undergone a convergence in their ideological stances (Gibson 1996), positioning the left-of-center FREPASO to attract votes away from them by proposing a more activist role for the state. It appealed primarily to young, educated, left-of-center voters interested in seeing more government intervention in the economy and in social policy.

FREPASO could conform readily to public opinion because of the flexibility afforded by not being tied down by a strong organization. Its lack of institutionalization also gave it the ability to form pragmatic electoral alliances, for example, with the *Unión Cívica Radical*. However, there were also drawbacks to the fact that FREPASO was a force with very little organization and territorial presence. For example, the lack of regularized mechanisms for consultation and decision making sometimes led to a serious disconnect within its various leadership factions, and between them and their respective bases. Throughout De la Rua's presidency (December 1999–2001) there were internal disagreements between the more conservative De la Rua and the center leftism of FREPASO. In addition, various independently issued media pronouncements by party leaders upset party militants. Although some of these limitations became clear over time, steps were not taken to build the party or subject it to greater institutionalization. Apparently none of the figures and groups that made up FREPASO wanted to lose the autonomy with which they had initially entered (Novaro and Palermo 1998: 106–109). The FREPASO paid the ultimate price for this when it encountered unforeseen challenges. The *Alianza* was badly hurt when Chacho Álvarez resigned from the Vice Presidency in October 2000 in protest over the government's failure to investigate allegations of bribery in the Senate (Levitsky 2003: 229). It collapsed altogether, and FREPASO along with it, when a massive wave of popular protest forced De la Rua to renounce the Presidency in December 2001. In contrast to the PT and the *Frente Amplio*, the circumstances of FREPASO's formation and its lack of institutionalization had allowed for strategic adaptation early on – thereby accelerating its rise – but at the same time reduced the likelihood that it would build a structure and support base solid and coherent enough to weather such crises. In the end, FREPASO's astonishing initial success proved short lived.

La Causa R: Ascent and Disintegration

Just as FREPASO's neuralgic point was its absence of organization, LCR suffered similarly from a lack of institutionalization. LCR was a left party that developed and campaigned explicitly against Venezuela's two established parties, the *Acción Democrática* and the Social Christian COPEI.[5] LCR rose to national visibility in 1989 when it won three seats in Venezuela's National Chamber of Deputies. This began its "truly meteoric" electoral rise (Crisp and Levine 1998: 39). A year later the party won a major state governorship (Bolívar State), in 1992 its own Aristóbulo Istúriz won the mayoralty of Caracas, and in 1993 it garnered over 20 percent of both the presidential and parliamentary votes.

---

[5] The letter *R* initially signified "*revolucionario.*" To avoid legal problems, however, the *R* was changed to "*radical*" (Salamanca 2004).

Candidate Andrés Velásquez won 21.97 percent of the presidential vote share, up from the less than 1 percent the party captured in 1983 and 1989.

Behind this rapid upward trajectory, however, was slow grassroots growth dating back to the 1970s. LCR was fashioned as a vanguard party in "permanent formation and construction" and an ideology always in movement that was organically connected to popular movements involving students, workers, and neighborhood associations (Salamanca 2004: 239). It was with workers at the *Siderúrgica del Orinoco* that Velásquez got his start, fighting the corruption of traditional syndicalism, promoting democratic participation in unions, and advocating workplace health and security. Insurgent workers' groups successfully took control of the labor unions dominated by *Acción Democrática* and then coalesced into a political movement. Crisp and Levine (1998) argue that LCR was noteworthy in that it was a movement generated from civil society. Different from FREPASO, LCR did sink roots in society, thanks largely to its *nuevo sindicalismo* success. Nevertheless, its lack of institutionalization over matters like how to make decisions and sort out internal differences undermined it crucially in the end.

LCR arose indirectly when a small group splintered from the *Partido Comunista de Venezuela* in 1970. Most went on to form the *Movimiento al Socialismo* in 1971; Alfredo Maneiro (a veteran guerrilla commander) and other ideological dissidents (such as Andrés Velásquez and Pablo Medina) left *Movimiento al Socialismo* to form the heterodox Marxist *Venezuela 83* group, which was the immediate antecedent to LCR. This reconfiguration of leftist parties was a product of the end of Venezuela's armed struggle in the 1960s, amnesty to the guerrillas, and the rise of the New Left in Europe (López Maya 1995).

The gradual conversion of LCR from an insurgent movement to a major party organization with the goal of governing began in 1983. Candidates started winning state and local governments as well as occupying positions of power in Congress. Decentralizing constitutional changes facilitated LCR's ability to springboard onto the national political arena via local elections (López Maya 1995; Molina and Pérez 1998). LCR transformed from a "*grupúsculo 'radical'*" into an organization that had shown "*honestidad y ponderación*" in its handling of regional and municipal governments (López Maya 1995). Andrés Velásquez was at the helm of this pragmatic transformation. Of the orienting guidelines he established in 1990, three are very reminiscent of the PT: the exercise of democracy not only as elections but also as governance; an end to corruption; and efficiency and transparency in government services, such as health, education, and personal security (López Maya 1995).

Under Velásquez, LCR grew exponentially and began to moderate and professionalize piecemeal. It also made a transition from being worker centered to being multiclass in its base, although it continued to have organic ties with some societal sectors. Given these similarities with the PT, why then did LCR not follow the PT's path? Instead it split in 1997; radical members of the party left to found *Patria Para Todos* (Fatherland for All) and aligned with Hugo Chávez, whereas others remained in the LCR only to see it become a fringe party. LCR's collapse is attributable to a number of factors, most prominently a lack of institutional and ideological definition, a struggle for internal control of the party, and most immediately the Chávez factor, which raised issues like whether to side with the 1992 coup and other attempts to capture power (Salamanca 2004). The core problem, however, was that LCR never really institutionalized as a party. Similar to FREPASO, the LCR's electoral successes did not result from party institutionalization but rather from the crisis of identification among Venezuelans with the *Acción Democrática*–COPEI establishment. Velásquez's engagement in "extremely radical anti-party rhetoric" during the 1993 presidential election reflects this dynamic (Alvarez 2006: 20). The two traditional parties were collapsing and, with the recent constitutional changes allowing for direct elections of governors and mayors, LCR was one of few viable options available to voters.

Exogenous forces helped the party grow too fast for its own good – the meteoric expansion of the party was accompanied neither by institutional consolidation nor by the fashioning of consistent programmatic policies (Salamanca 2004: 218). Thus, besides the alternative presented by Chávez, LCR failed because of the internal shock of its "organizational implosion" (Salamanca 2004: 222). The party never matured into a stable organization with a permanent programmatic base. It refused to develop a hierarchical structure, instead relying upon consensus over majority rule, even though that often meant political stalemate and interminable debates (Yépez Salas 1993). The priority it gave to pluralism and expression over discipline was extreme. According to Michael Coppedge, "[i]n reaction to the iron discipline of AD and COPEI, *La Causa R* in Venezuela was opposed, on principle, to requiring its activists to toe any party line" (2001: 189).[6] Why there was no party development or

---

[6] Notably, he goes on to observe that in Brazil, "where most parties – especially the PMDB – were notoriously uncohesive, one of the most successful emerging parties was

Analytical Implications and Comparative Perspectives 193

organizational coherence goes back to the fact that LCR was initially formed as a fluid, antipolitical, anti-ideological, nonparty "in permanent construction." This philosophy from its founding moments remained in place, unchanged even after it no longer served a purpose.

In addition, fortuitous timing precluded the need to do much besides not be *Acción Democrática* or COPEI. The LCR was a forever fluid, programmatically incoherent party that, through happenstance, found itself as the third largest party in Venezuela in 1993. There was much tension between LCR's moderate and radical camps, and the contradictions between Velásquez and Pablo Medina were too great to bridge. Those in the Velásquez camp were pragmatic, liberal-democratic, and not wedded to *estatismo*. The activists tied to Medina were ideological, open to non-democratic routes to power, and statist in orientation. Because LCR had never invested in efforts to party build or form an ideology, its hollow and incoherent organization was unable to hold together the party's disparate parts.

Izquierda Unida: Aborted Take Off

The *Izquierda Unida* or United Left in Peru was an electoral alliance of three fronts presided over by a popular independent, Alfonso Barrantes. Marxist left parties formed the IU in late 1980, opposing the government of Fernando Belaúnde (1980–1985). The *Izquierda Unida's* comparison with the PT and its "externally mobilized" origins is fitting because "[i]t was not surprising that parties which were formed in opposition to a military regime adopted Leninist modes of organization, with undisputed leaders and organizational hierarchy" (Sanborn 1991: 253). There were three major tendencies in the *Izquierda Unida*: a reformist block, headed by Barrantes; a revolutionary block; and a more "ambiguous grouping" in the center (Schmidt 1996: 322). The significant infighting that had hurt the left's chances in previous electoral contests, together with the setting of municipal elections in November 1980 and the prospect of significant electoral victories, had created urgency for unification among left forces in the country. The possibility of winning national office strengthened the inclination of reformist elements to pursue an institutional strategy and to try to convince their more revolutionary counterparts to follow suit.

 the PT, which achieved the tightest discipline of any party in the system" (Coppedge 2001: 189).

Indeed, the context was propitious for the left to rise in the 1980s. The growing conservatism of APRA (*Alianza Popular Revolucionaria Americana* or American Popular Revolutionary Alliance) had created a political opening for the left's expansion in the 1960s and 1970s while the military regime (1968–1980) had stimulated popular organization and social mobilization. Similar to what occurred with the PT in Brazil and *Frente Amplio* in Uruguay, democratization prompted left parties in Peru to engage in grassroots organizational work and build alliances between urban popular movements and local governments (Schönwälder 1996). By the late 1980s, the successive failures of conservative and center-left administrations to resolve various crises strengthened the possibility of attaining national power. According to Roberts (1998: 209), "[t]he context could hardly have been more ideal for an expansion of the radical Left."

In addition to the promise provided by these broad contextual factors, the *Izquierda Unida* had personal leadership and organization potentially on its side, even though it was not a single party like the PT but rather a confederation of different parties. For example, the principle of hierarchy that characterized the Marxist parties making up the IU would mean that discipline and loyalty from the base could be expected in line with the leadership's preferences. In addition, the revolutionary block had a strong organizational base in the union and peasant movements. Although this did not entail a large percentage of voters, it was a core group whose support could be relied on. At the same time, having independent socialist Alfonso Barrantes at the IU's helm promised to be an advantage. A labor lawyer of modest provincial origins who had migrated to the city and struggled to gain an education, Barrantes appealed to the informal sector poor in a way that his more militant and extremist counterparts within the left did not. His nickname was "El Frijolito" ("Little Bean") in reference to his dark complexion, facial characteristics, and short stature (Schmidt 1996: 232). If a historic problem of the Peruvian left was that it had not found a way to resonate with the informal poor (far more numerous than the organized working class), Barrantes' ability to speak "to the people" addressed this deficiency. Indeed, where the Peruvian left was gaining new voters, the charismatic appeal of individual leaders rather than ideology per se was generally involved (Sanborn 1991: 263). Nonetheless, the potential of organizational and personal leadership factors to come together as the building blocks of a steady and sustained expansion of national power was not realized. The left wing of the IU remained mired "in the trenches." Barrantes, strategic in orientation and popular among voters, was unable to lift the weight of history sufficiently to promote institutional change.

The municipal victories of the *Izquierda Unida*, beginning in 1980 but especially in 1983, strengthened the inclination of the reformists to pursue an institutional strategy. Barrantes's authority over the IU was fortified after he placed second in his bid for the mayorality of Lima in 1980 and then won mayoral office in 1983. His proven electoral appeal allowed him to gain a political stature above and beyond the *Izquierda Unida* parties. Many signs suggested that he might become like Lula, a figure who could take advantage of the front's organizational strengths while leveraging his broader popularity to tame recalcitrant elements within it.

However, the *Izquierda Unida* as a whole failed to make the strategic adaptations that were required to advance in Peruvian politics. Parties on the far left remained concerned about becoming overly "electoralist" and abandoning their focus on grassroots organization and labor activities. An even more serious problem was the refusal of radical elements of the *Izquierda Unida* to take an unequivocal stance against the armed insurgency of *Sendero Luminoso*. *Sendero*'s ability to attract support among the Andean peasantry and recent migrants in urban shantytowns caused radical factions of the IU to fear a loss of mass support if they renounced the option of revolutionary violence. This, in turn, hurt the goal of reformist elements to make a decisive and credible centrist shift as part of a broader strategy to achieve change from within the system (Schönwälder 2002: 98).

Barrantes proved unable to persuade elements outside his own wing to follow his lead. Unlike Lula, he could not manage to leverage his popularity into moderating the IU's platform and image to sustain it as a serious electoral contestant. Whereas Lula was a founding member of the PT and remained at the heart of the party, Barrantes did not enjoy this standing. His independence may have allowed him to "stay above the fray" but it also hindered his efforts to exert influence over parties within the *Izquierda Unida*. The parties of the far left never fully accepted Barrantes' leadership. Javier Diez Canseco of the *Partido Unificado Mariateguista* or Unified Mariateguista Party, a key component of IU's radical wing, even charged that Barrantes had reduced the *Izquierda Unida* to "an electoral front around a caudillo" (Sanborn 1991: 367–368).

Comparing the FREPASO and the *Izquierda Unida*, one can say that if the fluidity of FREPASO's organization and the pragmatism of its leadership allowed it to make rapid strategic adjustments (perhaps excessively so), the *Izquierda Unida* did not shed its organizational and ideological inheritance enough to reduce sectarianism and internal discord to levels deemed acceptable by large numbers of voters. Although it had a popular leader with the potential to become a Lula, Barrantes lacked sufficient authority to enact the institutional changes required to capitalize fully on his public appeal. He resigned as IU president in 1987, leading the left parties that comprised the alliance to engage in open irreparable conflict over what opposition strategy to adopt. The *Izquierda Unida* ended up self-destructing, badly dividing the left, and contributing to the victory of Alberto Fujimori in 1990 (Schmidt 1996).

ANALYSIS OF COMPARATIVE CASES

What broader insights does the comparative evidence yield? On the basis of an examination of a number of left parties and alliances in Latin America since democratization, one can say that the ideal preconditions for successful party adaptation rest on a balance of organizational–institutional and personal leadership strengths. For left parties, organizational solidity stems from historical inheritances and path dependence, as historical institutionalism illuminates. As seen by rational choice, individual leadership is conducive to promoting strategic adaptation. Although there is often tension between party organization and popular leadership, as historical institutionalism and rational choice would suggest, they serve as vital complements in a party's growth, evolution, and adaptation. Ideally there should be a certain balance between them. When the two are roughly equilibrated, parties are positioned to adapt strategically to exogenous circumstances and are likely to do so in a gradual, steady, and sustained fashion.

The PT and the *Frente Amplio* exemplify the benefits of a combination of organizational–institutional and personal leadership strengths. The existence of a single popular electoral leader (albeit more pronounced in the case of Lula than Tabaré Vázquez) motivated and facilitated the enactment of strategic adjustments to external circumstances and changes in them. Party organization and institutionalization, although sometimes slowing or distorting these adjustments, ultimately enhanced their staying power by granting them legitimacy and support. When militants in the PT and *Frente Amplio* blocked or threatened to block necessary adaptations, Lula and Vázquez sometimes used their electoral popularity to circumvent the party or leverage change within it. It is noteworthy that neither party ascended rapidly and neither presidential candidate won office in his initial attempts. The expansion of these parties and their eventual presidential victories were built on a solid foundation that still survives to this day.

Personality-based leadership in the absence of organization is more conducive to rapid strategic maneuvering and accelerated expansion. Unconstrained by party organizations, such leaders are generally better able to take advantage of political openings and other shifting opportunities. This is important because many left parties and fronts or alliances in Latin America in the 1980s and 1990s received their initial break by the decline of traditional parties or center-left parties moving rightward in the political spectrum. Other adaptations, such as moderating political platforms or responding to public opinion polls with relevant changes, are no doubt facilitated by the absence of organizational constraints. The success of left parties and fronts that conform to this profile may be short lived, however, as demonstrated by the demise of FREPASO in Argentina. Party institutionalization is important for various reasons, including having procedures and mechanisms for sorting out internal conflicts, holding together disparate elements in ways that allow for a reasonable level of coherence in platforms and policies, and increasing the depth and longevity of societal support for them. The disintegration of *La Causa R* in Venezuela testifies to these points. Especially because exogenously based challenges and possibilities change over time, fortuitous timing and opportunistic responses to immediate considerations – even when mediated by popular leaders – cannot form the basis of a lasting left party or front.

Although organizational strength is necessary for a party to endure, organizational rigidity makes it difficult for a party or alliance to take flight in the first place. Ultimately, it impedes compromise, coordination, and successful adaptation. The *Izquierda Unida* – especially its left wing – was composed of parties that were vanguardist in their basic orientation and inflexible in their internal organization. Although the alliance was headed by a popular leader, who like Lula was a pragmatist of humble origins with an ability to reach common people, this important electoral asset was insufficient to overcome internally based challenges. In a sense, its potential was thwarted before it could even be tried. If FREPASO and LCR made dramatic but short-lived appearances on the national political scene only to disintegrate as a result of their lack of organization and institutionalization, *Izquierda Unida* never really got off the ground because of the rigidity and sectarianism of the party organizations that comprised it.

In sum, a propitious context for the emergence of new parties is not sufficient to guarantee their longer-term success. Grassroots ties and organized networks of support, institutionalized mechanisms of decision making, and a leadership that enjoys authority within the party and popularity among the electorate are factors crucially associated with successful and sustained adaptation among the cases identified. These features undergirded the slow but steady upward trajectory of the PT and *Frente Amplio*. Lack of organization and institutionalization hurt the staying power of the more immediately successful FREPASO and LCR. Organizational rigidity, even in the presence of a leader with considerable popular appeal, aborted the takeoff of *Izquierda Unida* into national politics.

PONDERING THE PT'S FUTURE

A key question that lies ahead concerns how long a party can maintain a profile of uneven adaptation, with ample changes on some dimensions and limited modification on others. How viable is it to continue to balance a strong organizational legacy of the kind that externally mobilized parties typically have with a growing corps of pragmatic and strategic elected leaders? In the case of the PT, the *mensalão* scandal placed into especially stark relief the hazards of trying to balance competing external and internal pressures and maintain a status in between that of full normalization and the retention of differences. There are tensions that apply more generally to externally mobilized parties that normalize over time. For example, as a previously policy-seeking party waters down its programmatic orientation and broadens its alliance partners, it will no doubt encounter difficulties in commanding the same commitment from its elected officials as in the past. Why should a party's elected officials agree to abide by strict standards of discipline and loyalty for an organization whose platforms and policies are ever less distinguishable from parties that allow their politicians far more autonomy? Furthermore, clearly the more "normal" a party becomes the less it can call upon its militant base as a source of energy, mobilization, and even financial sacrifice, factors that are so crucial in the rise and development of most externally mobilized parties. Most parties that go the way of the PT do not replenish their ranks with a new generation of militants whose support parallels that of preceding generations. Given the tensions associated with maintaining an "in-between" status, at some point in a party's evolution the balance is likely to shift in one direction or the other. Will the

PT move more unequivocally in one direction or the other? Will it continue to assimilate further and adopt the ways of Brazil's conventional parties even more uniformly than it has until now? In other words, will change, which started on the external front, proceed internally? Or, especially once it returns to the opposition, will the party undergo an internal process of self-reflection and reconfiguration and recover many of the characteristics that once made it so distinctive?

Pondering this question warrants a return to the factors – both external and internal – that were so crucial in shaping the PT's development since its inception. If growing public support for the overall contours of market reform and economic opening induced the party to undergo a process of moderation in the 1990s, it stands to reason that Brazil's buoyant economic situation in the current era places significant limits on how far Brazilians would be willing to veer from a path that has brought considerable stability, reasonable growth, and appreciable poverty reduction. Similarly, the diminishing political fragmentation and growing institutionalization that contributed to the PT's centrist shift shows little sign of changing course, and therefore points to further normalization.

As for internal factors that reflect the PT's historical endowment, although some organizational features remain so deeply entrenched that they will not change immediately, the PT is undergoing a generational shift that may well modify or remove them eventually. Indeed, many of the individuals who valued and defended the party's historic features the most – those who joined the party in the early stages of its development – have either departed already or will surely do so in the next couple of decades. At the same time, many newcomers to the PT conform more readily to the vote-seeking organization that it has become. This group, whose members strongly supported direct elections of the party leadership by the rank and file instead of party bureaucrats (PED), is working behind the scenes to devise measures to further diminish the influence of the party bureaucracy and elevate the autonomy of elected officials. Members of this group intend to start building support for some of these proposals at future national meetings of the party. Turning back the clock is unlikely especially because the moderates enjoy greater electoral success than their radical counterparts and rise better to the challenges of officeholding. Stated through the idea of "increasing returns," the changes enacted with the PT's normalization – especially those that generated greater electoral success – may well induce further steps in this direction. According to Pierson (2000: 252), "[i]n an increasing returns process, the probability of further steps along the same path increases with each move down that path. This is because the *relative* benefits of the current activity compared with the other possible options increase over time."

In any event, reflecting back upon what Brazil, Lula, and the PT were like in 1989, it is clear that all have traveled a long way since then. Brazil is now a much more stable and consolidated political democracy with some significant policy achievements to its name, notwithstanding the serious social inequities it still needs to confront. All major parties on the right as well as the left have now experienced both government and opposition. Lula, the PT's popular leader, has served as a vital complement to the party's strong organization the whole time. However, by 2009 Lula was a very different figure from who he was in 1989. The moderate policies he has advocated in government could not be further from the radical platforms he endorsed in his first bid for the presidency. Although still singularly able to exercise influence within the party and win support among the electorate, he has put greater distance between himself and the party over time. Similarly, the core of his societal backing has shifted considerably, diverging ever more from that of the party. The PT itself has become a major party that is now an integral part of the political mainstream. As part of the system, it cannot credibly be against it anymore. Change within the party has been gradual, uneven, and layered in nature. Nevertheless, over time the PT has been transformed.

Appendix

TABLE A.1. *Lula's Record in Presidential Elections: 1989–2006*

Year	% of Votes	
	First Round	Second Round
1989	17.2	47.0
1994	27.0	–
1998	31.7	–
2002	46.4	61.3
2006	48.6	60.8

Source: Nicolau, Jairo. *Banco de Dados Eleitorais do Brasil (1982–2006).*

TABLE A.2. *Congressional Election Results: 1982–2006*

Year	PT Seats in Chamber	
	%	No.
1982	1.7	8
1986	3.3	16
1990	7	35
1994	9.6	49
1998	11.3	58
2002	17.7	91
2006	16.2	83

Source: Nicolau, Jairo. *Banco de Dados Eleitorais do Brasil (1982–2006).*

TABLE A.3. *Municipal Election Results: 1982–2008*

Year	PT Mayors
1982	2
1988	36
1992	54
1996	115
2000	187
2004	411
2008	551

Source: Tribunal Superior Eleitoral.

TABLE A.4. *PT Mayoral Victories by Region and City Size: 1988–2008*

Year and City Size	North	Northeast	Southeast	South	Center-West	Subtotal
1988						
<10,000	0	1	4	1	0	6
10–20,000	0	1	5	3	1	10
20–50,000	0	2	1	1	1	5
50–150,000	0	0	4	0	0	4
150,000+	0	0	9	2	0	11
SUBTOTAL	0	4	23	7	2	36
1992						
<10,000	2	0	4	5	2	13
10–20,000	4	2	2	2	0	10
20–50,000	0	2	10	0	0	12
50–150,000	2	2	2	0	0	6
150,000+	1	1	8	2	1	13
SUBTOTAL	9	7	26	9	3	54
1996						
<10,000	5	3	14	21	1	44
10–20,000	2	3	8	6	2	21
20–50,000	4	3	9	5	1	22
50–150,000	0	2	11	1	0	14
150,000+	1	1	6	6	0	14
SUBTOTAL	12	12	48	39	4	115
2000						
<10,000	5	1	20	23	5	54
10–20,000	8	5	11	9	5	38
20–50,000	6	5	15	7	1	34
50–150,000	1	4	12	6	1	24
150,000+	1	6	16	12	2	37
SUBTOTAL	21	21	74	57	14	187
2004						
<10,000	24	16	52	55	21	168
10–20,000	18	16	38	17	9	98
20–50,000	9	20	31	12	3	75
50–150,000	4	8	17	6	1	36
150,000+	4	5	19	5	1	34
SUBTOTAL	59	65	157	95	35	411
2008						
<10,000	21	39	64	69	25	218
10–20,000	12	35	42	23	10	122
20–50,000	22	45	32	16	4	119
50–150,000	6	11	24	14	1	56
150,000+	4	6	22	4	0	36
SUBTOTAL	65	136	184	126	40	551

Sources: Tribunal Superior Eleitoral; Instituto Brasileiro de Geografia e Estatística.

TABLE A.5. *Presidential Vote Intentions by Education Level: 1989–2006*

Year of Election	% Lula	% Main Competitor
1989: First round		
Up to basic	15	37
Secondary	24	18
Superior	16	14
Valid vote share	16	32
1989: Second round		
Up to basic	44	57
Secondary	62	38
Superior	59	41
Valid vote share	48	52
1994		
Up to basic	25	55
Secondary	27	51
Superior	32	46
Valid vote share	26	54
1998		
Up to basic	30	63
Secondary	30	56
Superior	29	51
Valid vote share	30	60
2002: First round		
Up to basic	43	21
Secondary	48	20
Superior	50	21
Total vote share	45	21
2002: Second round		
Up to basic	64	36
Secondary	69	31
Superior	67	33
Valid vote share	66	34
2006: First round		
Up to basic	59	34
Secondary	45	40
Superior	30	48
Valid vote share	50	38
2006: Second round		
Up to basic	67	33
Secondary	59	41
Superior	47	53
Valid vote share	61	39

Notes: Valid vote share excludes undecided voters and those intending to cast a blank or spoiled ballot. Note that in the first round of the 2002 elections, valid vote share was not available; hence, total vote share was used.

Sources: Instituto Brasileiro de Opinião Publica e Estatística (October 27–30, 1989; December 1989; September 29 to October 2, 1994; September 18, 1998) and Datafolha (October 2 and 23, 2002; September 29–30, 2006; and October 27–28, 2006).

TABLE A.6. *Presidential Vote Intentions by Income Level: 1989–2006*

Year of Election	% Lula	% Main Competitor
1989: First round		
<2 min. wages	15	42
2–5 min. wages	18	30
5–10 min. wages	17	22
>10 min. wages	18	12
Valid vote share	16	32
1989: Second round		
<2 min. wages	43	57
2–5 min. wages	50	50
5–10 min. wages	59	41
>10 min. wages	52	48
Valid vote share	48	52
1994		
<2 min. wages	27	55
2–5 min. wages	27	52
5–10 min. wages	23	55
>10 min. wages	27	53
Valid vote share	26	54
1998		
<2 min. wages	28	64
2–5 min. wages	30	59
5–10 min. wages	33	53
>10 min. wages	25	58
Valid vote share	29	60
2002: First round		
<5 min. wages	45	20
5–10 min. wages	50	21
>10 min. wages	48	24
Total vote share	45	21
2002: Second round		
<5 min. wages	66	34
5–10 min. wages	68	32
>10 min. wages	65	35
Valid vote share	66	34
2006: First round		
<2 min. wages	61	32
2–5 min. wages	46	41
5–10 min. wages	35	47
>10 min. wages	26	54
Valid vote share	50	38
2006: Second round		
<2 min. wages	69	31
2–5 min. wages	59	41
5–10 min. wages	49	51
>10 min. wages	44	56
Valid vote share	61	39

Notes: Valid vote share excludes undecided voters and those intending to cast a blank or spoiled ballot. Note that, in 2002, Datafolha collapsed the two lowest income brackets. Also note that, in the first round of the 2002 elections, valid vote share was not available; hence, total vote share was used.

Sources: Instituto Brasileiro de Opinião Pública e Estatística (October 27–30, 1989; December 1989; September 29 to October 2, 1994; September 18, 1998) and Datafolha (October 2 and 23, 2002; September 29–30, 2006; and October 27–28, 2006).

TABLE A.7. *Presidential Vote Intentions by City Size: 1994–2006*

Year of Election	% Lula	% Main Competitor
1994		
≤10,000	21	60
10,001–20,000	22	61
20,001–50,000	25	57
50,001–200,000	29	51
200,000+	32	50
Valid vote share	27	54
1998		
≤10,000	24	60
10,001–20,000	25	59
20,001–50,000	29	55
50,001–200,000	34	53
200,000+	25	65
Valid vote share	27	60
2002: First round		
≤10,000	42	33
10,001–20,000	42	30
20,001–50,000	44	26
50,001–200,000	48	21
200,000+	49	19
Valid vote share	46	23
2002: Second round		
≤10,000	52	43
10,001–20,000	53	47
20,001–50,000	57	43
50,001–200,000	64	36
200,000+	67	33
Valid vote share	61	39
2006: First round		
≤10,000	51	44
10,001–20,000	54	41
20,001–50,000	52	41
50,001–200,000	48	43
200,000+	45	40
Valid vote share	49	42
2006: Second round		
≤10,000	61	39
10,001–20,000	64	36
20,001–50,000	63	37
50,001–200,000	60	40
200,000+	59	41
Valid vote share	61	39

Notes: Valid vote share excludes undecided voters and those intending to cast a blank or spoiled ballot.
Source: Tribunal Superior Eleitoral.

TABLE A.8. *Cabinet Distribution among Coalition Members: The Cardoso and Lula Administrations Compared*

Coalition	No. Chamber Seats	% of Coalition	No. Cabinets	% of Cabinet
	Cardoso's First Term (1995–1998)			
1/95–4/96				
PSDB	63	21.7	5	27.8
PMDB	107	36.9	2	11.1
PFL	89	30.7	3	16.7
PTB	31	10.7	2	11.1
Nonpartisan	0	0.0	6	33.3
TOTAL	290	100.0	18	100.0
4/96–3/98				
PSDB	63	18.4	4	21.1
PMDB	107	31.2	2	10.5
PFL	89	25.9	3	15.8
PTB	31	9.0	2	10.5
PPB	51	14.9	1	5.3
PPS	2	0.6	1	5.3
Nonpartisan	0	0.0	6	31.6
TOTAL	343	100.0	19	100.0
3/98–12/98				
PSDB	63	18.4	4	21.1
PMDB	107	31.2	2	10.5
PFL	89	25.9	4	21.1
PTB	31	9.0	1	5.3
PPB	51	14.9	2	10.5
PPS	2	0.6	1	5.3
Nonpartisan	0	0.0	5	26.3
TOTAL	343	100.0	19	100.0
	Cardoso's Second Term (1999–2002)			
1/99–3/99				
PSDB	99	26.0	5	25.0
PMDB	83	21.8	3	15.0
PFL	105	27.6	4	20.0
PTB	31	8.1	1	5.0
PPB	60	15.7	2	10.0
PPS	3	0.8	1	5.0
Nonpartisan	0	0.0	4	20.0
TOTAL	381	100.0	20	100.0
3/99–10/01				
PSDB	99	28.3	4	20.0
PMDB	83	23.7	2	10.0
PFL	105	30.0	4	20.0
PPB	60	17.1	2	10.0

(*continued*)

TABLE A.8 (continued)

Coalition	No. Chamber Seats	% of Coalition	No. Cabinets	% of Cabinet
PPS	3	0.9	1	5.0
Nonpartisan	0	0.0	7	35.0
TOTAL	350	100.0	20	100.0
10/01–3/02				
PSDB	99	28.5	5	25.0
PMDB	83	23.9	3	15.0
PFL	105	30.3	4	20.0
PPB	60	17.3	2	10.0
Nonpartisan	0	0.0	6	30.0
TOTAL	347	100.0	20	100.0
3/02–12/02				
PSDB	99	40.9	4	20.0
PMDB	83	34.3	2	10.0
PPB	60	24.8	2	10.0
Nonpartisan	0	0.0	12	60.0
TOTAL	242	100.0	20	100.0
Lula's First Term (2003–2006)				
1/03–12/03				
PT	91	36.4	11	47.8
PSB	28	11.2	1	4.3
PDT	17	6.8	1	4.3
PPS	21	8.4	1	4.3
PCdoB	12	4.8	1	4.3
PV	6	2.	1	4.3
PL	34	13.	1	4.3
PTB	41	16.4	1	4.3
Nonpartisan	0	0.0	5	21.7
TOTAL	250	100.0	23	100.0
1/04–7/05				
PT	91	30.0	10	43.5
PSB	28	9.2	1	4.3
PPS	21	6.9	1	4.3
PCdoB	12	4.0	1	4.3
PV	6	2.0	1	4.3
PL	34	11.2	2	8.7
PTB	41	13.5	1	4.3
PMDB	70	23.1	2	8.7
Nonpartisan	0	0.0	4	17.4
TOTAL	303	100.0	23	100.0

TABLE A.8 *(continued)*

Coalition	No. Chamber Seats	% of Coalition	No. Cabinets	% of Cabinet
7/05–12/06				
PT	83	24.1	10	43.5
PSB	29	8.4	2	8.7
PCdoB	10	2.9	1	4.3
PL	38	11.0	1	4.3
PTB	44	12.8	1	4.3
PMDB	80	23.3	3	13.0
PP (former PPB)	54	15.7	1	4.3
PV	6	1.7	1	4.3
Nonpartisan	0	0.0	3	13.0
TOTAL	344	100.0	23	100.0
Lula's Second Term (2007)				
1/07–3/07				
PT	83	24.0	10	43.5
PSB	28	8.1	2	8.7
PCdoB	13	3.8	1	4.3
PR (former PL)	34	9.8	1	4.3
PTB	21	6.1	1	4.3
PMDB	90	26.0	3	13.0
PP (former PPB)	41	11.8	1	4.3
PDT	23	6.6	0	0.0
PV	13	3.8	1	4.3
Nonpartisan	0	0.0	3	13.0
TOTAL	346	100.0	23	100.0
3/07–9/07				
PT	79	22.1	9	39.1
PSB	29	8.1	1	4.3
PCdoB	12	3.4	1	4.3
PR (former PL)	42	11.7	1	4.3
PTB	23	6.4	0	0.0
PMDB	96	26.8	6	26.1
PP (former PPB)	38	10.6	1	4.3
PDT	25	7.0	1	4.3
PV	14	3.9	1	4.3
Nonpartisan	0	0.0	2	8.7
TOTAL	358	100.0	23	100.0

Notes: In Lula's first term, the Partido Verde left the governing coalition in May, 2005, returning in November, 2006.

Sources: Tribunal Superior Eleitoral; www.presidencia.gov.br; Amorim Neto and Coelho (2007); Meneguello (1998).

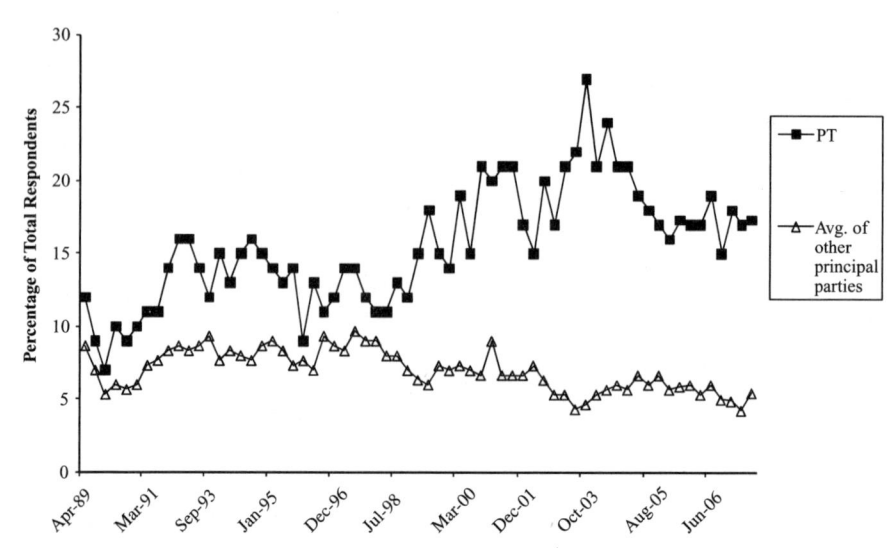

CHART A.1. Evolution of Party Preferences: 1988–2006. (*Sources:* Carreirão and Kinzo 2004; Carreirão 2007.)

References

Abers, Rebecca. 2000. *Inventing Local Democracy: Grassroots Politics in Brazil.* Boulder, CO: Lynne Rienner.
Abranches, Sérgio Henrique. 1988. "Presidencialismo de Coalizão: O Dilema Institucional Brasileiro." *DADOS* 31(1): 5–34.
Aguiar, Marcelo, and Carlos Henrique Araújo. 2002. *Bolsa-Escola: Education to Confront Poverty.* Brasília: UNESCO.
Albuquerque, Jose. 2007. "President Lula's Approach to Fragile States." *Carta Internacional* 2(1): 25–31.
Almeida, Alberto Carlos. 2008. *A Cabeça do Eleitor: Estratégia de Campanha, Pesquisa e Vitória Eleitoral.* Rio de Janeiro: Editora Record.
Almeida, Jorge. 1996. *Como Vota o Brasileiro.* São Paulo: Casa Amarela.
_____. 1997. "Esquerda, Pesquisas e Marketing Político." *Teoria e Debate* 34 (March–May): 12–15.
Almeida, Maria Hermínia Tavares de. 2004. "Privatization: Reform through Negotiation." In Mauricio A. Font and Anthony Peter Spanakos, eds., *Reforming Brazil* (pp. 53–70). Lanham, MD: Lexington Books.
Almeida, Maria Hermínia Tavares de, and Maurício Moya. 1997. "A Reforma Negociada: O Congresso e a Política de Privatização." *Revista Brasileira de Ciências Sociais* 12(34): 119–132.
Almeida, Paulo Roberto de. 2004. "Uma Política Externa Engajada: A Diplomacia do Governo Lula." *Revista Brasileira de Política Internacional* 47(1): 162–184.
_____. 2006. "A Diplomacia do Governo Lula: Balanço e Perspectivas." Unpublished paper (available at www.pralmeida.org).
Alvarez, Angel E. 2006. "Social Cleavage, Political Polarization and Democratic Breakdown in Venezuela." *Stockholm Review of Latin American Studies* 1(November): 18–28.
Alves, Brito. 2003. *A História de Lula: O Operário Presidente.* Rio de Janeiro: Espaço e Tempo.

Amann, Edmund, and Werner Baer. 2006. "Economic Orthodoxy versus Social Development? The Dilemmas Facing Brazil's Labour Government." *Oxford Development Studies* 34(2): 219–241.

Amaral, Aline Diniz, Peter Kingstone, and Jonathan Krieckhaus. 2008. "The Limits of Economic Reform in Brazil." In Peter Kingstone and Timothy J. Power, eds., *Democratic Brazil Revisited* (pp. 137–160). Pittsburgh, PA:. University of Pittsburgh Press.

Amaral, Oswaldo E. do. 2003. *A Estrela Não é Mais Vermelha: As Mudanças do Programa Petista nos Anos 90*. São Paulo: Editora Garçoni.

———. 2006. "Survey of the Participants in the Workers' Party 13th Annual National Convention." Unpublished paper (available from author upon request).

Ames, Barry. 2001. *The Deadlock of Democracy in Brazil: Interests, Identities, and Institutions in Comparative Perspective*. Ann Arbor: University of Michigan Press.

Amorim Neto, Octavio. 2005. "O Poder Executivo, Centro de Gravidade do Sistema Político Brasileiro." In Lúcia Avelar and Antônio Octávio Cintra, eds., *Sistema Político Brasileiro: Uma Introdução* (pp. 131–141). Rio de Janeiro: Fundação Konrad Adenauer Stiftung.

Amorim, Neto Octavio, and Carlos Frederico Coelho. 2007. "Un Año Inolvidable: Violencia Urbana, Crisis Política y el nuevo Triunfo de Lula en Brasil." *Revista de Ciencia Política* 27(Special Issue): 59–78.

Armijo, Leslie Elliott, Philippe Faucher, and Magdalena Dembinska. 2006. "Compared to What? Assessing Brazil's Political Institutions." *Comparative Political Studies* 39(6): 759–786.

Avritzer, Leonardo, and Zander Navarro, eds. 2002. *A Inovação Democrática: O Orçamento Participativo no Brasil*. São Paulo: Cortez Editora.

Azevedo, Clóvis Bueno de. 1995. *A Estrela Partida ao Meio: Ambigüidades do Pensamento Petista*. São Paulo: Editora Entrelinhas.

Baiocchi, Gianpaolo, ed. 2003. *Radicals in Power: The Workers' Party and Experiments in Urban Democracy in Brazil*. London and New York: Zed Books.

———. 2005. *Militants and Citizens: The Politics of Participatory Democracy in Porto Alegre*. Stanford, CA: Stanford University Press.

Baker, Andy. 2003. "Why is Trade Reform so Popular in Latin America? A Consumption-Based Theory of Trade Policy Preferences." *World Politics* 55(April): 423–455.

———. 2009. *The Market and the Masses in Latin America: Policy Reform and Consumption in Liberalizing Economies*. New York: Cambridge University Press.

Baker, Andy, Barry Ames, and Lúcio Rennó. 2006. "Social Context and Voter Volatility in New Democracies: Networks and Neighborhoods in Brazil's 2002 Elections." *American Journal of Political Science* 50(2): 382–399.

Barbosa, Rubens. 2008. "A Política Externa do Brasil para a América do Sul e o Ingresso da Venezuela no Mercosul." *Interesse Nacional* 1(1): 11–21.

Bates, Robert H., Avner Greif, Margaret Levi, Jean-Laurent Rosenthal, and Barry R. Weingast. 1998. *Analytic Narratives*. Princeton, NJ: Princeton University Press.

Baumgartner, Frank R., and Bryan D. Jones. 1993. *Agendas and Instability in American Politics*. Chicago: University of Chicago Press.

Bittar, Jorge, ed. 1992. *O Modo Petista de Governar*. São Paulo: Teoria e Debate.

Bourne, Richard. 2008. *Lula of Brazil: The Story So Far*. Berkeley: University of California Press.

Brazil Focus: Weekly Report. Issued by David Fleischer. Various issues.

Bremaeker, François E. J. 2000. *A Reeleição dos Prefeitos Municipais em 2000*. Rio de Janeiro: Instituto Brasileiro de Administração Municipal.

Burnham, Walter Dean. 1999. "Constitutional Moments and Punctuated Equilibria: A Political Scientist Confronts Bruce Ackerman's We the People." *The Yale Law Journal* 108(8): 2237–2277.

Campello, Daniela. 2007. "What is Left of the Brazilian Left?" Paper presented at the 65th meeting of the Midwest Political Science Association, April 14, Chicago, IL.

Cantanhêde, Eliane. 2001. *O PFL*. São Paulo: PubliFolha.

Carmine, E. G., and James Stimson. 1989. *Issue Evolution: Race and the Transformation of American Politics*. Princeton, NJ: Princeton University Press.

Carreirão, Yan de Souza. 2002. *A Decisão do Voto nas Eleições Presidencias Brasileiras*. Florianópolis/Rio de Janeiro: Editora da UFSC/Editora Fundação Getúlio Vargas.

Carreirão, Yan de Souza, and Maria D'Alva G. Kinzo. 2004. "Partidos Políticos, Preferência Partidária e Decisão Eleitoral no Brasil (1989/2002)." *DADOS* 47(1): 131–168.

Carvalho, Nelson Rojas de. 2003. "E no Início Eram as Bases: Geografia Política do Voto e Comportamento Legislativo no Brasil." Doctoral dissertation. Rio de Janeiro: IUPERJ.

Carvalho, Francisco Cristiano Noronha. 2006. "O Crescimento do PT na Câmara dos Deputados entre 1994 e 2002." Master's thesis. Brasília: Universidade de Brasília (UnB).

Cason, Jeffrey, and Timothy J. Power. 2009. "Presidentialization, Pluralization, and the Rollback of Itamaraty: Explaining Change in Brazilian Foreign Policy Making from Cardoso to Lula." *International Political Science Review* 30(2): 117–140.

Castañeda, Jorge G. 2006. "Latin America's Left Turn." *Foreign Affairs* 85(3): 28–43.

Centro de Estudos de Opinião Pública. 2002a. *Estudo Eleitoral Brasileiro: Relatório de Pesquisa*. Campinas: Universidade de Campinas.

———. 2002b. "Tendências." *Encarte da Revista do CESOP* 8(2): 341–393.

Checchi, Daniele, Massimo Florio, and Jorge Carrera. 2005. "Privatization Discontent and its Determinants." Discussion Paper No. 1587. Bonn: Institute for the Study of Labor.

Cleary, Matthew. 2006. "A 'Left Turn' in Latin America? Explaining the Left's Resurgence." *Journal of Democracy* 17(4): 35–49.

Confederação Nacional da Indústria–Instituto Brasileiro de Opinião Pública e Estatística. Opinion polls, 2009 and various years.

Confederação Nacional do Transporte–Sensus. Opinion polls, 2008.
Collier, David, and Ruth Collier. 1991. *Shaping the Political Arena: Critical Junctures, the Labor Movement, and Regime Dynamics in Latin America*. Princeton, NJ: Princeton University Press.
Colomer, Joseph M. 2005. "The Left-Right Dimension in Latin America." Working Paper No. 813. Barcelona: Universitat Pompeu Fabra – Department of Economic and Business Sciences.
Coppedge, Michael. 1997. A Classification of Latin American Parties. Working Paper No. 244. Notre Dame: The Helen Kellogg Institute of Latin American Studies.
_____. 2001. "Political Darwinism in Latin America's Lost Decade." In Larry Diamond and Richard Gunther, eds., *Political Parties and Democracy* (pp. 173–205). Baltimore: Johns Hopkins University Press.
Couto, Claudio Gonçalves. 2003. "The Second Time Around: Marta Suplicy's PT Administration in São Paulo." In Gianpaolo Baiocchi, ed., *Radicals in Power: The Workers' Party (PT) and Experiments in Urban Democracy in Brazil* (pp. 79–90). London and New York: Zed Books.
Cox, Gary. 1997. *Making Votes Count: Strategic Coordination in the World's Electoral Systems*. New York: Cambridge University Press.
Crisp, Brian F., and Daniel H. Levine. 1998. "Democratizing the Democracy? Crisis and Reform in Venezuela." *Journal of Interamerican Studies and World Affairs* 40(2): 27–61.
D'Araújo, Maria Celina, ed. 2007. *Governo Lula: Contornos Sociais e Políticos da Elite do Poder*. Rio de Janeiro: Editora Fundação Getúlio Vargas.
Datafolha Research Institute. Opinion polls, 1994 and various years.
Desposato, Scott W. 2006. "Parties for Rent? Ambition, Ideology, and Party Switching in Brazil's Chamber of Deputies." *American Journal of Political Science* 50(1): 62–80.
Deud, Cláudia Augusta Ferreira. 2007. "*Quadro Comparativo da Legislação Previdenciária*." Brasília: Consultoria Legislativa da Câmara dos Deputados.
Departamento Intersindical de Assessoria Parlamentar. 1999. *Os Cabeças do Congresso Nacional*. Brasília: DIAP.
_____. 2000. *Os Cabeças do Congresso Nacional*. Brasília: DIAP.
_____. 2001. *Os Cabeças do Congresso Nacional*. Brasília: DIAP.
_____. 2003. *Os Cabeças do Congresso Nacional*. Brasília: DIAP.
_____. 2004. *Os Cabeças do Congresso Nacional*. Brasília: DIAP.
Dirceu, José. 1999. "Governos Locais e Regionais e a Luta Política Nacional." In Inês Magalhães, Luiz Baretto, and Vicente Trevas, eds., *Governo e Cidadania* (pp. 18–25). São Paulo: Editora Fundação Perseu Abramo.
Downs, Anthony. 1957. *An Economic Theory of Democracy*. New York: Harper & Row.
Dulci, Luiz. 1997. "Por uma Nova Estratégia." *Teoria e Debate* 34(March–May): 25–28.
Duverger, Maurice. 1954. *Political Parties: Their Organization and Activity in the Modern State*. London: Metheun.
Encarnación, Omar G. 2003. *The Myth of Civil Society: Social Capital and Democratic Consolidation in Spain and Brazil*. New York: Palgrave Macmillan.

Epstein, Leon D. 1986. *Political Parties in the American Mold.* Madison: University of Wisconsin Press.
Farah, Marta Ferreira Santos, and Hélio Batista Barnoza, eds. 2000. *Novas Experiências de Gestão Pública e Cidadania.* Rio de Janeiro: Editora Fundação Getúlio Vargas.
Federação das Indústrias do Estado de São Paulo. 1994a. "Eleições 1994: Cenários Políticos." Proceedings from the meeting of the Conselho Superior de Orientação Política e Social da FIESP.
_____. 1994b. "Eleições 1994: Cenários Políticos Prováveis. Um Governo Lula." Proceedings from the meeting of the Conselho Superior de Orientação Política e Social da FIESP.
Fedozzi, Luciano. 1997. *Orçamento participativo: reflexões sobre a experiência de Porto Alegre.* Porto Alegre: Tomo Editoria.
Fernandes, Bernardo Mançano. 2000. *A formação do MST no Brasil.* Petrópolis: Editora Vozes.
Feuerwerker, Alon. 1994. "Eleições: Novos caminhos para chegar lá." *Teoria e Debate* 26 (September–November) (available at http://www.fpabramo.org.br/conteudo/eleioes-novo-caminhos).
Figueiredo, Argelina Cheibub, and Fernando Limongi. 1999. *Executivo e Legislativo na Nova Ordem Constitucional.* Rio de Janeiro: FAPESP/Editora Fundação Getúlio Vargas.
_____. 2008. *Política Orçamentária no Presidencialismo de Coalizão.* Rio de Janeiro: Editora Fundação Getúlio Vargas and Fundação Konrad Adenauer Stiftung.
Fleischer, David. 2002. "As Eleições Municipais no Brasil: Uma Análise Comparativa (1982–2000)." *Opinião Pública* 8(1): 80–105.
Flynn, Peter. 2005. "Brazil and Lula, 2005: Crisis, Corruption and Change in Political Perspective." *Third World Quarterly* 26(8): 1221–1267.
Folha de São Paulo. 1995. "Olho no Congresso." January 31.
_____. 1996. "Olho no Congresso." January 14.
_____. 1997. "Olho no Congresso." January 30.
_____. 1998. "Olho no Congresso." February 5.
_____. 2000. "Olho no Congresso." March 22.
_____. 2001. "Olho no Congresso." March 22.
Freston, Paul. 1994. "Os Trabalhadores e os Evangélicos." *Teoria e Debate* 25 (June–August): 23–26.
_____. 2001. *Evangelicals and Politics in Asia, Africa, and Latin America.* New York: Cambridge University Press.
Fundação Perseu Abramo. 2006. "*Pesquisa de Opinião Pública: Imagem Partidária e Cultura Política.*" São Paulo: Fundação Perseu Abramo.
Garcia, Maurício, and Helio Gastaldi. 2007. "A Participação do Estado Brasileiro na Sociedade – Percepções da População em Relação ao Processo de Privatização." Paper presented at the Primer Congreso Latinoamericano de Opinión Pública, WAPOR (World Association of Public Opinion Research), April 12–14, Colônia de Sacramento, Uruguay.
Geddes, Barbara, and Artur Ribeiro Neto. 1992. "Institutional Sources of Corruption in Brazil." *Third World Quarterly* 13(4): 641–661.

Genro, Tarso, and Ubiratan de Souza. 1997. *Orçamento Participativo: A Experiência de Porto Alegre.* São Paulo: Editora Fundação Perseu Abramo.

Giambiagi, Fabio. 2006. "A Política Fiscal do Governo Lula em Perspectiva Histórica: Qual é o Limite para o Aumento do Gasto Público?" Discussion Paper No. 1169 (March). Rio de Janeiro: Instituto de Pesquisa Econômica Aplicada (IPEA).

Gibson, Edward. 1996. *Class and Conservative Parties: Argentina in Comparative Perspective.* Baltimore: Johns Hopkins University Press.

Goldfrank, Benjamin. 2003. "Making Participation Work in Porto Alegre." In Gianpaolo Baiocchi, ed., *Radicals in Power: The Workers' Party (PT) and Experiments in Urban Democracy in Brazil* (pp. 27–52). London and New York: Zed Books.

———. 2007. "The Politics of Deepening Local Democracy: Decentralization, Party Institutionalization, and Participation." *Comparative Politics* 39(2): 147–168.

Goldfrank, Benjamin, and Aaron Schneider. 2006. "Competitive Institution Building: The PT and Participatory Budgeting in Rio Grande do Sul." *Latin American Politics and Society* 48(3): 1–31.

Greene, Kenneth F. 2007. *Why Dominant Parties Lose: Mexico's Democratization in Comparative Perspective.* New York: Cambridge University Press.

Grindle, Merilee S. 1996. *Challenging the State: Crisis and Innovation in Latin America and Africa.* New York: Cambridge University Press.

Guidry, John A., and Pere Petit. 2003. "Faith in What Will Change: Belém's Workers' Party Administration." In Gianpaolo Baiocchi, ed., *Radicals in Power: The Workers' Party (PT) and Experiments in Urban Democracy in Brazil* (pp. 53–78). London and New York: Zed Books.

Hagopian, Frances. 2005. "Economic Liberalization, Party Competition, and Political Representation: Brazil in Comparative (Latin American) Perspective." Unpublished manuscript (available from author upon request).

———. 2008. "Latin American Catholicism in an Age of Religious and Political Pluralism: A Framework for Analysis." *Comparative Politics* 40(2): 149–168.

Hall, Anthony. 2006. "From Fome Zero to Bolsa Família: Social Policies and Poverty Alleviation under Lula." *Journal of Latin American Studies* 38(4): 689–709.

Hall, Peter A., and Rosemary C. R. Taylor. 1996. "Political Science and the Three New Institutionalisms." *Political Studies* XLIV: 936–957.

Handlin, Samuel, and Ruth Berins Collier. Forthcoming. "Party Change and the Left in South America: Linkages through Partisanship, Direct Contact, and Social Organizations." In Steven Levitsky and Kenneth M. Roberts, eds., *Latin America's Left Turn: A Conceptual and Theoretical Overview.* Baltimore: Johns Hopkins University Press.

Harmel, Robert, and Kenneth Janda. 1994. "An Integrated Theory of Party Goals and Party Change." *Journal of Theoretical Politics* 6(3): 259–287.

Hunter, Wendy. 2006. "Growth and Transformation of the Workers' Party in Brazil, 1989–2002." Working Paper No. 326. Notre Dame: The Helen Kellogg Institute of International Studies.

_____. 2007a. "The Normalization of an Anomaly: The Workers' Party in Brazil." *World Politics* 59(3): 440–475.

_____. 2007b. "Corrupção no Partido dos Trabalhadores: O Dilema do 'Sistema'." In Jairo Nicolau and Timothy J. Power, eds., *Instituições Representativas no Brasil: Balanço e Reforma* (pp. 155–167). Belo Horizonte: Editora UFMG.

Hunter, Wendy, and Timothy J. Power. 2005. "Lula's Brazil at Midterm." *Journal of Democracy* 16(3): 127–139.

_____. 2007. "Rewarding Lula: Executive Power, Social Policy, and the Brazilian Elections of 2006." *Latin American Politics and Society* 49(1): 1–30.

Hunter, Wendy, and Natasha Borges Sugiyama. 2009. "Democracy and Social Policy in Brazil: Advancing Basic Needs, Preserving Privileged Interests." *Latin American Politics and Society* 51(2): 29–58.

Hurrell, Andrew. 2008. "Brazil on the World Stage." *Current History* 107(706): 51–57.

Instituto Brasileiro de Geografia e Estatística. 2000. *Indicadores Sociais Municipais*. Rio de Janeiro: IBGE.

Instituto Brasileiro de Opinião Pública e Estatística. Multiple years. Time series data (available at www.ibope.com.br).

Jacob, Cesar Romero, Dora Rodrigues Hees, Philippe Waniez, and Violette Brustlein. 1997. "A Eleição Presidencial de 1994 no Brasil: Uma Contribuição à Geografia Eleitoral." *Comunicação & Política* 4(3): 17–86.

Jensen, Nathan M., and Scott Schmith. 2005. "Market Responses to Politics: The Rise of Lula and the Decline of the Brazilian Stock Market." *Comparative Political Studies* 38(10): 1245–1270.

Kada, Naoko. 2003. "The Role of Investigative Committees in the Presidential Impeachment Processes in Brazil and Colombia." *Legislative Studies Quarterly* 28(1): 29–54.

Katznelson, Ira. 2003. "Periodization and Preferences: Reflections on Purposive Action in Comparative Historical Social Science." In James Mahoney and Dietrich Rueschemeyer, eds., *Comparative Historical Analysis in the Social Sciences* (pp. 270–301). New York: Cambridge University Press.

Katznelson, Ira, and Barry R. Weingast. 2005. "Intersections between Historical and Rational Choice Institutionalism." In Ira Katznelson and Barry R. Weingast, eds., *Preferences and Situations: Points of Intersection Between Historical and Rational Choice Institutionalism* (pp. 1–24). New York: Russell Sage Foundation.

Keck, Margaret. 1991. *PT: A Lógica da Diferença: O Partido dos Trabalhadores na Construção da Democracia Brasileira*. São Paulo: Editora Ática.

_____. 1992. *The Workers' Party and Democratization in Brazil*. New Haven, CT: Yale University Press.

Kingstone, Peter R. 2003a. "Privatizing Telebrás: Brazilian Political Institutions and Policy Performances." *Comparative Politics* 31(1): 21–40.

_____. 2003b. "Democratic Governance and the Dilemma of Social Security Reform in Brazil." In Ana Margheritis, ed., *Latin American Democracies in the New Global Economy* (pp. 221–240). Miami: North/South Center Press.

_____. 2004. *Critical Issues in Brazil's Energy Sector*. Houston: James A. Baker III Institute for Public Policy of Rice University.

Kingstone, Peter R., and Aldo F. Ponce. 2010. "From Cardoso to Lula: The Triumph of Pragmatic Neoliberalism in Brazil." In Kurt Weyland, Raúl L. Madrid, and Wendy Hunter, eds., *Leftist Governments in Latin America: Successes and Shortcomings* (pp. 140–180). New York: Cambridge University Press.

Kirchheimer, Otto. 1966. "The Transformation of the Western European Party Systems." In Joseph LaPalombara and Myron Weiner, eds., *Political Parties and Political Development* (pp. 177–200). Princeton, NJ: Princeton University Press.

Kitschelt, Herbert. 1989. *The Logic of Party Formation: Ecological Politics in Belgium and West Germany*. Ithaca, NY: Cornell University Press.

_____. 1994. *The Transformation of European Social Democracy*. New York: Cambridge University Press.

Krasner, Stephen D. 1988. "Sovereignty: An Institutional Perspective." *Comparative Political Studies* 21(1): 66–94.

Kucinski, Bernardo. 2000. *As Cartas Ácidas da Campanha de Lula de 1998*. São Paulo: Ateliê Editorial.

Lacerda, Alan Daniel Freire de. 2002. "O PT e a Unidade Partidária como Problema." *DADOS* 45(1): 39–76.

Lafer, Celso, and Fernando Kasinski Lottenberg. 1992. "Nacionalismo e Reestruturação da Economia." In Bolívar Lamounier, ed., *Ouvindo o Brasil: Uma Análise da Opinião Pública Brasileira Hoje* (pp. 72–73). São Paulo: Editora Sumaré.

Lamounier, Bolívar. 2003. "Brazil: An Assessment of the Cardoso Administration." In Jorge I. Domingues and Michael Shifter, eds., *Constructing Democratic Governance in Latin America* (2nd ed., pp. 269–291). Baltimore: Johns Hopkins University Press.

Lamounier, Bolívar, and Rubens Figueiredo, eds. 2002. *A Era FHC: Um Balanço*. São Paulo: Cultura Editores Associados.

Lanzaro, Jorge. 2010. "Uruguay: Persistence and Change in an Old Party Democracy." In Kay Lawson and Jorge Lanzaro, eds., *Political Parties and Democracy: The Americas* (pp. 195–217). New York: Praeger.

Latinobarómetro. 2005. *1995–2005: A Decade of Public Opinion*. Santiago de Chile: Corporación Latinobarómetro.

Leal, Paulo Roberto Figueira. 2005. *O PT e o Dilema da Representação Política*. Rio de Janeiro: Editora Fundação Getúlio Vargas.

Levitsky, Steven. 2001. "An 'Organised Disorganisation': Informal Organisation and the Persistence of Local Party Structures in Argentine Peronism." *Journal of Latin American Studies* 33(1): 29–65.

_____. 2003. *Transforming Labor-Based Parties in Latin America: Argentine Peronism in Comparative Perspective*. New York: Cambridge University Press.

Levitsky, Steven, and Kenneth Roberts, eds. Forthcoming. "Latin America's 'Left Turn': Causes and Implications." Unpublished manuscript. Baltimore: Johns Hopkins University Press.

Lima, Marcelo Oliveira Coutinho de, and Camilla Bustani. 1995. "The Brazilian Elections of 1994." *Electoral Studies* 14(2): 212–218.

Lindert, Kathy. 2006. "Brazil: Bolsa Família – Scaling-up Cash Transfers to the Poor." In *MfDR: Principles in Action: Sourcebook on Emerging Good Practices* (1st ed., pp. 67–74). OECD/World Bank (available at http://www.mfdr.org/Sourcebook/3-1stEdition.html).

Lipset, Seymour M., and Stein Rokkan. 1967. *Party Systems and Voter Alignments: Cross-National Perspectives*. New York: The Free Press.

López Maya, Margarita. 1995. "El Ascenso En Venezuela de la Causa R." *Revista Venezolana de Economía y Ciencias Sociales* 2–3 (April–September): 205–239.

Luna, Juan Pablo. 2005. *Programmatic and Non-Programmatic Party-Voter Linkages in Two Institutionalized Party Systems: Chile and Uruguay in Comparative Perspective*. Doctoral dissertation. Chapel Hill: University of North Carolina.

_____. 2007. "Frente Amplio and the Crafting of a Social Democratic Alternative in Uruguay." *Latin American Politics and Society* 49(4): 1–30.

Macaulay, Fiona. 1996. "'Governing for Everyone': The Workers' Party Administration in São Paulo, 1989–1992." *Bulletin of Latin American Research* 15(2): 211–229.

_____. 2003a. "The Purple in the Rainbow: Gender Politics in the PT." In Gianpaolo Baiocchi, ed., *Radicals in Power: The Workers' Party (PT) and Experiments in Urban Democracy in Brazil* (pp. 176–201). London and New York: Zed Books.

_____. 2003b. "Sexual Politics, Party Politics, and PT Government's Policies on Gender Equity and Equality." *Working Paper* No. CBS-46-03. University of Oxford: Centre for Brazilian Studies.

Macaulay, Fiona, and Guy Burton. 2003. "PT Never Again? Failure (and Success) in the PT's State Government in Espírito Santo and the Federal District." In Gianpaolo Baiocchi, ed., *Radicals in Power: The Workers' Party (PT) and Experiments in Urban Democracy in Brazil* (pp. 131–154). London and New York: Zed Books.

Machado, João, and Paulo Vannuchi. 1991. "Mãos à Obra." *Teoria e Debate* 13(February): 4–10.

Madrid, Raúl L. 2003. *Retiring the State: The Politics of Pension Privatization in Latin America and Beyond*. Stanford, CA: Stanford University Press.

Magalhães, Inês, Luiz Barreto, and Vicente Trevas, eds. 1999. *Governo e Cidadania: Balanço e Reflexões sobre o Modo Petista de Governar*. São Paulo: Editora Fundação Perseu Abramo.

Mahoney, James, and Kathleen Thelen. 2010. "A Theory of Gradual Institutional Change." In James Mahoney and Kathleen Thelen, eds., *Explaining Institutional Change: Ambiguity, Agency, and Power* (pp. 1–37). New York: Cambridge University Press.

Mahoney, James, and Celso M. Villegas. 2007. "Historical Enquiry and Comparative Politics." In Carles Boix and Susan C. Stokes, eds., *The Oxford Handbook of Comparative Politics* (pp. 73–89). Oxford: Oxford University Press.

Mainwaring, Scott. 1993. "Presidentialism, Multipartism, and Democracy: The Difficult Combination." *Comparative Political Studies* 26(2): 198–228.

_____. 1997. "Multipartism, Robust Federalism, and Presidentialism in Brazil." In Scott Mainwaring and Matthew Soberg Shugart, eds., *Presidentialism and*

Democracy in Latin America (pp. 55–109). New York: Cambridge University Press.

———. 1999. *Rethinking Party Systems in the Third Wave of Democratization: The Case of Brazil.* Stanford, CA: Stanford University Press.

Mainwaring, Scott, and Aníbal Pérez-Liñan. 1998. "Party Discipline in the Brazilian Constitutional Congress." *Legislative Studies Quarterly* 22(4): 453–483.

Mainwaring, Scott, Rachel Meneguello, and Timothy J. Power. 1999. "Conservative Parties, Democracy, and Economic Reform in Contemporary Brazil." Working Paper No. 264. Notre Dame: The Helen Kellogg Institute of International Studies.

Manzetti, Luigi. 1999. *Privatization South American Style.* New York: Oxford University Press.

March, James G., and Johan P. Olsen. 1984. "The New Institutionalism: Organizational Factors in Political Life." *American Political Science Review* 78(3): 734–749.

Maxwell, Kenneth. 2010. "Lula's Last Year." *Current History* 109(724): 43–46.

McDonough, Peter, Doh C. Shin, and José Alvaro Moisés. 1998. "Democratization and Participation: Comparing Spain, Brazil, and Korea." *Journal of Politics* 60(4): 919–953.

Melo, Marcus André. 2002. *Reformas Constitucionais no Brasil.* Rio de Janeiro: Editora Revan.

Melo, Carlos Ranulfo Felix de. 2000. "Partidos e Migração Partidária na Câmara dos Deputados." *DADOS* 43(2): 207–239.

Melo, Carlo Ranulfo Felix de, and Geralda Luiza de Miranda. 2006. "Migrações e partidos no governo Lula." Paper presented at the 5th Meeting of the Brazilian Political Science Association, June 26–29, Belo Horizonte, Brazil.

Mendes, Antonio Manuel Teixeira, and Gustavo Venturi. 1994. "Eleição Presidencial: Plano Real na Sucessão de Itamar Franco." *Opinião Pública* 2(2): 39–82.

Mendes, Gabriel. 2004. "Da Frente Brasil Popular à Aliança Capital/Trabalho: As Campanhas de Lula a Presidente de 1989 a 2002." Master's thesis. Rio de Janeiro: IUPERJ.

Meneguello, Rachel. 1989. *PT: A Formação de um Partido, 1979–1982.* São Paulo: Paz e Terra.

———. 1995. "Electoral Behavior in Brazil: The 1994 Presidential Elections." *International Social Science Journal* 146(4): 627–641.

———. 1998. *Partidos e Governos no Brasil Contemporâneo (1985–1997).* São Paulo: Paz e Terra.

———. 2005. "Government Popularity and Public Attitudes to Social Security Reform in Brazil." *International Journal of Public Opinion Research* 17(2): 173–189.

Ministério do Desenvolvimento Social. 2006. *Programa Bolsa Família, Guia do Gestor.* Brasília: Ministério do Desenvolvimento Social.

Molina, José E., and Carmen Pérez. 1998. "Evolution of the Party System in Venezuela, 1946–1993." *Journal of Interamerican Studies and World Affairs* 40(2): 1–26.

Nassif, Maria Inês. 2002. "Previdência Social." In Bolívar Lamounier and Rubens Figueiredo, eds., *A Era FHC: Um Balanço* (pp. 569–598). São Paulo: Cultura Editores Associados.

Nelson, Roy C. 2003. "Harnessing Globalization: Rio Grande do Sul's Successful Effort to Attract Dell Computer Corporation." *Journal of Developing Societies* 19(2/3): 268–307.

Neri, Marcelo Côrtes, ed. 2006. *Poverty, Inequality and Labor Dynamics: The Second Real.*" Rio de Janeiro: Centro de Políticas Sociais da Fundação Getulio Vargas (available at http://www.fgv.br/cps/pesquisas/site_ret_port/).

Nicolau, Jairo. *Banco de Dados Eleitorais do Brasil* (1982–2006). Rio de Janeiro: IUPERJ (available at http://jaironicolau.iuperj.br/banco2004.html).

————. 2000. "Disciplina Partidária e Base Parlamentar na Câmara dos Deputados no Primeiro Governo Fernando Henrique Cardoso (1995–1998)." *DADOS* 43(4): 709–734.

————. 2006. "O Sistema Eleitoral de Lista Aberta no Brasil." Working Paper No. CBS-70-06. University of Oxford: Centre for Brazilian Studies.

Nicolau, Jairo, and Vitor Peixoto. 2007. "As Bases Municipais da Votação de Lula em 2006." In João Paulo dos Reis Velloso, ed., *Quem Elegeu Lula?* Cadernos do Fórum Nacional No. 6 (pp. 15–25). Rio de Janeiro: INAE (Instituto Nacional de Altos Estudos).

Nóbrega, Maílson da. 1992. "Presença do Estado na Economia e na Sociedade." In Bolívar Lamounier, ed., *Ouvindo o Brasil: Uma Análise da Opinião Pública Brasileira Hoje* (pp. 33–34). São Paulo: Editora Sumaré.

Novaes, Carlos. 1993. "PT: Dilemas da Burocratização." *Novos Estudos CEBRAP* 35(March): 217–237.

Novaro, Marcos, and Vicente Palermo. 1998. *Los caminos de la centroizquierda: Dilemas y desafíos del FREPASO y de la Alianza*. Buenos Aires: Editorial Losada.

Nylen, William R. 2003. *Participatory Democracy versus Elitist Democracy: Lessons from Brazil*. New York: Palgrave Macmillan.

Oliveira, Vanessa de Elias. 2005. "Judiciário e Privatizacões no Brasil: Existe uma Judicialização da Política?" *DADOS* 48(3): 559–587.

Ondetti, Gabriel. 2006. "Lula and Land Reform: How Much Progress?" Paper prepared for delivery at the 2006 Congress of the Latin American Studies Association, March 15–18, San Juan, Puerto Rico.

————. 2008. *Land, Protest, and Politics: The Landless Movement and the Struggle for Agrarian Reform in Brazil*. University Park: Pennsylvania State University Press.

Ondetti, Gabriel, and Sybil Rhodes. 2007. "Courting the Third World: Lula's South-South Trade Diplomacy." Paper prepared for delivery at the 2007 Congress of the Latin American Studies Association, September 5–8, Montréal, Canada.

Pacheco, Regina Silvia. 2004. "Public Management as a Non-Policy Field in Lula's Administration." Paper presented at the Conference on Generation Reform in Brazil and Other Nations, organized by the International Public Management Network and the Escola Brasileira de Administração Pública e Empresa, Fundação Getúlio Vargas, November 17–19, Rio de Janeiro, Brazil.

Panizza, Francisco. 2000. "Is Brazil becoming a 'Boring Country'?" *Bulletin of Latin American Research* 19(4): 501–525.
Panebianco, Angelo. 1988. *Political Parties: Organization and Power*. New York: Cambridge University Press.
Paraná, Denise. 2002. *Lula: O Filho do Brasil*. São Paulo: Editora Fundação Perseu Abramo.
Partido dos Trabalhadores. 1986. *Programa, Manifesto, Estatuto e Discurso da Convenção de 1981*. São Paulo: Companhia Editora Joruês.
———. 1989. *Programa de Governo 1989, Coligação Frente Brasil Popular. Brasil Urgente: Lula Presidente – Democracia*. São Bernardo do Campo, SP: Gráfica e Editora FG.
———. 1992. *Resoluções do 1º Congresso*. São Paulo: Partido dos Trabalhadores, Diretório Nacional.
———. 1994. *Programa de Governo 1994, Coligação Frente Brasil Popular Pela Cidadania. Lula Presidente: Uma Revolução Democrática no Brasil – Bases do Programa de Governo*. São Paulo: Teoria e Debate.
———. 1998a. *Programa de Governo 1998, Coligação União do Povo Muda Brasil. União do Povo Muda Brasil – Diretrizes do Programa de Governo*. São Paulo: Fundação Perseu Abramo.
———. 1998b. *Partido dos Trabalhadores: Resoluções de Encontros e Congressos, 1979–1998*. São Paulo: Editora Fundação Perseu Abramo.
———. 2001a. *O PT faz História*. São Paulo: Partido dos Trabalhadores, Diretório Nacional.
———. 2001b. *Estatuto do Partido dos Trabalhadores*. São Paulo: Editora Fundação Perseu Abramo.
———. 2002a. *Partido dos Trabalhadores: Resoluções de Encontros e Congressos & Programas de Governo do PT, 1979–2002*. São Paulo: Editora Fundação Perseu Abramo (available at http://www2.fpa.org.br/portal/modules/news/index.php?storytopic=622).
———. 2002b. *Concepcão e Diretrizes do Programa de Governo do PT para o Brasil*. São Paulo: Comitê Lula Presidente, 2002.
———. 2003. *Caderno Informativo de junho de 2003, Secretaria Nacional de Finanças & Planejamento*. São Paulo: Partido dos Trabalhadores, Diretório Nacional.
———. 2006. *Resoluções do 13º Encontro Nacional do PT*. São Paulo: Partido dos Trabalhadores, Diretório Nacional.
———. 2007a. *Resoluções do 3º Congresso*. São Paulo: Partido dos Trabalhadores, Diretório Nacional.
———. 2007b. *Deputados Federais do PT: Resumo Biográfico 2003–2007*. Brasília, DF: Liderança do PT na Câmara dos Deputados.
Payne, Mark J., Daniel Zovatto, and Mercedes Mateo Díaz. 2007. *Politics Matters: Democracy and Development in Latin America*. Washington, DC: Inter-American Development Bank and the International Institute for Democracy and Electoral Assistance.
Pereira, Carlos, and Timothy J. Power. 2005. "Governo de Coalizão ou Monopólio Político?" *Valor Econômico* 30 (June).
Petkoff, Teodoro. 2005. "Las dos Izquierdas." *Nueva Sociedad* 197 (May–June): 114–128.

Pierson, Paul. 2003. "Big, Slow–Moving, and...Invisible: Macrosocial Processes in the Study of Comparative Politics." In James Mahoney and Dietrich Rueschemeyer, eds., *Comparative Historical Analysis in the Social Sciences* (pp. 177–207). New York: Cambridge University Press.

_____. 2000. "Increasing Returns, Path Dependence, and the Study of Politics." *American Political Science Review* 94(2): 251–267.

Pierucci, Antônio Flávio, and Reginaldo Prandi. 1995. "Religões e Voto: A Eleição Presidencial de 1994." *Opinião Pública* 3(1): 20–44.

Power, Timothy J. 1998. "Brazilian Politicians and Neoliberalism: Mapping Support for the Cardoso Reforms, 1995–1997." *Journal of Interamerican Studies and World Affairs* 40(4): 51–72.

_____. 2000. *The Political Right in Post-Authoritarian Brazil*. University Park: Pennsylvania State University Press.

_____. 2008. "Centering Democracy? Ideological Cleavages and Convergence in the Brazilian Political Class." In Peter Kingstone and Timothy J. Power, eds., *Democratic Brazil Revisited* (pp. 81–106). Pittsburgh, PA: University of Pittsburgh Press.

_____. Forthcoming. "Brazilian Democracy as a Late Bloomer: Reevaluating the Regime in the Cardoso-Lula Era." *Latin American Research Review*.

Power, Timothy J., and César Zucco Jr. 2009. "Estimating Ideology of Brazilian Legislative Parties, 1990–2005." *Latin American Research Review* 44(1): 218–240.

Pribble, Jennifer. 2008. *Protecting the Poor: Welfare Politics in Latin America's Free Market Era*. Doctoral dissertation. Chapel Hill: University of North Carolina.

Przeworski, Adam, and John Sprague. 1986. *Paper Stones: A History of Electoral Socialism*. Chicago: University of Chicago Press.

Roberts, Kenneth M. 1998. *Deepening Democracy? The Modern Left and Social Movements in Chile and Peru*. Stanford, CA: Stanford University Press.

_____. Forthcoming. *Changing Course: Party Systems in Latin America's Neoliberal Era*. New York: Cambridge University Press.

Rodrigues, Leôncio Martins. 1987. *Quem É Quem na Constituinte: Uma Análise Sócio-Política dos Partidos e Deputados*. São Paulo: OESP-Maltese.

_____. 2002. *Partidos, Ideologia e Composição Social: Um Estudo das Bancadas Partidárias na Câmara dos Deputados*. São Paulo: EdUSP.

_____. 2006. *Mudanças na Classe Política Brasileira*. São Paulo: PubliFolha.

Roett, Riordan. 2010. "How Reform Has Powered Brazil's Rise." *Current History* 109(724): 47–52.

Roma, Celso. 2005. "Atores, Preferências e Instituição na Câmara dos Deputados." Doctoral dissertation. São Paulo: Universidade de São Paulo (USP), Department of Political Science.

_____. 2006. "Organizaciones de Partido en Brasil: El PT y el PSDB bajo Perspectiva Comparada." *América Latina Hoy* 44: 153–184.

Rosas, Guillermo, and Elizabeth Zechmeister. 2000. "Ideological Dimensions and Left-Right Semantics in Latin America." Paper presented at the Latin American Studies Association Congress, March 16–18, Miami, FL.

Sader, Emir, and Ken Silverstein. 1991. *Without Fear of Being Happy: Lula, the Workers' Party and Brazil*. New York: Verso.

Salamanca, Luis. 2004. "La Causa Radical: Auge y Caída." In José Enrique Molina Vega and Ángel Eduardo Álvarez Díaz, eds., *Los partidos políticos venezolanos en el siglo XXI* (pp. 217–261). Caracas: Vadell Hermano Editores.

Sampaio, Plínio de Arruda. 1989. "Depende da Gente." *Teoria e Debate* 6 (April–June): 2–4.

Samuels, David J. 1999. "Incentives to Cultivate a Party Vote in Candidate-Centric Electoral Systems: Evidence from Brazil." *Comparative Political Studies* 32(4): 487–518.

———. 2001. "Money, Elections, and Democracy in Brazil." *Latin American Politics and Society* 43(2): 27–48.

———. 2003. *Ambition, Federalism, and Legislative Politics in Brazil*. New York: Cambridge University Press.

———. 2004. "From Socialism to Social Democracy: Party Organization and the Transformation of the Workers' Party in Brazil." *Comparative Political Studies* 37(9): 999–1024.

———. 2006a. "Sources of Mass Partisanship in Brazil." *Latin American Politics and Society* 48(2): 1–27.

———. 2006b. "Financiamento de Campanhas no Brasil e Propostas de Reforma." In Gláucio Ary Dillon Soares and Lúcio Rennó, eds., *Reforma Política: Lições da História Recente* (pp. 133–153). Rio de Janeiro: Editora Fundação Getúlio Vargas.

———. 2008. "Brazilian Democracy under Lula and the PT." In Vitor Amorim de Angelo and Marco Antonio Villa, eds., *Uma História Revisitada: O Partido dos Trabalhadores e a Política Brasileira (1980–2006)* (pp. 203–229). São Carlos: EdUSCar.

Sanborn, Cynthia Ann. 1991. *The Democratic Left and the Persistence of Populism in Peru: 1975–1990*. Doctoral dissertation. Cambridge, MA: Harvard University.

Santander. 2010. Latin American Equity Research, Strategy Report (January).

Santos, Boaventura de Souza. 1998. "Participatory Budgeting in Porto Alegre: Toward a Redistributive Democracy." *Politics and Society* 26(4): 461–510.

Santos, Fabiano. 2006. "Em Defesa do Presidencialismo de Coalizão." In Gláucio Ary Dillon Soares and Lúcio Rennó, eds., *Reforma Política: Lições da História Recente* (pp. 281–295). Rio de Janeiro: Editora Fundação Getúlio Vargas.

Schickler, Eric. 2001. *Disjointed Pluralism: Institutional Innovation and the Development of the U.S. Congress*. Princeton, NJ: Princeton University Press.

Schlesinger, Joseph A. 1991. *Political Parties and the Winning of Office*. Ann Arbor: University of Michigan Press.

Schmidt, Gregory D. 1996. "Fujimori's 1990 Upset Victory in Peru: Electoral Rules, Contingencies, and Adaptive Strategies." *Comparative Politics* 28(3): 321–254.

Schönwälder, Gerd. 2002. *Linking Civil Society and the State: Urban Popular Movements, the Left, and Local Government in Peru, 1980–1992*. University Park: Pennsylvania State University Press.

Seligson, Amber. 2003. "Disentangling the Roles of Ideology and Issue Positions in the Rise of Third Parties: The Case of Argentina." *Political Research Quarterly* 56(4): 465–475.

Share, Donald. 1999. "From Policy-Seeking to Office-Seeking: The Metamorphosis of the Spanish Socialist Workers Party." In Wolfgang C. Müller and Kaare Strøm, eds., *Policy, Office, or Votes? How Political Parties in Western Europe Make Hard Decisions* (pp. 89–111). New York: Cambridge University Press.
Shefter, Martin. 1994. *Political Parties and the State: The American Historical Experience*. Princeton, NJ: Princeton University Press.
Shugart, Matthew Soberg, and John M. Carey. 1992. *Presidents and Assemblies: Constitutional Design and Electoral Dynamics*. New York: Cambridge University Press.
Silva, Luis Inácio Lula da. 2002. *Letter to the Brazilian People* (available at http://www.pt.org.br).
Silva, Rodrigo Freire de Carvalho e. 2007. "Caminhando para o Centro: Uma Análise da Conjuntura Interna do Partido dos Trabalhadores no Processo de Eleições Diretas de 2007." *Revista Espaço Acadêmico* 78(November) (available at http://www.espacoacademico.com.br/078/78silva.htm).
Singer, Paul. 1996. *Um Governo de Esquerda para Todos: Luiza Erundina na Prefeitura de São Paulo (1989–1992)*. São Paulo: Editora Brasiliense.
Singer, André. 1990. "Collor na Periferia: A Volta por Cima do Populismo?" In Bolívar Lamounier, ed., *De Geisel a Collor: O Balanço da Transição* (pp. 135–152). São Paulo: Editora Sumaré.
———. 2001. *O PT*. São Paulo: PubliFolha.
Snyder, Richard, and David Samuels. 2001. "Devaluing the Vote in Latin America." *Journal of Democracy* 12(1): 146–159.
Soares, Fábio Veras, Sergei Soares, Marcelo Medeiros, and Rafael Guerreiro Osório. 2006. "Programas de Transferência de Renda no Brasil: Impactos sobre a Desigualdade." Discussion Paper No. 1228 (October). Rio de Janeiro: Instituto de Pesquisa Econômica Aplicada (IPEA).
Soares, Gláucio Ary Dillon, and Sonia Luzia Terron. 2008. "Dois Lulas: a geografia eleitoral da reeleição (explorando conceitos, métodos e técnicas de analise geoespacial." *Opinião Pública* 14(2): 269–301.
Sola, Lourdes. 2008. "Politics, Markets, and Society in Lula's Brazil." *Journal of Democracy* 19(2): 31–45.
Souza, Amaury de. 2004. "Political Reform in Brazil: Promises and Pitfalls." In *Policy Papers on the Americas*, Volume XV, Study 3 (April). Washington, DC: Center for Strategic and International Studies.
Souza, Celina. 1996. "Redemocratization and Decentralization in Brazil: The Strength of the Member States." *Development and Change* 27(3): 529–555.
———. 1997. *Constitutional Engineering in Brazil: The Politics of Federalism and Decentralization*. New York: St. Martin's Press.
Streeck, Wolfgang, and Kathleen Thelen. 2005. "Introduction: Institutional Change in Advanced Political Economies." In Wolfgang Streeck and Kathleen Thelen, eds., *Beyond Continuity: Institutional Change in Advanced Political Economies* (pp. 1–39). Oxford: Oxford University Press.
Strøm, Kaare, and Wolfgang C. Müller. 1999. "Political Parties and Hard Choices." In Wolfgang C. Müller and Kaare Strøm, eds., *Policy, Office, or Votes? How Political Parties in Western Europe Make Hard Decisions* (pp. 1–35). New York: Cambridge University Press.

Sugiyama, Natasha Borges. 2007. *Ideology and Social Networks: The Politics of Social Policy Diffusion in Brazil*. Doctoral dissertation. Austin: University of Texas.

Suplicy, Eduardo Matarazzo. 2002. *Renda de Cidadania: A Saída é pela Porta*. São Paulo: Cortez Editora and Editora Fundação Perseu Abramo.

Taylor, Matthew M. 2008. *Judging Policy: Courts and Policy Reform in Democratic Brazil*. Stanford, CA: Stanford University Press.

Thelen, Kathleen. 1999. "Historical Institutionalism in Comparative Politics." *Annual Review of Political Science* 2(June): 369–404.

_____. 2003. "How Institutions Evolve: Insights from Comparative Historical Analysis." In James Mahoney and Dietrich Rueschemeyer, eds., *Comparative Historical Analysis in the Social Sciences* (pp. 240–280). New York: Cambridge University Press.

_____. 2004. *How Institutions Evolve: The Political Economy of Skills in Germany, Britain, the United States, and Japan*. New York: Cambridge University Press.

Transparency International. 1997 and previous years. "Corruption Perception Index" (available at http://www.transparency.org/policy_research/surveys_indices/cpi).

Tribunal Superior Eleitoral. 2002. "Estatística do Eleitorado" (available at http://www.tse.com.br).

Tribunal Superior Eleitoral. Electoral data. Various years (available at http://www.tse.com.br).

Turner, Frederick C., and John D. Martz. 1997. "Institutional Confidence and Democratic Consolidation in Latin America." *Studies in Comparative International Development* 32(3): 65–84.

Venturi, Gustavo. 2006. "A Opinião Pública diante da Crise." *Teoria e Debate* 66(April–June): 20–26.

Wampler, Brian. 2004. "Expanding Accountability through Participatory Institutions: Mayors, Citizens, and Budgeting in Three Brazilian Municipalities." *Latin American Politics and Society* 46(2): 73–100.

_____. 2007. *Participatory Budgeting in Brazil: Contestation, Cooperation, and Accountability*. University Park: Pennsylvania State University Press.

Weber, Max. 1976. *Wirtschaft and Gessellschaft* [Economy and Society], 5th ed. Tübingen: J.C.B. Mohr.

Weffort, Francisco. 1994. "Eleições: Nossa trajetória é de vitórias." *Teoria e Debate* 26 (September–November) (available at http://www.f[abramo.org.br/node/1526).

Weingast, Barry R. 2002. "Rational Choice Institutionalism." In Ira Katznelson and Helen V. Milner, eds., *Political Science: The State of the Discipline* (pp. 660–692). New York: American Political Science Association–Norton.

Weyland, Kurt. 2002. *The Politics of Market Reform in Fragile Democracies: Argentina, Brazil, Peru, and Venezuela*. Princeton, NJ: Princeton University Press.

_____. 2006. *Bounded Rationality and Policy Diffusion: Social Sector Reform in Latin America*. Princeton, NJ: Princeton University Press.

_____. 2009. "The Rise of Latin America's Two Lefts? Insights from Rentier State Theory." *Comparative Politics* 41(2): 145–164.

Weyland, Kurt, Raúl L. Madrid, and Wendy Hunter, eds. 2010. *Leftist Governments in Latin America: Successes and Shortcomings*. New York: Cambridge University Press.
Wilson, Frank L. 1994. "The Sources of Party Change: The Social Democratic Parties of Britain, France, Germany, and Spain." In Kay Lawson, ed., *How Political Parties Work* (pp. 233–283). Westport, CT: Praeger.
Wright, William E. 1971. "Comparative Party Models: Rational Efficient and Party Democracy." In William E. Wright, ed., *A Comparative Study of Party Organization* (pp. 17–54). Columbus, OH: Charles E. Merrill.
Yaffé, Jaime. 2005. *Al centro y adentro: la renovación de la izquierda y el triunfo del Frente Amplio en Uruguay*. Montevideo: Librería Linardi y Risso.
Yépez Salas, Guillermo. 1993. *La Causa R: Origen y poder*. Caracas: Editorial Tropykos.
Zucco, Cesar. 2008. "The President's 'New' Constituency: Lula and the Pragmatic Vote in Brazil's 2006 Presidential Elections." *Journal of Latin American Studies* 40(1): 29–49.

Interviews

Araújo, João Batista Oliveira de (Babá). Former PT deputy, Brasília, August 6, 2003
Arbix, Glauco. Party activist and social policy advisor, São Paulo, August 1, 2006
Arns, Flávio. Former PT senator, Brasília, August 12, 2003
Azevedo, Clovis Bueno de. Member of São Paulo city government under former PT mayor Luiza Erundina, São Paulo, July 31, 2006
Buarque, Cristovam. Former PT governor of the Federal District, Austin, TX, April 18, 2009
Campos, Antonio Claret. Social policy expert, *Ministério do Desenvolvimento Social – Bolsa Família* division, Brasília, August 16, 2006
Cardoso, Fernando Henrique. Former President of Brazil, Austin, TX, September 13, 2006
Cardozo, José Eduardo. PT deputy, Brasília, August 14, 2003
Carepa, Ana Julia. Former PT senator and former PT governor, Brasília, August 12, 2003
Cantalice, Alberto. PT president of the state of Rio Janeiro, Rio de Janeiro, June 9, 2009
Drummond, José. Party affiliate and CUT labor leader, São Paulo, August 8, 2006
Garcez, Máximiliano Nagl. Legal advisor to the PT in the Chamber of Deputies, Brasília, August 15, 2003
Genoino, José. Former party president and several term PT deputy, São Paulo, August 7, 2006
Greenhalgh, Luiz Eduardo. Former legal advisor to the *Movimento dos Trabalhadores Rurais Sem Terra*, and several term PT deputy, São Paulo, August 8, 2006
Gushiken, Luis. Former party president and several term PT deputy, Brasília, August 14, 2006
Júnior, Raimundo. Former assistant to José Genoino (PT deputy and former party president), Brasília, July 29, 2003
Kucinski, Bernardo. PT advisor and media coordinator, Brasília, July 31, 2003

Mendes, Tânia. Former adviser to José Dirceu (three-term PT president), São Paulo, August 8, 2006

Moisés, José Alvaro. Founding member of the PT and researcher, São Paulo, August 2, 2006

Paiva, Paulo. Former Minister of Labor, Austin, TX, May 24, 2005

Pereira, Athos. Chief of Staff, Leadership of the PT in the Chamber of Deputies, Brasília, August 1, 2003 and August 14, 2006

Peixoto, Edmar Coelho. Secretariat of Mobilization, Rio de Janeiro office of the PT, Rio de Janeiro, June 9, 2009

Pereira, Hamilton. PT activist and former candidate for party president, Brasília, August 15, 2006

Pomar, Valter. High-ranking party militant and cadre, São Paulo, August 3, 2006

Rodrigues, Ricardo José Pereira. Director of the Parliamentary Assistance Office, Brasília, August 11, 2003

Sandroni, Paulo. Head of the Department of Metropolitan Transportation under former PT mayor Luiza Erundina, São Paulo, July 14, 2003

Silva, Benedita da. Former PT senator and former PT governor of Rio de Janeiro, Austin, Texas, February 11, 2006

Silva, Márcio Luiz. PT activist and official in the Ministry of Culture, Brasília, August 18, 2006

Singer, André. Former presidential spokesperson for Lula, Brasília, August 14, 2003

Singer, Paulo. PT intellectual and economic advisor, Brasília, August 16, 2006

Sokol, Markus. High-ranking party militant and cadre, São Paulo, August 8, 2006

Souza, Marcio. Founding member of the PT and novelist, Austin, TX, April 10, 2003

Suplicy, Eduardo Matarazzo. Several term PT senator, Brasília, August 5, 2003

Vannuchi, Paulo. Founding member of the PT and Special Minister of Human Rights under the Lula Government, Brasília, August 17, 2006

Venturi, Gustavo. Pollster and PT adviser, São Paulo, August 9, 2006

Weffort, Francisco. Founding member of the PT and former party intellectual, various conversations since the early 1990s

Index

Agrarian reform, 26, 32, 34, 60, 111, 112, 118, 119, 122, 125, 132, 139, 153–154, 175, 176
Alckmin, Geraldo, 168, 169
Alencar, José, 140
Araújo, João Batista Oliveira de (Babá), 56, 98, 151
Arns, Flávio, 174

Baker, Andy, 32, 67
Berzoini, Ricardo, 172, 174
Bittar, Jacó, 91
Bolsa Escola, 7, 71, 80, 85–86, 97–98
Bolsa Família, 86, 148, 154–156, 169, 170, 175
　criticism of, 155
Bornhausen, Jorge, 51
Brazilian Labor Party (PTB), 52, 67, 140, 164, 165, 168
Brazilian Progressive Party, 54, 69
Brazilian Progressive Party (PPB), 50, 51, 69, 98
Brazilian Socialist Party (PSB), 50, 64, 69, 99, 111, 119, 140
Brizola, Leonel, 47, 52, 111, 114, 120, 133, 134
Broad Front (Uruguay), 6, 156, 178, 185, 186–188, 196–197
Buaiz, Vitor, 67
Buarque, Cristovam, 66, 86

campaign finance
　PT difficulties with, 41–42, 103, 120, 124, 125, 130, 181
Cardoso, Fernando Henrique, 107, 119, 123, 132
　1994 election, 123–125
　1998 election, 130
　incumbency advantage, 134
　as Finance Minister, 118, 124
　campaign contributions, 42, 120
　coalitional presidentialism and, 161, 166
　declining popularity of, 61, 101, 135–137
　improved governance and, 8, 35, 123, 145, 178–179
　neoliberal reforms, 26, 48
　pension reform, 67–69
　Plano Real, 34, 125
　privatization, 72–73, 77
Cardozo, José Eduardo, 85
Catchall parties, 10, 11, 13, 23, 43, 52, 55, 75, 83, 106, 108, 135, 143, 144, 148, 160–161, 179, 181–183, 186, 188
Center-West, 114, 141, 170
Chávez, Hugo, 156, 158–159, 192
Christian base communities, 22, 29, 30, 117
Citizenship Institute (IC), 128, 133, 144
Civil society, 23, 29, 83, 85, 88

231

Coalitional presidentialism
  Cardoso Administration and, 161, 166
  PT difficulties with, 161–162, 165–166
  rationale behind, 160–161
Collor de Mello, Fernando, 1, 8, 26, 34,
    110, 113, 116, 117, 119
  impeachment of, 61–62
Communist Party of Brazil (PCdoB), 64,
    69, 99, 111, 119, 133, 140
Corruption
  budgetary scandal of 1993, 62, 63
  caixa dois, 4, 43, 103–104, 120
  mensalão scandal, 4, 104, 147–148, 163,
    165, 167–169
Critical junctures, 17
CUT. *See* Unified Workers' Confederation

Daniel, Celso, 43
Decentralization, 83
Delgado, Paulo, 75
Democratic Labor Party (PDT), 27, 47, 50,
    52, 64, 99, 111, 121, 130, 133, 140
Dirceu, José, 29, 67, 79, 93, 116, 121, 122,
    127, 129, 135, 140, 165, 167, 175
Downs, Anthony, 18, 183
Dutra, José Eduardo, 75, 175
Dutra, Olívio de Oliveira, 33, 88, 90, 100,
    162
Duverger, Maurice, 15, 16

electoral competition, 3, 19, 178
  stabilization of, 145
electoral system, 55–60, 86–87
  open-list proportional representation,
    55–57
electoral volatility, 29, 31, 35, 116, 118,
    179
Erundina, Luiza, 87, 89–93, 95, 117,
    125–126
evangelicals, 115, 140
externally mobilized parties, 15–17, 99,
    108, 147, 167, 180, 185, 193, 198

FA. *See* Broad Front (Uruguay)
Federation of Industries of the State of São
    Paulo (FIESP), 113–114, 120, 122
FIESP. *See* Federation of Industries of the
    State of São Paulo
Franco, Itamar, 117, 118, 133, 137, 140
FREPASO. *See* Front for a Country in
    Solidarity (Argentina)

Front for a Country in Solidarity
    (Argentina), 4, 143, 145, 178, 185,
    186, 188–190, 196, 197, 198
Fundação Perseu Abramo, 38, 129

Garcia, Marco Aurélio, 158–159
Garotinho, Anthony, 134, 137
Genoino, José, 34, 63, 68, 75–76, 121,
    126, 129, 168, 171
Genro, Luciana, 56, 151
Genro, Tarso, 101
Gomes, Ciro, 133, 134, 137, 143
Green Party (PV), 99, 119
Greenhalgh, Luiz Eduardo, 76
Gubernatorial elections
  1994, 34
Guimarães, Samuel Pinheiro, 158
Gushiken, Luis, 29, 167

Hall, Peter and Taylor, Rosemary, 4, 181
Helena, Heloísa, 139, 151, 168
Historical institutionalism, 39, 104, 107,
    144, 147, 163
  contrasts with rational choice
    institutionalism, 15
  institutional stickiness, 5, 15, 17, 18, 21,
    44, 179, 183–185
  integrating with rational choice
    institutionalism, 4–5, 20–21, 37, 44,
    181–185
  view of change, 17–18
    institutional layering, 5, 18, 183
    punctuated change, 14, 17, 183

Import Substitution Industrialization, 32
Inflation, 28, 109, 118, 123–125, 130,
    131, 136, 149–150
Institutional Revolutionary Party (Mexico),
    20
International financial institutions, 13, 68,
    98, 111, 151, 155, 157
IU. *See* United Left (Peru)

Jefferson, Roberto, 165, 168
Jorge, Eduardo, 68, 75, 121
Judicialization of politics, 65
Justicialist Party (Argentina), 20, 189

Katznelson, Ira and Weingast, Barry, 4,
    181
Keck, Margaret, 7, 31

Index

Kirchheimer, Otto, 19, 141, 188
Kitschelt, Herbert, 20, 26–27, 36

Laura, Maria, 64
LCR. *See* The Radical Cause (Venezuela)
Liberal Party (PL), 39, 99, 140, 161
Lulismo vs. *Petismo*, 171–172, 175

Magalhães, Antônio Carlos, 51
Mainwaring, Scott, 23, 24, 55, 56
Maluf, Paulo, 93, 110
Mantega, Guido, 74
mass bureaucratic parties, 20, 22, 45, 144, 163
Mendonça, Duda, 38, 138, 139
Mercadante, Aloizio, 63, 76, 122, 175
Minas Gerais, 81, 101, 140, 155
minimum wage negotiations
   Cardoso Administration, 70–71, 74
Movement of Landless Rural Workers (MST), 22, 76, 112, 117, 128, 132, 153, 154
Multilateral trade negotiations, 156–158
Multiparty presidentialism, 147, 160, 166
Municipal elections
   1988
      São Paulo, 87
   1992, 93
   1996, 98–100
      alliances, 99
   2000, 100–102
      alliances, 99, 101

National Action Party (Mexico), 20
neoliberal reforms, 48
   PT opposition to, 48–50, 63–69
   public support for, 32–33, 72, 130
North, 114, 141, 170
Northeast, 36, 75, 102, 109, 110, 114, 119–120, 132–134, 141, 142, 155, 170, 171

Paim, Paulo, 64, 70
Palocci, Antônio, 66, 76, 149, 162, 167
PAN. *See* National Action Party (Mexico)
Panebianco, Angelo, 15, 16, 38, 40, 45, 144
Pará
   Belém, 81, 90, 98, 100
Participatory budgeting, 1, 7, 26, 80, 84–85, 95–96, 98, 105
Partisan identification, 28

Party adaptation, 13, 21, 177–178, 181, 196–198
   sequencing of, 5
Party discipline, 16, 192, 193
Party for Socialism and Liberty (PSOL), 76, 151, 168
Party loyalty, 52, 194
Party of Brazilian Social Democracy (PSDB), 27, 35, 39, 51–52, 54, 61, 62, 67, 75, 77, 98, 99, 111, 119, 121, 124, 137, 145, 151, 161, 166
Party of the Brazilian Democratic Movement (PMDB), 30, 39, 51, 52, 55, 69, 112, 121, 140, 164, 165, 166, 168, 173–174
Party of the Democratic Revolution (Mexico), 20
Party of the Liberal Front (PFL), 27, 35, 50–52, 54, 55, 67, 74, 101, 119, 124, 134, 166
Party switching, 26, 40, 50, 52, 147, 160–161
Party system fragmentation, 24, 110, 147, 160, 199
Party system institutionalization, 8, 28, 29, 106, 178, 187, 199
Party-label votes, 58
PCdoB. *See* Communist Party of Brazil
PDT. *See* Democratic Labor Party
Pension reform, 73
   Cardoso Administration, 67–69
   Lula Administration, 150–152
PFL. *See* Party of the Liberal Front
Pierson, Paul, 17, 105, 199–200
Pinheiro, Walter, 65
PJ. *See* Justicialist Party (Argentina)
PL. *See* Liberal Party
PMDB. *See* Party of the Brazilian Democratic Movement
Political-institutional context, 24–25
Pont, Raul, 88, 162, 172
Popular Socialist Party (PPS), 64, 99, 119
PPB. *See* Brazilian Progressive Party
PPS. *See* Popular Socialist Party
PRD. *See* Party of the Democratic Revolution (Mexico)
Presidential elections
   1989, 1, 8, 28–29, 34
      advantages held by Collor, 113–114
      context of, 109–110
      Lula's support base, 114–116

Presidential elections (*cont.*)
  postelection analysis, 116–117
  PT strategy of polarization, 110–112
 1994, 31, 34
  Cardoso's Plano Real, 123
  context of, 117–118
  Lula's support base, 30, 123–124
  postelection analysis, 124–126
  PT strategy, 118–123
 1998
  context of, 130–131
  postelection analysis, 134–135
  PT strategy, 131–134
 2002, 1, 8, 39, 61, 77
  context of, 136–138
  Lula's moderation, 38
  Lula's support base, 140–143
  PT strategy, 138–140
 2006
  Bolsa Família and, 169
  Lula's distancing from PT, 169
  Lula's support base, 169–170
  mensalão scandal and, 168–169
PRI. *See* Institutional Revolutionary Party (Mexico)
privatization, 63–67
  Lula and, 131–132
  waning support for, 72–73
PSB. *See* Brazilian Socialist Party
PSDB. *See* Party of Brazilian Social Democracy
PSOL. *See* Party for Socialism and Liberty
PSTU. *See* Unified Socialist Workers' Party
PTB. *See* Brazilian Labor Party
PV. *See* Green Party

Rational choice institutionalism, 104, 106, 107, 126, 143, 147, 163
  integrating with historical institutionalism, 4–5, 20–21, 37, 44, 181–185
  view of change, 18–19
Real Plan, 8, 30, 34, 48, 106, 123–125, 130, 131, 136
Rio Grande do Sul, 52, 99, 100, 124
  Porto Alegre, 10, 81, 84, 88, 90, 95–96, 98, 100, 105, 109
Rodrigues, Edmilson, 88, 95
Rousseff, Dilma, 173, 175

Sampaio, Plínio de Arruda, 87
São Paulo, 76, 81, 85, 87, 88, 93, 100, 101, 105, 112, 124
  ABC district, 36, 80, 101, 110
  Erundina Administration, 89–92, 125
  Marta Suplicy Administration, 95, 96
  moving PT headquarters to Brasília, 129
  PT base, 103, 109
  PT losses, 98, 99–100
Sarney, José, 109, 112, 113, 173–174
Serra, José, 8, 137, 140, 141, 145, 168
Shefter, Martin, 16, 22
Shugart, Matthew and Carey, John, 24
Silva, Benedita da, 139
Silva, Luiz Inácio Lula da
  ambition of, 7, 14, 60, 106, 143
  Articulação and, 25
  as PT president, 122–123
  background of, 7, 36, 110, 111, 119, 133
  Bolsa Família and, 71, 86
  business and, 42, 114, 120, 128, 137, 148–149
  circumventing the party bureaucracy, 107, 108, 121–122
  Carta ao Povo Brasileiro, 137–138, 144, 179
  Instituto Cidadania, 128, 144
  evolving support base of, 108–109, 114–116, 140–144, 148, 169–171, 176, 200
  image of, 1, 107, 111, 119, 126, 132–133, 168–169
  in the presidency
    approval ratings of, 150, 176, 179
    cabinet of, 66, 149, 163–166
    executive–legislative relations, 147–148, 159–167
    moderation by, 8, 105, 179
    multilateral trade negotiations and, 156–158
    pension reform and, 69
    politicization of foreign policy by, 158–159

Index

leadership of, 3, 7, 36, 108
moderation of, 121–122, 131–133, 137, 200
popularity of, 30, 116, 117, 171
technocrats and, 133
the consensus candidate, 106, 108, 111, 116, 122, 128
women and, 139–140
Silva, Marina, 139, 174
Social movements, 23, 29, 55, 57, 83, 88–90, 95, 96, 109, 113, 161, 188
Social policy, 11, 146, 148, 150, 152–156, 171, 175, 189
Sokol, Markus, 98, 127
South, 28, 34, 36, 47, 81, 108–109, 114, 141, 170, 171
Southeast, 28, 34, 47, 81, 108–109, 114, 141, 170, 171
Souza, Telma de, 76
Suplicy, Eduardo, 63, 71, 75, 85, 93, 108
Suplicy, Marta, 95, 96, 101, 139

tax reform, 84, 90
Temer, Milton, 65, 127, 134
The Radical Cause (Venezuela), 6, 185, 186, 192–193, 197, 198
Thelen, Kathleen, 4, 15, 17, 18, 184

Unemployment, 8, 30, 33, 61, 64, 70, 73, 77, 124, 125, 130, 131, 134–136
Unified Socialist Workers' Party (PSTU), 99, 119
Unified Workers' Confederation (CUT), 64–68, 70, 72, 92, 96, 100, 130
Unions, 36, 89, 188, 191, 194
  as PT's traditional base, 8, 23, 29, 64, 95, 96, 100, 101, 117, 165, 180
  opposition to privatization, 65–67
  tensions with PT, 87, 90–92, 95–96
United Left (Peru), 6, 83, 178, 185, 186, 193–198

Valente, Ivan, 76, 162
Vázquez, Tabaré, 178, 186–188, 196
Vigilante, Chico, 63

Wagner, Jacques, 65, 76
women, 54, 139–140
Workers' Party (PT)
  absolving Sarney, 175
  adaptation by, 2, 7, 14, 21, 44, 106, 107–108, 144–145
  2002 presidential campaign, 137–143
  capacity for, 36
  economic constraints and, 8, 13, 31–33, 178
  in comparative perspective, 5–6
  in municipal government, 103–105
  in the presidency, 147–148
  institutional incentives, 24–25, 126, 178, 179
  obstacles encountered, 175–176, 183, 184
  post-1994, 127–130
  rationale behind, 31, 145, 181–184
  spatial dynamics and, 35
  summary of, 177
  unevenness of, 182, 198
  anticorruption efforts by, 27
  broadening alliances, 39, 129–130, 140
  caixa dois and, 4, 43, 103–104, 120, 167
  campaign finance and, 41–42, 58, 103, 120, 125, 130, 181
  candidate selection, 26, 57, 87, 180
  citizen participation and, 27, 179
  Commitment to PT Principles, 23
  Congressional delegation
    cohesion of, 2, 26, 40, 48, 50, 55, 56, 60, 67
    conflicts with *petista* executives, 67
    demographic characteristics of, 53–55
    electoral system and, 55–60
    ethical image of, 61–63
    growth of, 1, 46–47
    in comparison with other parties, 50–53
    Lula's pension reform and, 151
    moderates within, 34, 76–77
    organizational strength, 45, 48, 77
    party discipline of, 2, 3, 9, 26, 37, 40, 45, 48, 50, 55, 60, 77, 144, 151, 161, 177, 180, 182, 183, 198
    party loyalty of, 26, 37, 40, 50, 55, 58–60, 180, 198
    programmatic economic orientation of, 47–50
    public image of, 71–75
    spatial distribution of constituents, 55

Workers' Party (PT) (*cont.*)
  support base of, 170–171
  the Senate, 45
  distinctiveness of, 21, 25–27, 39–41, 50, 55, 180–181
    limitations to, 33–35
    logic of difference, 27–31
  economic orientation of, 26, 28
    criticizing the status quo, 110–111
    limitations of, 33–34
    moderation of, 38, 76–77, 118–119, 131–132, 136–137, 180
    opposition to the status quo, 117–118
    popularity of, 30
  ethical image of, 179
  expulsion by, 57, 93, 151
  factions of, 107, 180
    Articulação, 25, 32, 87, 95, 121, 162, 167
    Campo Majoritário, 162, 167, 171, 172, 175
    Construindo um Novo Brasil, 175
    Democracia Socialista, 122, 130, 162, 171
    Força Socialista, 95, 130, 162
    ideological pluralism and, 36
  financial contribution requirement of, 17, 25, 37, 40, 161, 181, 198
  formation of, 22
  future of, 178, 198–200
  generational shift, 199
  high barrier to entry, 39, 147, 161, 180
  image of, 148, 168, 173, 176, 180
  in municipal government, 1, 78
    alliances, 91, 95
    anticorruption efforts, 85
    appointing party militants, 88–89
    growth of, 81
    innovation, 81–86
    internal tensions, 79–80, 90–91
    lessons learned, 92–102
    media and, 85, 88, 92, 96–98
    modo petista de governar, 80, 84–86, 94
    pragmatism of, 79, 86–88, 94–95
    problems encountered, 89–93
    reelection, 80, 81, 88, 93, 98, 101
    São Paulo (1989–92), 89–92
    Stepping-stone to the presidency, 80, 94, 102
  in opposition, 60–71
  in the presidency
    economic growth, 150, 179
    economic moderation of, 147, 148–156, 175
    executive–legislative relations and, 147–148, 159–167
    foreign policy, 156–159, 175
    institutional constraints, 146–147, 160
    internal tensions, 146, 152, 155–156, 171–172, 173
    macroeconomic policy, 149–150, 175
    overrepresentation of *petistas* in the bureaucracy, 163–165
    pension reform, 150–152
    social policy, 152–153
  institutional legacies of, 22–23
  internal tensions, 106–108, 120–123, 144, 145
  layering and, 14, 37, 128, 144, 200
    dysfunctionalties, 43
  mensalão scandal and, 104, 147–148, 163, 165, 167–169, 176, 198
  minimum wage negotiations, 70–71, 74
  neoliberal reforms and
    opposition to, 26
  organizational change and, 3, 127–129
    Process of Direct Elections (PED), 40–41, 135, 144
  organizational continuity of, 3, 14, 37, 39–40, 44, 151, 179–181
  organizational structure of, 22, 23
  party bureaucracy, 21, 23, 39, 40, 63, 92, 95, 107, 108, 121–123, 125, 127, 128, 135, 140, 144, 162, 171, 175, 180, 199
  party label votes and, 58
  political marketing and, 39, 129
  restricted alliance policy of, 27, 111–112, 119–120, 125, 133–134
  support base of, 29